I0450678

IMMODEST PROPOSALS

IMMODEST PROPOSALS

THROUGH THE PORNOGRAPHIC LOOKING GLASS

Tom Slattery

Writers Club Press
San Jose New York Lincoln Shanghai

Immodest Proposals
Through the Pornographic Looking Glass

All Rights Reserved © 2001 by Matthew Thomas Slattery; III

No part of this book may be reproduced or transmitted in any form or by any means, graphic, electronic, or mechanical, including photocopying, recording, taping, or by any information storage or retrieval system, without the permission in writing from the publisher.

Writers Club Press
an imprint of iUniverse.com, Inc.

For information address:
iUniverse.com, Inc.
5220 S 16th, Ste. 200
Lincoln, NE 68512
www.iuniverse.com

ISBN: 0-595-15974-5

Printed in the United States of America

To all those who dared, and bared.

Contents

Preface

While coincidentally tracing camera-based pornography's history and social causes-effects, this book probes pornography, not history or sociology. In occasional graphic descriptions of obscene events and images, and in sometimes capturing pornographic flavor with its specialized terminology set apart as lewd or obscene, there is in it language that will offend some.

Pornographic terminology is often used as pejorative vulgarity to purposely offend people. At best, it is antisocial terminology and used by those who want to appear antisocial, including, of course, pornographers. But the terminology is also that of sexuality, especially sexual aggression, sexual dominance, and sexual submission. I felt that a book probing pornography might not be able to fully communicate ambiances, settings, and attitudes without using some of its terminology. So I used smatterings.

Those who may be offended by this terminology and the topic of pornography should cease reading right here.

Those who may continue reading will find this inquiry into pornography presented against the backdrop of the invention of photography. It first contemplates ways in which this invention seems to have changed perception and society. Then pornography is juxtaposed against an awareness of our planet's sex-derived overpopulation, with suggestions that pornography may have positive roles to play in encouraging sex while limiting reproduction.

The "presidential sex-scandal" cast light on a deep division in American society and by extension world society. We appear to be on a threshold of new sexual values. I have coined a concept of a "Great Social Beast," a word-based entity composed of human integers that reacts against threats to its survival like a living organism. Reacting to technological change, the "Beast" is agonizingly reprogramming its sexual-survival mechanisms, old battling new.

But these brushes on technological, social, and historical backdrop aside, this book is about pornography and all of the lewd images and obscenities that the word may conjure.

Before tackling the text from Chapter One, a quick reading of the three-part "Introduction" may help readers to understand the book's purposes and allow subsequent text to fall into a context.

Bay Village, Ohio, September 1989 (revised October 2000)

Introduction

INTRODUCTION:

POPULATION, PHOTOGRAPHY, AND PORNOGRAPHY

Part One: Emergency

The content of our hearts and minds slowly evolved. Billions of years later, we thinking creatures have control of our one and only planet and are on the verge of destroying its thin, precious, and delicate biosphere. We have arrived at the threshold of destruction and mass extinction, and the decisive ingredient will be reversal of overpopulation.

The oceans are over-fished. The landmass is farmed to its limits. Topsoil erodes away. Deforestation to increase food crop area is changing the global climate and ironically reducing fertile productive land area.

For the greater part of our million-or-more-year human existence— a tiny fraction of the total billions of years of life on earth—there were only a marginal few of us, and at times in our proto-human and human beginnings we risked extinction.

To counter these ancient threats of human species extinction, cultural contexts evolved that placed premiums on procreation and family-rearing and placed stigmas on sexual pleasures. Religion and law growing gradually but directly out of proto-human survival formulas came to define procreation as the sole purpose of sex.

But if it once was, it should not be now—or into the distant future. There are too many of us, and the biosphere is about to collapse under the weight. And when it collapses, it will take civilization with it—perhaps the human species itself and much of the present bio-diversity.

A global crisis looms. And we have to quickly alter our attitudes and break links between sex and procreation.

The emergency demands exploration—even unconventional exploration approaching the bizarre, grotesque, and outlandish.

We have been deeply programmed, biologically and socially, into accepting a now unacceptable sexual norm and into considering other approaches weird and deviant. But it is now the weird and deviant that must become the normal.

The technology of birth control is ready and waiting. Population could have been reduced years ago if that were the only problem.

But population control now flounders on dangerous ingrained ancient social attitudes toward sex, reproduction, and family originally meant for species propagation and survival and often cloaked in our most deeply unquestioning religious and philosophical views of ourselves.

Those attitudes now restrain present planet-saving human-birth-limiting technology and threaten to overturn even present meager population-control progress and force the imminent runaway overpopulation disaster.

So it is the attitudes that we must question and change. One tool for change emerged just as the population explosion began. That tool was photographed pornography.

It raised questions about our attitudes toward not only our sexuality but toward one another and gave us a new dimension for exploring our "humanness" through our sexuality.

Introduction, Part Two: Formation of Attitudes

Return to a time when our proto-human ancestors had no tools and ran naked in the wild grasses near the security of forests.

We have no records because records require language and archeology requires artifacts. There were neither. Fragments of bones that anthropologists find only give clues to body shape and structure.

After humans chipped stones to use as tools we get hints at mental processes and even imagination, but before the invention of first stone tools, we lack even the scantiest clues to human mental and social growth.

As a result, glimpses of our proto-human and then early ancestral human mental and social development start with tool-using creatures. It is a crucial point, where we modern humans can both begin to see our mental and cultural development and where we can begin to identify with our remote ancestors.

The ancient industry of shaping stone tools lasted millions of years and permanently shaped our culture and language.

The Stone Age actually predates human beings. Proto-humans chipped crude tools from small hard rocks.

Humans evolved physically over eons—actually evolved several times in the proto-human phase of the Stone Age. Fortunately for researchers now, this vast ultra-ancient stone-age culture and language, which predated our human physical evolution, lasted right up to our own technological time. Tribal peoples who made and exclusively depended upon carefully manufactured sharp flaked-flint arrowheads and cutting tools are preserved in early photographs.

Whether language preceded or followed the first use of stone tools, it certainly grew and developed subsequent to it, an accumulation of linguistic symbols and structures going back a million-plus years.

When the metals-ages began a mere five to seven thousand years ago, language and its resulting cultural values were deeply ingrained in our human being.

The invention of written language at that point only attached itself like a tail to something so old and deep that our very physical body structure and posture has changed since we began using it: clothing.

Clothing probably followed stone tools. Even the roughest animal-skin garb could not have been fabricated without them.

Clothes, language, and tools are so terribly ancient and so deeply part of us that our ancestral proto-human and human pre-language natural nakedness cannot be reconstructed. We now can only imagine those tool, clothing, and language inputs that began to affect thought and develop the attitudes we hold today.

Amid major climate changes of the ice ages, clothing would have become vital for survival. But attitudes toward clothing and its resultant new conceptual counterpart "nakedness" had hardened ages earlier.

As the great ice sheets of the last ice age began retreating a mere 11,000 years ago, agriculture and animal raising gave rise to early cities, and civilization created its own written record. We need less imagination to picture our ancestors at this point. We have hand-rendered pictures and sculptures as well as records and written-word descriptions.

That time-phase represented a great social change. People were tied to a place, lived on farms around cities and towns, or in them. To govern resulting large populations whose individuals slipped increasingly into anonymity, people were literally assigned different values, and as the concept of money took hold, they were assigned monetary value as reflected in pay for goods and services and worth of agricultural output.

A social stratification developed. And out of the stratification came institutionalized disrespect for those in lower strata and contempt for those in the lowest—servants, serfs, slaves, and prostitutes.

Then very recently mechanical engines replaced human and animal power. Things could go faster than a human or a horse could run, and continue going without wearing out. Machines could do the work of many people.

Farms no longer needed human labor. Cities grew in size and in population as a result of distance-covering powered vehicles and increased agricultural productivity.

So when we look at the long line of human mental and social development, the world had changed considerably—but over eons—as a result of the tool-clothing-language revolution. Then it changed dramatically with the introduction of agriculture, the creation of cities, and the use of written language.

Then it suddenly and dramatically changed again—after less than ten millennia—into our present industrialized, mechanical, technological context of huge cities and rapid communication.

And at the moment it began to change to this, photography was invented to objectively preserve a few images of the old ways along with revelations of attitudes not tainted by the subjectivity of contemporary written biases and interpretations.

The million-year-old tool-clothing-language revolution is now so deep in our psyche that we accept it as "us." Present social, religious, and even legal values go back to those of early metals-age civilizations and written language.

And we have had less than two hundred years to assimilate the last great dramatic change, much of it recorded by photography, then motion pictures. During the last century of growing into massive overpopulation we have those all too familiar photographed, filmed, televised and videotaped social-breakdown horrors.

Introduction, Part Three, The Way We Were

Native Peoples of the Americas were being photographed, filmed and recorded even as their cultural and national identities were being annihilated.

In 1842, three years after the invention of photography, population pressures forced the white American invasion across the Mississippi River.

In less than forty years the last of the several remaining significant Native American nations were gone, their lands confiscated. The buffalo were slaughtered for more efficient domestic animal grazing, and the prairies were plowed for food crops to feed the growing and already gigantic eastern cities.

Four centuries earlier, Aztec Mexico, technologically in the Stone Age that had dominated the greatest part of proto-human and then human prehistory, was on the verge of a metals-age when Europeans arrived. Though still in the Stone Age, the nations of Mexico were civilized, had their own modern language, writing, great cities, unique foods and agriculture, and complex social structure.

Being civilized, they had social stratification that included social classes of servants, serfs, slaves, and prostitutes. But the Europeans, while instantly recognizing the civilized institutions and even admiring the Mexican cities, had both a two-or-three-millennia technological edge and the deadly disease of smallpox, and, only a couple weeks away by ship, a vast supporting population hungry for land.

Elsewhere in the Americas five hundred years ago most of the Native American nations were just barely emerging from the million-year-old Stone Age. Their values were quite different. Rather than looking down at lower social status, they looked up to those with vital skills, leadership qualities, and records of heroism.

A North American Ojibwa culture and language still hangs on, infiltrated with European culture and language impurities. Ojibwa language gives great relative importance to concepts of sharp (*giin*) and dull (*azhiw*) and virtually discounts all arithmetic and counting concepts that we find so vital to the functioning of civilized societies.[1] Might this reflect an importance of stone-age tools in protecting and preserving tribal society? Words like "sharp" and "dull," as with stone tools, were vastly more linguistically and culturally important than number-related concepts of "amount" and thus numerical social "ranking."

Would it not have been more the case as we go back in time in the million-plus-year length of the human race's Stone Age? Most likely it was.

And therefore until civilization came along a mere several thousand years ago—with its arithmetic needs and subsequent monetary valuing of people—values like "sharp" and "dull," and many other tribal survival values, may have been applied to tribal individuals for over a million years of human prehistory and additional millions of years of proto-human prehistory. And only in the half of a percent of that vast amount of time, during which we have been "civilized," have we assigned numerical-based social-strata rankings and monetary values to ourselves.

As stone and non-stone industry and resultant trade grew, mathematics for transactions and manufacture-planning gained increasing language importance. And as concepts of number gained linguistic importance over million-year-old discernments, individual human beings began to be assigned differential number-based amounts of personal "value."

As civilized societies became increasingly complex and work and social standing became specialized, people themselves were ranked by the services they could sell and thus were assigned a relative value and social status. The butcher, baker, and candlestick maker were worth less, usually, in pay, but always lower in social standing, than the scribe, the tax collector, the district administrator. Below them, of course, were the servant, serf, slave, and prostitute.

Dichotomy defined interpersonal relationships in all but the uppermost civilized society classes, master-servant, higher servant-lower servant, buyer-seller, servant-slave, and ultimately procurer-prostitute.

In stone-age cultures, a respected master craftsman very individually and independently "pahs" and "tecs" away (*tecpatl* is the Aztec-Nahuat word for flint) at a piece of flint rock to make a tool.

As society increased in complexity and permitted larger and denser populations, those skills in human organizing needed to assure food, water, housing, social order, and manufactured implements became more vital than skills needed for crafts and technologies. Skilled craftspeople fell in rank below government authorities, regulators, planners, and merchants and effectively became subservient to them. But skilled craftspeople continued to require capital-intensive training and education and as a result came to secure a mid-level social and economic ranking or "value." Thus they were likely to have their own servants, laborers, apprentices, or craftspeople of lesser rank performing more mundane or rudimentary tasks.

In this complex structure, mere barter became too clumsy, and pay and accounting became necessary. Arithmetic and money replaced the independent stone-age flint craftsman's value-system. "Sharp" or "keen," weighted though these words remained deep in the verbal-based human psyche, mattered only in so far as they affected business transactions.

An ever-increasing stream of new technologies (a word derived from ancient Greek *techne*, the "tec" sound of the stone-age craftsman?) emerged to further complicate and stratify society.

Old values slipped away as technology changed culture. But note how language is conservative, going back to very ancient cultural values.

"Sharp" still connotes value. A good mind may be a "sharp" one. A person may look "sharp." "Dull" still has negative value. It is a "dull" day. He or she has a "dull" mind. We had a "dull" time.

This conservative nature of language works in support of fading cultural values and fuels change-resisting attitudes. Thus until very recently, use of spoken and written language in social protest always contained foundations of that being protested and worked to caution, soften, and slow changes brought about by its use.

Then something truly revolutionary and earthshaking happened. New technology created sharp evanescent images that spoke for themselves and bypassed language. These images and resulting nonverbal languages and protests speaking for themselves have speeded change and often made it harsh. The invention of photography in 1839 quickly worked to undercut thoughtful verbal deliberation, raise levels of social anxieties, and prove a great challenge to ancient word-based systems of social order.

And no sooner did we have photography than we had camera-based pornography, both the phenomenon and the word itself.

CHAPTER ONE

Advent of Photography

In 1839, barely before the last of the multimillion-year-long line of stone-age craftsmen tec-tecked the last stone tool in a genuine stone-age culture, Louis Jacques Mande Daguerre combined the *techne* of physics and chemistry to create the first commercially viable photographs. Borderline successful attempts at preserving objective images had gone back to Nicéphore Niepce's experiments in 1814, but Daguerre, a Basque, then fifty years old, discovered the first practical photographic process.

It is difficult if not impossible for us to appreciate what a world without photography was like. The effects and consequences of the invention of photography are so ubiquitous and pervasive and have so thoroughly influenced human life, culture, and thought—possibly like no other since the inventions of language, stone tools, and clothing—that those of us born a mere four or five generations later may find comprehending a world without photography as difficult as comprehending our proto-human ancestors' worlds before the inventions of language, clothing, and tools.

Still, we may try. All around us in museums, libraries, and even in our homes are artifacts and writings as recent as some of our great great grandparents, who were alive when the invention of photography suddenly struck. And they were living in what we might find a recognizable modern world.

A steam railroad was already operating between Paris and Versailles in 1839. Gaslights were illuminating homes and streets. People of Europe and America wore clothing similar to modern. And daily newspapers and periodical magazines hardly different from modern ones were published and circulated.

And the population crisis was beginning.

The seventeenth century discoveries of Jenner and van Leeuwenhoek had begun to curb and provide scientific answers to disease. Louis Pasteur would make his discovery less than two decades after Daguerre's discovery. Disease was about to give way to the new threat: the end of civilization and possibly mass extinction from overpopulation.

There was a fleeting moment in 1839 when there was perhaps only one working camera in the world. Only a handful of people had actually seen a genuine photograph at that moment of transition, and they, even more than Daguerre and the new photographers, were the first participants in what would fast become a new era.

Like all inventions, photography created anxiety.

One widely quoted immediate response was in a Leipzig newspaper, the *Leipziger Stadtanzeiger.*

The wish to capture evanescent reflections is not only impossible, as has been shown by thorough German investigation, but the mere desire alone, the will to do so, is blasphemy. God created man in His own image, and no man-made machinery may fix the image of God. Is it possible that God should have abandoned His eternal principles, and allowed a Frenchman in Paris to give the world the invention of the Devil?

The newspaper editorial compares Daguerre's discovery to Napoleon's dreams of conquering and uniting Europe, then goes on.

If this thing were at all possible, it would have been done long ago in antiquity by men like Archimedes or Moses. But if these wise men knew nothing of mirror pictures made permanent, then one can straightaway call the Frenchman Daguerre, who boasts of such unheard things, a fool of fools.[2]

We can smile and forgive the newspaper editor now. In all too few years he would come to see the science and art of the photograph profoundly change his and everyone's way of life. The Frankenstienian creation of captured soulless lifelike images frozen in time has haunted civilization ever since. A hundred years later an evil Austrian would use the invention to create a mass-image of himself and justify a war for *Lebensraum* (living space), then lead Germany into it with devastating consequences and previously unimagined horrors, among them the Hellish firebombing of that newspaper's city of Leipzig and the mind-boggling population-reducing depravity of the Holocaust.

Mary Shelley's novel *Frankenstein* had been in print and widely translated for two decades by the time Daguerre stunned the world with his invention. Even prior to it, intellectuals like her viewed the new age of science and invention with similar anxieties.

Daguerre the inventor did not.

In a broadsheet to raise money a few days after he announced his invention, he predicted in what may almost seem a television-age sales pitch:

Everyone, with the aid of a Daguerreotype, will make a view of his castle or country house: people will form collections of all kinds, which will be the more precious because art cannot imitate their accuracy and perfection of detail; besides they are unalterable by light. Even portraits will be made, though unsteadiness of the model presents, it is true, some difficulties in order to succeed completely.[3]

The extreme difficulty in photographing living individuals would be overcome as increasingly faster film was invented.

The modern promotional text betrays attitudes already in place as the invention was revealed.

Commercial advertising grabbed the invention and ran with it. The invention initiated great social changes, permitted outrageous political parties to seize power, created new sciences, and widely disseminated knowledge.

And it created the completely new human experience of photographed pornography, very likely from its first moments, possibly even prior to public disclosure.

As the excerpt from Daguerre's text continues, we see an interesting shift in viewpoint.

A Daguerreotype is first promoted to preserve a view of a home, an understandable appeal to well-healed French homeowners for a yet expensive process.

The text, however, does not continue by promoting taking of Daguerreotypes of middle and upper class "family members." It shifts and specifically employs the word "model," as if a promotional appeal to the thriving Paris artist community.

A successful artist with a studio himself, Daguerre certainly knew the market and the appeal.

And there were prosperous artists' studios all over Paris, and resultantly a thriving business in modeling.

When news of the invention of photography broke, Eugéne Delacroix (1798-1863) had a Paris studio and models. Among his paintings is an "Odalisque" female nude, circa 1845. Jean Auguste Dominique Ingres (1780-1867), painter of the most famous "Odalisque," had another and painted this female nude model twenty-five years before the invention of photography. And there were numerous less skilled and artistically incisive imitators painting models in Parisian studios. At the moment of the invention of photography's disclosure, there was a demand for painters of nudes and thus a demand for nude models, and there quickly evolved another extension of the dichotomous boss-employee, master-servant, artist-model bonding of complex civilized societies.

It is not surprising, then, that a number of the early Daguerreotypes are of nude models. One original, titled *Académie*, a photographed live-model odalisque dated 1845, can be seen in the George Eastman House collection in Rochester[4].

Another, simply called *Nude*, dated 1854, is in the Webb collection.

The captured image of that young woman at that moment in her life, in all her youth and beauty, is still with us over a century and a half later and long after her old age and death[5]. There are a number of other surviving early-post-invention nude photographs.

Early photography of live individuals, dressed or undressed, was tedious and complicated. Exposure times were painfully long and required professional model-level skills at stillness. Photography of them required expensive equipment and studio-level skills, as much skill input as drawing, sculpting, or painting models.

Daguerre's text-shift from photography of homes to an appeal to artists to photograph of models had its predictable effect. And being an artist with a studio himself, Daguerre surely knew what the studios would begin photographing.

Possibly because it began in the confines and context of artists' studios in Paris in the heyday of sensuous odalisque and other nude posed paintings, the photography of nudes came to be viewed as art.

After a century and a half of discussion, laws, trials in court and their precedents, and changes in popular attitudes there are still questions as to where to draw the line between art and photographic pornography, which is not to condemn pornography, but rather to consider it as just another category of human endeavor like art.

Interestingly, the English language word "pornography" is influenced by, if not derived from, the two most important communications inventions of our time. It evolved first from the word "telegraph" (from the Greek "distant writing," first used for the optical telegraph invented by Claude Chappe in 1792 and later adopted for the electrical telegraph). The reader may note that the direct technological successors to the telegraph, the telephone system and the Internet, present the latest adaptations and outlets of pornography—phone-sex, Internet sex literature, sex chat-rooms, and M-PEGS.

The already coined "telegraph" prompted the coining of "photograph" in 1839 by Sir John Herschel. The new coined word was quickly utilized by English photography inventor and pioneer William Henry Fox Talbot in 1841 for his process, while Daguerre was pressing for "Daguerreotype" in France. Thus the word "photography" entered the English language and spread worldwide in time to allow the coining of another word for one of its significant applications, pornography.

The word pornography, which comes from the Greek *porne* (whore) and *graph* or *graphos* (writing, writings), first enters English language use in the 1850s, subsequent to photography, the derogatory word-coining following the invention of photography and the use of that word for the new invention by at least a decade.

In the early confines and context of Paris artists' studios, there would seem to have been something descriptively "pornographic" in the photography of nude models. A relationship between prosperous Paris art studio owner and less affluent nude model insinuates both psychological and actual prostitution. Those early nude photographs approach being graphs of prostitutes, thus literally "porno-graphs."

And undoubtedly some of those nude photographs were actually of some of the numerous Paris prostitutes.

Seven years prior to Daguerre's proclamation of the invention of photography, Dr. Alexander Jean Baptiste Parent-Duchatelet, a French governmental public health officer, published his study of prostitution in Paris, *De la prostitution dans la Ville de Paris*,[6] which was so thorough that it included (in those days prior to photographs) a hair-eye-eyebrow measurement chart derived from the 12,600 prostitutes registered in that city between 1816 and 1831, and further included tables for ages and length of time involved in prostitution for the 3,517 known prostitutes in Paris as of December 31, 1831.

Of Parent-Duchatelet's 3,517 prostitutes, 2,100 had worked for four years-and-under while only 704 had been prostitutes for nine-to-twenty years. Of the 3,230 for whom there were birth certificates, roughly half were between the ages of twenty and twenty-seven. Only 128 were under eighteen, including 27 between the ages of twelve and fifteen (only one of them actually twelve), and 34 were fifty-and-over.

Parent-Duchatelet's statistics included occupations of fathers of 828 of the prostitutes. The majority were artisans ("working poor"), 113 were day-laborers, 64 were without a trade ("chronically unemployed"), 50 were shoemakers. At an apparent other end of the social (if not economic) scale, four fathers were doctors or lawyers, three were teachers, and nine were musicians.

Prior to prostitution, most of the women appear to have worked in factories or as domestics. In other words, at the moment Daguerre disclosed his invention that would powerfully impact perception, society, science, and art, the prostitutes of Paris, one of the world's largest cities and global focal point for art and science, were basically lower-end working class young women from working class families—with a very few rebellious higher-bracket daughters tossed in. His invention, and other marvels of the last industrial-society century-and-a-half, seems to have altered these statistics little, if at all.

As we have seen in our own time with cyberspace, some people cannot resist sexual possibilities inherent in some new technologies. The early nineteenth century invention of photography offered a new challenge to the human sexual imagination. As a result we see not only the beginnings of camera-based pornography as a social phenomenon but the coining of a word to describe, connote, and express its origins, attractions, and retail niches.

That the introduction of the word "pornography" so closely follows the coining of the word "photography" and the widespread use of the word "telegraph" as the electric telegraph system went global leads one to conclude that the original coining was in reference to literal "whore graphs," pictures of nude prostitutes utilizing the by then at least decade-old invention. "Pornography" apparently began to replace "obscenity" and other terms in reference to written-word sexual literature only following the invention of photography.

The word is not "model graphs" or any other similar possibility that might have been coined and stuck, but "whore graphs," aptly conveying of origins, procurement, processes, and retail attractions. Even those of later years who never knew the Greek-word derivation of "pornography" knew the connotations, implications, innuendo, and subtexts conjured by the word as a result of its deliberate coining and expected to see "whore graphs" or read "whore writings."

That the word "pornography" continues in use may reflect how little has changed. Human business and pleasure associations to produce nude photographs in Paris a century-and-a-half ago were probably not unlike those producing camera-based pornography today. Nor would the relationships between those people and their nude models appear to have much changed.

Few modern upper-class debutantes pose for nude photos. And at the other end of the social spectrum, few of the mostly lower-class nude models permit their nakedness to be captured without being paid, and few are not in some need of the pay they get.

Whether in need of the money or not, nude models are obliged to endure an insinuated social censure. Models in general are paid for turning themselves into visual objects. Nude models, who do not require skills in projecting appearances and demonstrating apparel, are also paid for becoming visual objects, but paid less because they simply undress. The money that nude models are paid would seem more to compensate them for consenting to community-standards taint more than for actual mental or physical work.

And this is all the more so for nude photography, film, and video models, who are not required to work at maintaining still poses. They are being compensated for far more lasting and significantly distributed and exhibited taints to their characters—far more than for any mental or physical work or skills. If you look at it from the "anyone else" point of view, anyone else might sue for libel, invasion of privacy, defamation of character, and the slander that would accompany the exhibition and distribution of such nude photographs, films, or videotapes.

At the moment of initiating a first interview to pose undressed, a person becomes subjectively debased and stigmatized into a new, lower, and, at least momentarily unfamiliar, social status. The nature of the nude modeling and the inferences of the poses or performances may create internal layers of nude-model rankings, but even prior to the moment of written or unwritten modeling contract, signed or not-yet-signed model release, virtually all nude models are cast into lower social ranking than their interviewers, camera people, and employers.

Anyone who has ever been interviewed for an everyday job may feel some parallels, but the social fabric of propriety protects a person's social status, however low it may be or browbeaten he or she may feel. In contrast, by its very nature a prospective nude model slips through the cracks of the protections of propriety and is automatically re-ranked as the interview begins.

Nude photography models, in addition to this initial social re-ranking of all nude models, further anticipate at the point of interview—and then experience—the results of likeness reproduction-multiplicity, and subsequent publication of the images of their bare flesh that invades a privacy of their integrity going beyond the conspicuous revocation of privacy of their bodily private parts.

There is a similarity with a young woman who may—like a nude non-photography model posing a few times—turn a very private trick once or twice, but once having become known as a prostitute, is socially stigmatized. Photographed nudes, like known prostitutes, are inherently relegated to enduring permanent lowered social standing. Their paying "employers," from the moment of procuring their disrobed services, begin looking down on them from a resulting vantage point of higher social strata.

Decently dressed photographers, cinematographers, or videographers who intend to capture their models' bare flesh usually arrive at the studio or location from higher economic brackets. Except for a few notable exceptions of star-quality mega-models, they stand to gain far more financially—and in status following the publication and distribution of their naked models' photographs, movies, or videos—than the lowered-status naked models themselves.

In a general sense, then, the naked models prostituted their flesh for pay. Even if not outright lewd or obscene, the resulting renderings and objective captured images constitute "pornography" (prostitute graphs) in an etymological sense of the word. Whether they are also art can only be judged by nebulous precepts of art.

Pornography is, then, a highly charged but descriptive word—in our time connotative but not necessarily totally derogatory. It describes not only a finished product but infers relationships and processes that created it.

In the early and difficult days of photography, an image was genuinely exhausting to capture. Reproduction and multiplicity of images were still some years into the future.

These early photographers of nudes were not very different from the early painters or sculptors of odalisques. The single resulting Daguerreotype was the end product in itself.

The shutter, lens, and developing pans may have replaced the brush and chisel, but early nude photography models would have viewed their employment as hardly much different than posing for painters.

In those days the technique of image capture was all-important and the art of photography had yet to develop. Those photographers were heirs to eons-old tradition that respected craftsmanship going back to those proto-human technicians "tec-tecking" at rough stones to create sharp tools.

They concentrated on "sharpness" of image, precision of product. But we can also sense the master-servant relationship in these early photographs.

In the 1845 odalisque photograph, the undoubtedly decently dressed master—probably wearing stuffy middle-class male attire of the time—clearly manipulated the posing naked servant for the best artistically and erotically enticing views. The servant, working for pay, complied. By its very nature, suggestive sexual connotations permeate the view. The almost hidden bare breasts, exposed buttocks, and general amount of flesh presented might have censored it out of American men's magazines a century later. Culture creates and defines obscenity. This 1845 nude photograph would clearly have been regarded as legally obscene in North America in 1945.

In 1845 in France, it was most likely just an artist's model posing for pay and an artist-become-photographer laboring to produce an artistic product.

The new twist that neither the photographer nor the model could have fully realized was that the camera recorded, permanently, objectively, revealingly. The photograph had authenticity.

The model is seen exactly as she had looked, precisely how she had posed and permitted herself to be captured at the time, without the convenient escape-clause excuse of subjective interpretation of the artist or his possible imaginary invention of the scene.

Even with the primitive photographic techniques of 1845 there is an accuracy of detail. In looking over this accurate detail back then, the woman and her photographer may have viewed the photograph as a perfected drawing. But it wasn't, even then. As a photograph it could reveal more in its accurate and objective frozen image than might have been gained from looking at the actual living presence at the fleeting moment, the very freezing of the instant allowing inspections that cannot take place in real time—a useful aspect of photography that would soon come into great use in scientific and other investigations.

And that calls attention to an important deception.

Even as the image of the young woman's bare body was being captured, chronicled, and acquired as a property unto itself, time moved on. The image remained, but the person aged and changed—first in seconds, then hours, days, weeks, months, years. More than a century later we can view the image of the moment, long after the living person has passed away.

And thus the photographed nude gained something the photographer lost.

With modern photographic techniques, the image of the ancient young nude has been duplicated, published, and duplicated again—forever young. Neither the early photographer nor his nude model is likely to have even vaguely suspected this at that moment of photographic capture back at the advent of photography.

CHAPTER TWO

Debaucher-Debauchee

The first photographers were artists or technicians interested in the accuracy of detail that the new invention allowed.

Early viewers may have approached viewing photographs as drawings with more accuracy of detail. But immediately everyone recognized the difference. The photograph was an authentic representation of a scene or event, a captured instant. The disinterested camera captured the image the way it was.

Early photographers were burdened by long exposure times, expensive handmade cameras, and expensive and difficult development processes. So their images of what really was were few and limited.

But the difference between a photograph and a subjective painting or drawing—even those wood-block or lithograph mass-produced in print media—was obvious. And a public demand to view events and scenes as "authentic news" of how they really appeared applied constant pressure for improvement.

A legion of experimenters dove in and over the decades improved exposure times, simplified development processes, added clarity, lowered costs, and added color. Capture of images was made ever cheaper and easier. Authenticity was enhanced by briefer exposure time, clarity, and color.

Increasingly cheaper photographs, movies, and finally camcorder videotapes allowed more and more photographers, cinematographers, and videographers, and just plain rank amateurs to capture ever wider human experience, from the dramatic and sublime to the mundane and banal.

As it were, it allowed increasingly larger numbers of people to become pornographers. And these pornographers could pursue increasingly authentic situations and accurate views of naked human bodies engaging in sexual acts.

An expanding availability of increasingly less expensive visual recording technology drew in larger and larger numbers of participants—on both sides of the camera—to pornography. Increasing numbers of buyers bought as the product price decreased. Aficionados could vicariously or actually participate—on both sides of the camera—as costs came down.

Needs for exceptionally attractive naked models decreased as low cost productions needed only marginal sales to turn profits, and "amateur porn videos" brought in average-looking but thus more authentic-looking situations, locations, and naked models.

From the fairly robust sales of often poor quality videotapes done with totally unskilled camera-operator techniques in bad lighting with very average-looking naked models with virtually no acting talent, the saving grace of authenticity would appear to have enhanced the pornographic imagination.

From the time of the earliest pornographic photographs, the viewer could see naked bodies exactly as they had been "seen" by the camera and presumably seen by the camera operator and any other audience.

Moreover, a viewer could not only browse sex-organs and bare flesh, but also could detect intentional and unintentional responses in the unclothed models being photographed.

Still-photographs allowed careful and even detached examination of not only body parts and facial identities but also communicated expressions and body language. Color photographs expanded realistic presentation of whatever reality had been photographed.

But the invention of motion pictures let the viewer see not only the activity but implied more of the context in which the capturing camera had been placed.

And context, with respect to both camera people and naked models, added to the fascination and excitement of pornography, the more authentic the better.

In celluloid or videotaped motion pictures, the viewer can see not only what the naked body or bodies did, but what they "are doing"— how personalities and bodies "are responding" to one another, to the presence of the camera, to both the audience and demands of camera operators and directors, to both the actual and the pornographic environments, and to the pornographic presentation situation itself.

Viewers become spectators to physical action and emotional interaction and can see and interpret—far more comprehensibly than in still photographs—responses of the naked models, how the camera person chooses to present views of them, and their private parts or sex acts.

And more dramatically than in still photographs, the spectators to motion picture pornography see "story." While close-ups of sex organs and their activity in sex acts genuinely add to pornographic stimulation and interest, it is "story" that creates genuine pornographic entertainment.

Whether a scripted feature-length porn production or an amateur home video, pornographic "story" is basically about "who"—"who" was compensated to publicly strip and exhibit sex organs, all the more titillating when about "who" was paid to exhibit them while publicly engaging in sex acts.

New facial identities are thus in constant demand because faces are more important in pornography than sex organs, which, after all, may be seen very unarousing in medical textbooks. If pornographers merely presented sex organs after sex organs and more sex organs, the market for pornography would evaporate. There is naturally some variation in sex organs, but basically when viewers have seen one male and female sex organ, they have seen them all. Faces that go with those sex organs, on the other hand, possess infinite variety and disclose the bare model's identity, and pornographers continuously seek new faces for their photographs, films, and videos.

Pornographic "story" fundamentally pertains to "who," to facial identities of those who exposed skin and sex organs and/or publicly performed sex acts, and this story-fundamental is present in still photographs as well as in celluloid or videotape motion pictures.

While still pornographic photographs present both facial identities and news reportage contexts in which those people's bare flesh and private parts have been captured, it is in motion picture pornography that nonverbal—and also often verbal—narrative "story" can be seen unfolding. And the story is not always the one intended by the bare models or sought by the pornographic producers/directors.

For instance, in virtually all porno movies or porn videos, average and untutored viewers may detect and enjoy occasional hints of embarrassment or resentment that models may betray when being photographed or videotaped naked or performing sex acts.

That is to say, basically viewers of pornography want to see an accurate depiction, a "news" story with all its "dirty gossip" recorded. They want to see an authentic record showing that it really happened, and these bare naked people actually did it on-camera.

If viewers psychologically identify with the pornographic depiction or the naked models, some of the "story" they identify with must be the cultural defiance—possibly including a defiance of that ancient sex-for-reproduction-only commandment.

This defiance of cultural norms manifests itself in both the authentic photographic representation of naked bodies by pornographers, and in the acts of nude modeling or pornographic portrayal of sexual acts by models. Not so long ago in most places, all pornography was in defiance of the very laws of society, and thus society itself. Viewers defied the laws of society by illegally viewing camera-based pornography, and producers and naked porno models defied those laws by producing or appearing in it.

That defiance made up a considerable part of its "story" and entertainment value. The bare models—as they have always done and continue to do—defied society's castigations and censure, and the camera operators and producers, and even the consumers, defied criminal penalties. Pornography is far less criminalized now, but obvious social restrictions, valuations, and condemnations remain in place and continue to invite defiance. So intrinsic to every porn photograph and porn production is a story of defiance.

The rebelliousness imbedded in overt pornographic story and undercurrent scandalous subtext may have some roots in infantile pre-acquisition of speech, but would seem also to reach back into our pre-clothing and pre-language proto-human past.

In all celluloid or videotape pornographic motion pictures, and not always confined to the intervals of sexual excitement, one can find a deep proto-human psychological defiance against learned language symbols, something the human race has not been without in over a million years. Even in silent pornographic films, and of course in still pornographic photographs, there is an inherent viewer and porno-model rebellion against language-based social definitions of propriety and suitable behavior.

In all pornographic motion pictures with sound tracks the audience can hear pre-language guttural grunts, moans, groans, slurps, sucks, squawks, and cries. While these pre-language communications issue from sexually related exertions by the porno models, none of these sounds are entirely involuntary in the sense that the porno models making them have been struck severe enough impacts to drive bursts of air past the vocal chords. The grunts, moans, groans, whimpers, slurps, sucks, squishes, licks, pants, squawks, and cries amount to authentic pre-speech and anti-language assertions. Pornography producers go to some lengths to pick-up and record these pre-language communications with hidden and directional microphones.

Early silent-era porno movies, following the pattern of early mainstream silent movies, intercut filmed action with dialogue and narrative subtitle boxes, but rarely superimposed written subtitles onto the action. Unless intended as humor, verbal representations were virtually never utilized in the midst of sex-acts—where the visualized pre-language guttural grunts, moans, groans, slurps, sucks, squawks, and cries required little auditory imagination.

By the time of silent 8-mm and 16-mm porno movie "loops" shown in peep-shows beginning in the 1960s and their "girl-only" predecessors beginning in the 1950s, pornographers saw no need for verbal representations other than occasionally introducing ostensible personal names to accompany the facial identities of the naked or quasi-naked models, clearly at least suspecting this pornographic language-defiance axiom in supplying for the demand of the marketplace.

In addition to this noticeable defiance of learned language, there is intrinsic in all pornography the blatantly obvious defiance against wearing clothing, something humans have been doing since near the advent of stone tools. And proceeding from that, there is the conspicuous defiance of social restrictions concerning public nudity and public sex.

Unquestionably other areas of defiance, like unconscious Freudian defiances, political-statement defiances, anti-prejudice defiances, and anti-cultural-sham defiances, can be effortlessly deciphered in pornography. The point being made here, though, is that defiance is a large part of the "story" entertainment being acted-out, film-and-video recorded, and subsequently enjoyed by viewers and spectators.

Both the producer of pornography and the models explicitly depicted in it flaunt this defiance, taking part in making something that is culturally censured if not actually illegal.

But there is a more indispensable "story" than defiance permeating pornography. Defiance, after all, can be acted out, communicated, and appreciated in mediums other than pornography. Guttural sounds in defiance of learned language can be heard at spectator sporting events. Non-pornographic nudity can defy the wearing of clothing in a number of public and private ways, from prancing naked around the living room to baring it all at a nude beach or in a gym or health club locker room.

In addition to defiance, a more important debaucher-debauchee role-playing—as a consequence of social dichotomies brought about by civilization—always lurks as the story behind the story in pornography and is integral to the appetite for, appreciation of, and participation in it.

Minimal mutual interests and motivations that camera operators/producers/distributors share with naked models in pay-for-modeling and producing a product for profit invariably diverge even prior to the actual on-camera production of pornographic entertainment, and the debaucher-debauchee dichotomy emerges at the initial meeting of the cameraperson or producer and the prospective naked model.

Pornography's entertainment value is plainly not wholly in pictorial representation as such, even in authentic pictorial representation of actual gossipy nude sex-model antics on-camera. Pictures in medical or other textbooks will be instructive, but they are hardly ever entertaining. Interest, amusement, and entertainment stems from "story," and "story behind story," and "story" sought lurking behind those.

And audiovisual pornographic "story" entertainment value is not so much the contrived, superficial, and sometimes scripted story surrounding the bare bodies and their on-camera sex-acts as in the intended and unintended "story" that can be read into the actual modeling and picture-taking session.

Viewers of pornography enter into looking at it in much the same way as sports spectators enter into looking at sporting events or readers of mystery novels enter into reading those stories. They know the rules of the game or story genre beforehand and have expectations of being amused and entertained by the play around those rules.

Underlying sport and story in pornography are debaucher-debauchee rules and dictates, and viewers prowl through the obvious given on-camera debaucher-debauchee machinations and their many and always present nonverbal subtexts to fulfill their amusement and entertainment expectations. The obvious "given" is the social dichotomy instituted and enacted between models and non-model personnel and spectators.

The naked porno models have been—and as seen on-camera, are being—debased and debauched by the camera operators, and by extension the producers/distributors, and eventually by the public customer/viewers themselves, without whom the pornographic production would simply be an ineffectual museum piece. But other debaucher-debauchee stories lurk under the surface.

Contact spectator sports, notably boxing, are not about fine uplifting human qualities. They are about brutality and power inflicting wills and goals. Murder mysteries may have more refined qualities, but the genre draws on power plays to impose ambitions, resolves, and the ultimate human brutality of murder for entertainment. Pornography is no more meant to be uplifting and refined than these.

Camera-based pornography is relatively new to human experience. Studies made of it have thus far tended to be scientized, objective-ized, statistical, measurement-oriented. Sports, literature, and drama, on the other hand, have been colored, refined, and influenced by accumulating subjective analyses from sports writers, drama critics, book reviewers, and others.

A great many people may be offended by graphic blow-by-blow accounts of boxers attempting to brutally beat opponents into unconsciousness while spectators cheer them on. But there is a wealth of sports literature subjectively rating the fine nuances of the sport.

A pornographic film or live-sex-show reviewer's blow-by-blow critical rating of a blowjob, however, lacks a needed accumulation of subjective reviews. As a result, even a serious attempt will end up sounding ridiculous—at best, humorous. This inadequacy would not seem inherent in scandalism of pornography, but rather resulting from a lack of history and field of subjective pornographic criticism. Whether one ever develops and grows, only time may tell.

In some ways, pornography seems a composite of disturbing dramatic story and brutal spectator sport. It is about the more audacious, ambitious and powerful imposing contemptuous profit-making goals on the acquiescent, imprudent, and powerless by inflicting indignities and defilement on them for public amusement and entertainment.

There also seems an element of a clown-show in pornography, with clowns accepting indignities to bring audiences back to the common reality of being just one more species in the biosphere by poking fun at our foolish human vanities and pretentious dignities. But whatever it is, like fans at a boxing match, audiences of gory murder movies, or spectators at a clown-show, pornography consumers may rightfully savor some merciless porno-model character-ravagement, but are equally interested in following the unfolding of events, the "story" and all the little gossipy "sub-stories" that weave in and out of it.

Story fragments are divulged in expressions a porno model might reveal while performing an oral or coital sex act. What might a viewer detect and enjoy, for instance, in the interplay between one porno model performing oral sex on another? What might he or she perceive and find amusing in a naked sex model's momentary heed of the capturing camera and fleeting facial expression betraying misgivings of the public indecency and enduring debasement?

What might he or she notice and enjoy from the bare porno model's interaction with the cameraperson recording and watching and with other production personnel and spectators observing. What might a viewer detect and find intriguing in a naked porno model giving himself or herself to sexual arousal in public and on-camera? And how much consciousness, during the excitement of a sex act, are the bare porno models reserving for awareness of doing it in front of a camera and audience—at very least the cameraperson as audience?

There are hundreds if not thousands of such subtle—and some pretty unsubtle—stories being played out for the interest of viewers in every pornographic production.

Sometimes one may see an unedited scowl of objection or reluctance. A naked porno model is told to perform something and betrays a momentary resisting. It may simply be a mild personality-conflict resentment at being told what to do. It may be a momentary aversion to performing a sex act in public on-camera, into which a viewer might read a sudden recognition of future social consequences and thus a trace of regret or shame. Or it may be annoyance at having to break off a sex-act at a stage of high sexual excitement.

The mini-story contained in this balking or fleeting annoyance by a porno model may be all the more stimulating to the viewer when the porno model acquiesces to his or her debauched and effectively prostituted employment-dictates and enacts on-camera what he or she had momentarily balked at performing.

A viewer may catch a "story" in a porno model's suppressed pouting glower followed by being perceivably debauched into grudgingly performing, continuing, or discontinuing a sex act. And the eye of a beholder may notice a fleeting facial expression realizing shame and embarrassing consequences in posing an obscene exhibit of private parts or engaging in a lewd sex-act for public amusement on-camera.

Or the viewer may be amused by the occasional unintended story of a debauched naked porno model's awareness of status, camera, and the ever present audience of at very least a camera person, but almost always including additional production personnel and often invited spectators. Sometimes pornography viewers notice this when a naked porno model looks directly at the camera, sometimes by audience's unintentional on-camera-visible or off-camera-auditory presence or reaction, sometimes when a porno model glances self-consciously at his or her undressed flesh and no longer private parts on-camera and in front of an audience.

Both in porno-model portrayal and in the backdrop on-camera reality, the viewer examines a master-subordinate relationship, a creative-artist vis-à-vis manipulable-human-object relationship, and a debaucher-deb-auchee relationship for their story amusements and entertainments.

As in prostitution, the paymaster becomes the overt debaucher. The naked models, only slightly extending definitions, literally portray themselves as debauched prostitutes, flesh for sale, sex acts for pay—but in portrayal. And this portrayal needs a brief paragraph of explanation before continuing.

Unlike prostitution itself—which many porno models quite likely take part in off the set—the porno models are clearly not offering actual sex to viewer-customers for pay, but rather portraying themselves as willing whores who strip and engage in sex on-camera for pay. To crim-inally charge porno models and porn producers with engaging in pros-titution—as has been done—is as legally absurd as charging an actor who also happened to be known as a car thief with thievery as the result of a movie-set car-theft scene. Sure the actor stole the car—and a not-too-clever prosecutor could stretch the facts and make a case that he or she actually did—right their on-camera. But pressing such absurd cases could have chilling effects on art and story in all motion pictures.

The prostitution being portrayed on-screen—either prostitution as part of a motion picture storyline, or when porno models invariably por-tray themselves as prostitutes on-camera—is performance portrayal, a form of Constitutionally protected expression. It could not reasonably be called anything else.

The real prostitution that porno models and sex-performers may as performers be portraying on-camera or in live-sex-shows, even, as it were, portraying themselves as willing paid whores, is an interesting two-way street. The prostitute's client buys into the whore's culturally classified debauchedness and gets as much satisfaction from the ease with which a little money can debauch as from the sex-act. But the prostitute, acceptive of degraded relative social standing, gets large satisfaction from the price so easily seduced from the purchaser.

Often consciously and intentionally in early pornography—and still in present low budget porn—the person-procurer behind the camera did the same thing. The cameraperson paid to debauch the effectively thus prostituted nude model or models as much as to profitably photograph them. Why otherwise would they bother with it, especially back when it was illegal, if it did not contain these perks? They could make better and more reliable money selling used cars.

In the 1970s there was a tangential illustration of this in the burlesque-show scene in Chicago. A strip-show theater there advertised in newspaper theater sections that they allowed all photographers, amateur or professional, to photograph totally nude female strippers during their erotic and suggestive performance routines. The photographers merely had to buy a slightly higher priced ticket. These were not art photographers hiring nude female art models to do nude art poses. There were always about a dozen of them, and they were there solely to photograph the more debasing and scandalous naked sexually suggestive gyrations of the strippers. And they were free to sell and exhibit their photos.

And the decently dressed audience could watch them with amusement as they mocked the paid naked female strippers with their cameras. It was, indeed, some of the advertised attraction.

Virtually by definition pornographers, the photographers plainly got a greater malicious delight and amusement than the audience from actually taking part in defaming and debauching the strippers—who for their pay virtually prostituted themselves by exhibiting their genitals, breasts, buttocks, and anuses to cameras and the audience in general, and with an awareness of wide commercial distribution.

While more public, the scene and milieu were not unlike early pornography creation. And it was, in fact, a form of contemporary low-budget pornography creation. The adult male and female public could watch the blatant social division of decently dressed pornographers who had paid specifically to take photographs scandalizing debauched naked strippers. It was only a half-step removed from pornographers actually physically paying the porno models themselves to debauch them naked on-camera.

In later and more commercialized pornography, where camerapersons and naked models are paid from the same corporate funds and thus have common interests in satisfying an employment-management apparatus, the dichotomy continues.

The decently dressed camera person still "shoots" the naked models, "captures" them on film of videotape, and "takes" the pictures he or she chooses of their bare bodies, their "private" parts, and thus participates in their debauchery.

The paid naked models, on the other hand, "submit" to the demands of the photography, filming, or videotaping session, "surrender" to its social consequences and social ranking aftermaths, and "acquiesce" to their present and future debauched status on-camera and off. They pose to publicly expose bare flesh and "private" parts, consent to being positioned to obscenely exhibit them for commercial publication, and await the pleasure of the camera person to award them permanent disrepute.

Right up to the pornographic corporate boardroom, the dichotomy is as clear as the profit-margin bottom line.

The first pornographic photographs may have been a kind of sexual experimentation in themselves. With the first one, and with a number of others who did not know about the first or subsequent ones, the experience may have been somewhere between a scientific experiment and masturbation. No one had ever before captured a sex act. What does it feel like?

Even with primitive equipment and long exposure times, it must have been tried in the early years of photography.

Almost that soon, and even given poor depiction quality, photographs of naked people engaging in sex acts must have been found to have commercial value. And very soon after that, befuddled legal systems acted to suppress it.

And why? Because in its sudden arrival in human affairs, photographed pornography seemed to pose a threat to cultural values— cultural values designed around procreation for species survival. The great word-based social beast saw a threat and reacted to it with one of its more powerful responses, legislation.

But with each new image-capture and image-reproduction invention in the last century-and-a-half-plus came necessities for social change that required more than the blunt legislation and law-enforcement tool.

Consider what happened after the invention of the home video camera. It totally bypassed the need for rank amateur pornographers to submit camera-recorded material to others for developing and printing. The Internet went a step farther, bypassing the need for local retail porn stores. Shop, download, and view. Even view a live and unedited sex-performance if you want.

Neither legislation nor law-enforcement could any longer keep pace with it. Barring brutal and socially stifling legislation and law-enforcement—that would effectively be more harmful and dehumanizing than pornography it sought to control—the genii of pornography has now completely slipped out of the social beast's bottle.

Not a few articles have now found their way into adult and mainstream periodicals about those video cameras surreptitiously glimpsed in yuppie bedrooms. But are they there in the interests of adding more people to the overpopulated planet? Are they there to record sex acts leading to procreation for family video albums? "Here, Junior, is when we had sexual intercourse to make you."

No way!

Those home video cameras are in the bedrooms for new sexual pleasures.

There is sexual pleasure in pornography. Both history and the size of the present industry proves that.

But it is not derived from sex for procreation, in fact, quite the opposite.

The widely admired "cum shot" of commercial pornography portrays the very antithesis of a sex act leading to procreation. Sperm visibly ejected onto a sex partner's epithelium are highly unlikely to lead to the addition of another member of our species.

Moreover, there is very little, if any, commercial heterosexual pornography exclusively limited to sexual intercourse in the missionary position, the one most likely to lead to human reproduction.

In fact, the percentage of film or video time devoted to this particular sex-act position in any given X-rated production is remarkably small.

The greatest portion of any given porno movie or porn video depicts various oral sex acts, by their very nature anti-reproductive.

And following that, the virtually required "doggie-style" copulation either terminates with a "cum shot," or reverts to oral sex.

Pornography, as the great social beast seems to have anticipated, is anything but instruction in sex techniques for reproduction. These are not manuals and training films for procreation.

Just the opposite. Pornography enlightens about the sexual enjoyments without their necessarily leading to procreation.

And more. Photographed pornography clearly represents a different and distinct sexual pleasure—in itself—something relatively new.

And even beyond that—if there may be anything to those camcorders in yuppie bedrooms—there is clearly a separate and distinct sexual pleasure derived from participation in the production of photographed pornography, from either side of the camera.

And if we extend that consideration into the commercial pornography industry and its "amateur" offshoots, the decently dressed camera people and the naked models must both be partaking in this different and distinct sexual pleasure made available by the invention of the photography and its subsequent enhancements.

Participation in the production of pornography—whether by camerapersons or naked models—including the yuppie couples in front of a private camcorder in their bedrooms, who are both—is a powerful new form of sexual pleasure and expression.

The new sexual pleasures of viewing and participating in pornography would appear to require no encouragement and need only to be left alone.

As the planet begins to cascade from overpopulation into whatever its terrible irreversible consequences may be, the fabric of our social programming must shift from sex for reproduction to expressions of our natural sexuality that do not lead to it. Visual pornography is one.

At the heart of it is sexually and visually stimulating photographed, filmed, and videotaped debaucher-debauchee stories, whore stories, the definition of pornography.

Sometimes dressed in contrived superficial story lines and badly acted, sometimes left to themselves with their own infinite subtle sex stories, they arrived with the invention of the camera.

Not only is visual pornography entertainingly presenting anti-procreational sex, it clearly motivates new attitude-formation necessary to planetary population stabilization.

And for whatever reasons, in whatever grand plan, it has arrived at this time in our history when members of the great human family have to find ways to reduce their numbers.

Traditional cultural, religious, and political leaders will continue to thrive on upholding conservative values initiated by our proto-human ancestors at the beginning of the Stone Age. It is always safe.

"Madonna and Child" (not the actress-singer and her kid!) is a touching pre-Christian image going way back into the mists of human beginnings, long before ancient Egyptian Isis and Osiris prototypes. "Motherhood" is a touching concept bandied by political hacks for eons.

But even as we are touched, we must stop and ask ourselves why. Is it appropriate now?

Might we be doing our human race and the planet's bio-diversity a great disservice by pandering to these ancient sentiments thoughtlessly taken to be so wholesome?

Traditional religious and political types will harp the ancient sentiments with increasing intensity as fears grow that the old ways may vanish—which they must if civilization is to survive, perhaps if our species and the whole of the bio-diversity is to survive.

But let no one be deluded that li'l ole pornography can defeat the monster of ancient cultural values. It is just one possible timely tool that may be useful in prying necessary change from the jaws of impending overpopulation disaster.

CHAPTER THREE

Birds, Bees, and Bare Behinds

"Birds do it. Bees do it. Even little fleas do it," goes the song.

Consider this. Virtually alone in the world of life forms, and as a direct result of wearing clothing, humans are sexually stirred by the viewing of sex-organs and sexually associated private parts.

In the rest of the animal and plant world, scents, sounds, and signals excite sexual interest. Seeing sex organs does not turn on bugs, beasts, or creatures. Only humans are turned on by it, females probably as much as males, as evidenced by the recent successes of all-male strip-shows for liberated females and female-oriented pornography productions.

The initial primeval acts of our proto-human ancestors first donning rudimentary pseudo-clothes and concealing sex-organs created a new and perhaps unnatural visual sexuality. Prior to clothes, our primate-like ancestors would have gone through life like tribes of chimpanzees, with uninteresting and totally unexciting sex-organs exposed all around them. Proto-human acquisition of language and language-based word-images and abstracting abilities wrested this new clothing-generated visual sexuality from its natural role in reproduction and began to endow it with an erotic mystique and new word-based social symbolism.

So sexual interest generated by seeing naked human beings, their sex-organs, and other associated private parts, is socially generated rather than instinctually generated. People who are publicly or para-publicly stripped and exhibited naked are involved in social statements. People who, largely in anonymity, pay to see live stripped-naked people and their sex-organs and associated private parts on exhibit, or who pay to see their images in publications and on screens, or who risk social censure and legal penalties to view unsuspecting people who remove clothes for non-sexual purposes in their normal life-processes, are also engaged in social statements.

Ever present at the root of these social statements, however, is normal biology. The sexual drive itself differs little from other functions like eating or going to the bathroom—an urge, satisfying it, and a going on to other things.

One-celled plants and animals have no trouble with sexual urges. When they feel like dividing, they divide.

Higher up on the evolutionary ladder it becomes more complex. It takes two to tango. Sex displaces cell-dividing simplicity.

As central nervous systems advance up the evolutionary scale, sex and sexual rituals become more intricate and enigmatic.

Lazy August days buzz with the clackings of cicadas. August nights are lush with the symphonies of crickets. But what are these millions of little critters vibrating their sound organs or rubbing their legs together saying? What are they communicating with one another all night long? Sex sex sex!

All that monumental effort and clamor goes into just one word, the sole word "spoken" by billions of insects in millions of different insect species: sex!

It gains in complexity with higher animals, but it is the same. In all animals a great percentage of central nervous system matter must be devoted to communicating sex, and those found lacking lose in the game of natural selection.

In highly complex human society a high value is placed on the sexual urge, and this artificial social value plays its own part in the natural selection of successful social organizations.

Unlike even the highest of other animal species, social selection has replaced natural selection in the survival of human genetic lines. Sex is more socially—rather than biologically—bound up with reproduction and generating the future of our species.

And the societal analogy to the DNA molecule is language. Words, the building blocks of language, create human society.

Higher primate species like chimpanzees—from which our own species branched-off after our common ancestor's invention of tools and acquisition of rudimentary language, but before inventing clothing—have small vocabularies. But these are nothing compared to huge human vocabularies and their vast complex contexts.

And now, some thirty to fifty million years after separating from the chimpanzees, we as a species simply could not survive without the use of words and the language-based use of highly evolved tools.

We are, for all practical purposes, nothing if we are not words. Our very names are words. Everything we do, everything we think, everything we wish, and everything we attain is made up of words, and even our dreams may have words.

So that while chimpanzees as well as other animals use tools, no other earthly species has utilized the vast stores of word-based memory data to create and use tools with the complexity of human ones. And as a result, animals have not had to adapt their societies to the interrelationships of constantly created vocabulary, text input, and increasingly complex tools and their uses.

Since unlike all other animals, humans wear clothing, and since unlike all other animals we have a large vocabulary and a resultant enormous capacity to generate symbolic structures and meanings, these two exclusively human qualities naturally converge in the roots of what we are. Extensive word-based and story-based social values have grown around the human wearing of clothing.

For example, the most influential religious-social word basis of Western civilization, the Bible, virtually begins with an ancient story about the first donning of garments, the Adam and Eve tale.

At first, like the animals in the Garden of Eden, Adam and Eve were naked in nature and unashamed of it. After they had tasted the forbidden fruit of the tree of knowledge of good and evil, they covered their genitals and behinds in shame. And this symbolic donning of apparel to conceal body areas associated with sexuality is the defining moment in Western and other civilization where humans become separate from animals.

From most ancient times then, clothing has had as at least much to do with our word-based concept of shame as it has with protection from climate.

Clothing evolved to indicate status and station, command respect, and offer degrees of socially defined dignity based on appearance.

Lack of clothing also indicated status. As in many ancient societies, Aztec lower classes were only permitted to wear minimal amounts of garb and to reveal much more leg and body flesh than upper classes. Slaves and captives had to submit to going naked in public as an indication of social status.

Like the Aztecs, upper classes in all societies throughout history have attired themselves in fine and beautiful clothing. In our modern Western society the fashion industry strives to artificially create high value for creative stylish clothing to signify status, dignity, and respectability.

Apparel, or the lack of it, does not, however, create dignity or shame. Society defines those.

And human society is language. Our entire highly evolved and complex social structure would instantly collapse without language.

Language binds people together in societies, but it also separates one society from another in commercial competition, religious righteousness, political conflicts, feuds, and wars.

Languages freely translate. But the words in context that bind people into societies also separate societies into competing groups even when languages are the same. These society-defining words in context are called laws, constitutions, myths, word-based religions, technical information transferences, histories, and favorite stories.

In short, we are what we are as humans because of words and stories. As a result, we are what we are as sexually reproducing animals due to both biological evolution and word-based social evolution.

Just as Adam and Eve draped symbolic coverings to thwart a natural visual revealing of their private parts, pretensions in languages prohibit the auditory revealing of certain words and terminology contexts surrounding sexuality. Every human society seems to have its forbidden words revolving around sex.

In an ironic twist around the use of off-color words, a fourth-grade teacher in Spokane, Washington was recently suspended because she had her students each write one of these forbidden sexually loaded words to try to analyze the handwriting and discover which of them was the brat who dared to write it on a school table.

Why should society fear a word and punish a teacher who had her students write it for whatever reasons? And why should society regard a sexually-loaded word as more important than basic living needs of an all too human teacher?

Teachers have a special place in the learning of words and stories of that form the fundamental bases of societies.

Consider that the school board and administration would probably not have criticized her if she had taken her prepubescent students to a zoo and they had witnessed animals engaging in sex, even if they had seen our nearest ancestral relatives—who may have broken away from our evolutionary line as our common ancestor was experimenting with stone tools and language—a couple of the zoo's chimpanzees, engaging all too human-like in sexual activity.

The same parents, board members, and school administrators probably encourage these same students to watch "nature shows" on public television, where each episode as a rule shows and explains animal sexual activity.

Animal biological processes do not provoke the same deep fears and resulting confrontations, criticisms, and punishments as words and word-based assertions do. Social judgment weighs down when word-based human values and story-based human social processes are called into question and threaten social continuities.

The Spokane incident not only focuses on sex, words, learning, and the story base of society, it calls attention to a whole range of concepts surrounding propriety, reputation, social standing, public appearances, and private lives that serve to maintain the amorphous beast of any given society.

Social rewards and punishments revolve around words and the stories behind their definitions: honor, dishonor, proper, improper, decent, indecent, praise, shame, reputation, debasement or degradation. All these words are entangled in perceptions of pornography, and a subtext running through them is reproductive sex.

For instance, family "honor" has to do with economic and status values in mate selection, procreation, child rearing, and in completion of the circle in filial piety leading to "proper" mate selection again.

Relationships of the negative words to associated with "improper" sex are well known and can speak for themselves: dishonor, improper, indecent, shame, and debasement or degradation and thus shed light on their positive counterparts.

Supermarket tabloids accumulate great wealth from these words and their social story-based definitions.

A politician at the pinnacle of power may suddenly fall based on associations of words. Such was the case with the late Congressman Wilbur Mills who was caught behaving in a bizarre manner one night with a striptease dancer stage-named Fanny Foxe.

The event resulted in political disaster for poor Mills. It meant a loss of power, eventual loss of job and sacrifice of income, and a lowering of esteem and personal value among his peers, apparently punctuated, as I recall it was reported somewhere, when his Masonic brothers considered ousting him.

On the other hand, publicity surrounding the same event seems to have promoted Foxe's stripping career.

Why the contradictions?

At first glance we see that two people whose lives were defined by different sets of social values had become entwined in a relationship that was doomed unless one or the other of them adopted the other's values and lived by that code.

If Fanny Foxe had repudiated her lifelong career and pledged allegiance to the Beltway social circuit, she and Mills might have had a fine clandestine relationship not uncommon in the Washington scene.

Or, if Mills had slowly eased himself into publicly disowning the stilted Bible Belt values that had gotten him not only elected but reelected and reelected into a virtual Congressional career, the shock would not have been so severe and he may have weathered it.

But he could not. And indeed, he had been elected and reelected to represent those very word-based values. His real or seeming betrayal of them led to his downfall.

Foxe, on the other hand, was caught in the act of representing her career values of publicly flaunted sexual "indecency," and she reaped a few rewards of her value-system as a result.

But the tradeoff was that Arkansas voters would never have elected Foxe to Congress, where their cherished, if stagnant, social values had to be guarded with all those carefully chosen words of legislation.

Foxe, as long as she elected to hold values surrounding flaunted sexual "indecency," could never expect to get her hands near the awesome levers of power and appropriated money that Mills did. You have to have "respect" in the eyes of the voters, and even if, in order to gain that socially defined "respect," Foxe had renounced her old values, she would not have been able to extract herself from a socially defined "fallen woman" stigma.

Foxe would not have been able to convince voters in Mills's Bible Belt constituency of her worthiness to represent them. She would have had a "reputation," a word with a lot of social baggage and weight—and all the more so in politics, policing, and education, which more than other aspects guard to word-context fabric of the great amorphous beast of society.

Curious words, reputation and respect.

Note how the military utilizes one word, respect, to get young men to hurl their bodies into volleys of machine-gun bullets.

Military society is virtually constructed around it. Without this word, military organizations could not exist.

And it is a fear-based word and concept. Internal fears are carefully inculcated to counter the fears of charging into machine guns.

Respect is routinized and tied to clothing appearance. Soldiers salute officers. Even unintentional shows of disrespect or inadequate appearances in military clothing mean punishment.

Civilian societies allow more personal leeway, but concepts build around the words "respect" and "reputation" still grow out of instilled fears and feed the amorphous word-based beasts.

And "respect" is a two-way street. Those whom the beast of society holds worthy of it hold power. Holding of power carries with it comfort and insulation from some of the discomforts and dangers always lurking out there.

"Reputation" grows out of "respect." The great intangible social beast rewards those who function as preservers of social order and therefore in need of "respect" with "reputation."

But cross the beast and put the social order in danger of change, and "reputation" can be obliterated. And the eons-evolved social beast most fears those who advocate changes that affect reproduction of its integers, the human individuals.

In other words, the great intangible social animal most fears changes in attitudes toward sex, and exacts punishment in the form of sacrifice of reputation to those who threaten it.

Every now and then a police person finds himself or herself unemployed as a result of posing nude in a sexually explicit magazine spread.

Very infrequently a school teacher turns up on page one of the local daily arrested for prostitution.

There go their "reputations," and invariably as a result, there go their livelihoods. Status in society is reduced. Pay and position, with their levels of comfort and insulation, are generally sacrificed.

The word-based social beast wins. Its individual human integers retreat in fear, cower and comply. "Ain't it awful" both feeds the fear and supports the censure.

As society slowly evolves, both genders are increasingly represented in these losses of "respect" and status, but even so the teachers or police persons involved in these incidents represent only a tiny fraction of the great masses of people in their professions.

They make news where accountants, seamstresses, or sales people would not because their professions require respect in order to function.

Police have a need for respect on the streets in order to function, and teachers need it in classrooms. Both professions are on the front lines of identifying and fighting those thoughts, words, and deeds that might disrupt and infect any given word-based society.

But societies, like animal species, adapt and evolve.

Our own is no exception. For instance, recently politicians and teachers have made the front pages as a result of financing or producing pornographic films. Disclosures like these are always good gossipy pseudo-news stories, examples of how society puts its aberrant and wayward members in the spotlight of threat of discomfort to force conformity on them, and others. But they also reveal undercurrents of adapting and evolving social change

The amorphous word-based beast of society clearly must adapt to changes going on within it as a means of survival. But it does so slowly at the pace of generations, taking no chances on what works and what does not.

A generation ago to be exposed as a homosexual was a death-knell for a politician and the end of a teaching career. Now there are openly gay politicians and teachers, but a stigma remains.

A contemporary conservative former college professor's run for the presidency of the United States was not cut short by revelations that he helped finance soft-core pornographic films, but it clearly cost him some direly needed Christian Coalition votes, and after a vigorous and even admirable political campaign he was forced to drop out.

And every now and then a teacher caught producing pornography can find a way back to his or her job after a suspension commotion. The same may even be true from time to time of a teacher found to have appeared in the buff in something that at least used to be called pornography, a *Playboy* or *Playgirl* or similar centerfold.

So while society adapts slowly, often far more slowly than wise or necessary as technology-induced change takes place within it, society is constantly evolving.

Eventually old stigmas fade away.

Playboy and *Playgirl* magazine centerfold men and women have gone on to significant and lucrative careers in this country.

And other undercurrents hinting at social evolution keep surfacing.

While hardcore pornography models and performers may have more trouble achieving social status here in America, in Italy, a brazenly hardcore pornographic performer was elected to a significant political office as a member of their parliament.

But successful centerfolds and elected hardcore porn performers are still newsworthy exceptions.

Prevailing reality continues along lines that, for example, the late hardcore pornographic performer Linda Lovelace's famous early 1970's bid for the presidency of the United States could not have been anything else than a publicity-related prank. And it, of course, was. But the prevailing reality would seem to be experimenting with allowing hardcore sex performers access to sincerely sought political offices.

The success of 1987 Italian Radical Party candidate Ilona Staller, whose hardcore porn stage name is Cicciolina, prods a little reflection. "Cicciolina" Staller was elected to a seat in the Italian parliament after blatantly flaunting her hardcore pornography-acting career in the campaign.

Following that success, in 1992 she made another political office try with two other hardcore porn actresses, Virna Bonina, whose porn-performing name is Barbarella, and Luisa Pistarino, whose porn name is Eva Orlovsky. The three of them formed the Love Party and ran as flagrant hardcore pornographic performers.

As I recall, one or more of them again won seats in the Italian parliament. At very least, all of them made a tolerably good showing and drew significant numbers of votes.

"Cicciolina" Staller's election to Italian Parliament was something of a fluke, of course, a cynical protest vote, a commentary on the Italian electorate's disenchantment with the whole Italian political system. In a field of off-color and even blatantly corrupt candidates, it could hardly have mattered much to the voters which one of them won.

This rejection of "the system" at the ballot box by at least one riding of Italian voters highlighted social protest. And social protest runs as an essential element, as we have seen, through pornography, a commentary questioning the relevance of values. One may have served to enhance the other.

Note a hint of slight social progress in it. The great amorphous beast of word-based society learned and adapted out of painful experience.

Hardcore porno-star "Cicciolina" Staller's election was certainly an improvement over the way that the Italian electorate registered disenchantment with politics and politicians in the mid-1920's and brought Benito Mussolini and the Fascist Party to power, with eventual painful social and military disaster.

Even if we accept that the election of Staller to the parliament was done with humor and that in the next election a large number of voters cast their ballots for her and her two pornographic colleagues to make jesting statements about the political system, there probably was a certain undercurrent of seriousness of desire for change in social attitudes.

There were, after all, other candidates protesting other things. And the voters had options of not voting at all, and they refused those options and elected at least one nationally known and openly hardcore porno star.

The Lovelace candidacy for president in the United States during the Vietnam-protest years over a decade earlier was, of course, never meant to be serious. The very running of this nationally famous hardcore porno star under her stage name rather than her birth name Linda Marchiano (or, then married: Linda Marchiano Traynor) was intended as high alternative political theater and as a publicity stunt for her feature-length porno movie, *Deep Throat*, released that election year.

At that dawn of decriminalized public pornography in America, and to put it in the thought-context of the times, Lovelace's candidacy was meant to call publicity-related attention to her laughingstock shamelessness and public scandal in order to derogate and de-mystify the awesome imperial office of President of the United States at the height of the Vietnam War. And it additionally chided American political values in general in this time of unwanted war and resulting protest.

The blatant publicity stunt enhanced box-office receipts for the entire new X-rated industry profiting from these new out-of-the-closet debaucher-debauchee amusements of "nationally paraded laughing-stock shame and disgrace."

But to put it in proper perspective, the publicity protest included subtexts that shed light on war profiteering and other corruption tolerated by the body politic. These were days when young men, paid less than minimum wage, were goaded by values of military respect, honor, and glory to be senselessly slaughtered in battles of dubious value in Vietnam—like the charge up infamous Hamburger Hill—to gratify perverse officer-soldier (master-subordinate) pleasures, while back on the home front military-industrial-complex potentates raked in enormous sums from taxpayers in master-servant assertions. Profits and perversions of porn pale when compared to the profits and perversions of cold or hot war.

Memories of Lovelace's notorious burlesque run for high public office would seem to have influenced Ilona "Cicciolina" Staller and her supporters in Italy a decade-and-a-half later. And Staller made an authentic political run for office, and won.

This non-Italian (Hungarian immigrant) woman flaunted her "Cicciolina" pornographic film identity and even utilized her peeled public sex performances and reels of porno film performances tangential to her campaign, but she ran under her real name and made it plain that she was a serious candidate for public office. By statement and implication she advertised her candidacy as an opposition to old stagnant sexual values. And, fluke protest or not, she got elected.

What, then, might have been the case if Lovelace had otherwise accumulated the political background and other credentials necessary to the office of president—which she of course clearly did not. Why should appearing in pornography have deemed her unfit?

And in retrospect, and to ask with tongue in cheek, if she had miraculously won the 1972 election and become President Lovelace, would she have turned out to have been any greater embarrassment than President Nixon?

In fact an investigation of this distortion in comparing "embarrassments" would seem pertinent here since "embarrassment," as an offshoot of "shame" and a reflection on "reputation," seems an integral part in pornography.

Large portions of the American public may have been "embarrassed" by Nixon's attempts to establish a police state. But that is different.

Pornography customers, in and of themselves, were never "embarrassed" by—in the attitudes of her heyday—Linda Lovelace's lewd nakedness, obscene filmed fellatio, and other public "dirty movie" sex acts. They paid; they viewed; they were entertained and often delighted.

Unlike these porn customers, though, Lovelace herself appears to have been, or become, "embarrassed." Many years after she had appeared in the buff to all appearances playfully performing sex-acts on-camera, she publicly reversed herself and denounced both pornography in general and her immodest appearance and erotic acts on-camera in particular, claiming she had been forced.

At some level of her understanding she knew that this would strike back at the porn industry—not from making criminal accusations, which she ultimately failed to adequately support, but from implying that the debaucher-debauchee entertainments intrinsic in pornography had been fraudulently obtained. By and large porn customers are more like news readers than drama patrons. They want authenticity of image and honesty of performance as opposed to carefully crafted dramatic and story fictions seen in mainstream movies and television, and Lovelace was implying artistic fraud and performance fiction.

Even that peripheral small minority of porn consumers who relish experiencing aspects of force in sexuality and seeing representations of force and coercion in pornography would have been later disappointed at not having been honestly shown the force alleged to have been involved Lovelace's otherwise manifestly voluntarily naked on-camera sex-acts. There were no juicy whips, chains, slave collars, or manacles. Thus, either way, Lovelace was implying the pornographic equivalent of artistic dishonesty, possibly more damaging to porn—should it have been shown to be true—than virtual criminal accusations.

If this many-years-after-the-fact turnabout was honest, it touches on "embarrassment," and related concepts of "respect" and "reputation." Unlike the porn customers who viewed her X-rated movies, Lovelace later implied that she was "embarrassed" even at the time of her nude sex-performances on-camera. And even if her belated comments may have been less-than-honest, they betray belated embarrassment.

Clearly in later years she agonized over what she considered her shame. Society had defined it. If she had not voluntarily defied the great social beast, she had been compelled to defy it, and she had subsequently found the defiance had become too uncomfortable, too "embarrassing," and either retreated into the great den of propriety and denounced it, or sought to salvage "respect" by revealing that she had been coerced.

Eve prior to eating the forbidden fruit thought little of cavorting naked. While Scripture is silent on the subject, we can only imagine that naked Eve, prior to tasting the fruit of knowledge of good and evil, would not have considered public sex with naked Adam any more shameful than the animals in Eden did, nor even, if there had been cameras in those days, doing it on-camera for public and permanently preserved images.

The birds and the bees, and even the little fleas of the Garden of Eden were doing it. There was no shame or embarrassment.

In fabled Eden, which symbolizes enormously ancient proto-human transitions to clothes, tools, and words and stories, we may detect ancient preserved memories and moments. In fact as well as in fiction, we descended from proto-human "Adams and Eves" who lived before clothes, tools, and language were to become part of the agglomeration of human knowledge.

And the very first human knowledge following clothing, according to the enormously influential story, was the knowledge of shame and its offshoot expression, embarrassment. Somewhere way back in the mists of our human beginnings there was a moment when the new clothing-generated visual sexuality went off on a tangent from its natural role in reproduction and our proto-human ancestors began to endow it with socio-erotic complexities growing out of word-based symbols.

Eons later symbolic thought and knowledge led to cameras and photography, and sex led to overpopulation of the tiny garden of Spaceship Earth as it zoomed through the great cruel dark void.

Sex, cameras, knowledge, and undoubtedly a certain amount of shame came together while Linda Lovelace and Ilona Staller flaunted their nakedness on-camera while engaging in sex in public like the animals of Eden.

CHAPTER FOUR

Pedestals, Prostitution, and Pornography

Throughout history, and probably throughout the span of proto-human and human social-structure existence, women have played second fiddle to men in society.

In more ancient times this had some justification in biological realities.

Women nurtured their children and did the greater part of the uninspiring hard grungy work while men concocted the military-political strategies for survival and made the decisions and fought the battles to protect the tribe and increase its margins of safety against acts of nature and other tribes.

But the great amorphous social beast balanced it with small social compensations, and one of the more successful ones is the pedestal.

Women were granted an artificial "respect" as long as they stayed "female" and avoided treading on male aspiration toes or opposing the great social animal itself.

And it had ancient practical survival roots. Women get pregnant and require protection for several months, and the children they bear need special nurturing, protection, and attention for years.

Proto-human survival societies that disowned this died out. The surviving amorphous social beasts survive partly by rewarding their life-giving female integers with, among other things, contrived pedestal statuses.

But this has always been truer for leadership class upper strata women than lower class females. The former wear the aristocratic styled finery and are addressed with elaborate social conventions of respect, while the latter sweat at the hard grungy work, some of it raising children, much of it work going into supporting those elaborate upper class life styles and their artificial conventions. Still, even for lower class "proper" women there is a degree of lip-service respect.

Below them in every society are the "fallen women," the whores, who serve as fine examples of socially defined degradation and humiliation to keep those females only slightly above them in line and doing all that necessary child bearing, child rearing, housekeeping, and other hard monotonous uninspiring grungy women's work.

The very word "whore" connotes degradation, disgrace, and shame.

Unlike words for any other occupation, the word "whore," or even its nicer and more refined designation, "prostitute," is more often used in a pejorative sense than to describe employment.

To call someone "You electrician!" clearly falls short of arousing the same fighting passions as to say "You whore!" to a man or woman, or even to imply that a person "prostitutes" himself or herself.

And yet the job requirements of a whore do not, in themselves, involve work as intrinsically dirty as that of a sewage treatment plant engineer, or a knee-deep-in-mud rice-paddy stoop laborer, or even a garbage collector.

It is simply a word that describes an occupation that needs a social stigma.

Without the confinements of socially defined stigma, degradation, and shame, the female whore could have a big easy. Other than a slightly greater risk of sexually transmitted disease, whores traditionally faced fewer hazards and discomforts than the average lower class respectable female.

If a few of a prostitute's clientele might sometimes get violent, respectable lower class husbands also tended to be violent with their wives.

On the other hand, the employment requirements for a whore were not terribly demanding as compared to respectable female work like, say, less-than-minimum-wage sweat-shop sewing twelve hours a day meeting heavy production quotas.

Unlike "respectable" lower class women, the nature of a whore's employment allowed her some ease and time for thinking and reflection, even, as a result, occasional contributions to art and literature.

And instead of backbreaking work that made painful blisters and calluses, there was sexuality pleasure in whoring. Some clients may have been odorous, obnoxious, detestable, and horrible to briefly be with, but most of them were upper-class gentlemen and generally were not. And as a rule, even episodes with undesirable clients resulted not in hours of painful raw bleeding hands or ankle deep dirt as much respectable lower class female work did, but brief periods where the stimulation of sexual pleasure nerve endings came into play.

To counterbalance the manifest draw, successful societies evolved scorn, shame, disgrace, and degradation commentaries. They defined these "fallen women" into rock bottom social strata classifications, and when that did not wholly suffice, the social control that goes with criminal penalties and criminal records and reputations was added.

Society needed degraded whores as examples to keep lower class women in line, but it did not need too many of them dropping out of the "respectable" work force and thus driving up wage expectations, not to mention reducing the numbers involved in birthing and child raising.

To keep the great majority of respectable women in their proper places, and away from levers of social power and control that might accrue from consorting with wealthy and influential gentlemen, these "fallen women" needed defining nomenclature so strongly loaded with connotations of shame, degradation, disgrace, and humiliation that even it had to be prettified in "decent" conversation. If, for instance, the topic of prostitution should be brought up by accident at upper class cocktail parties, one might snickeringly refer to "ladies of the night," but it would have been considered beneath one's "dignity" to use the word "prostitute," let alone "whore," especially in the company of upper class "respectable" women.

And yet the very upper class men who prettified the word whore in parlor titter frequently slipped out to "houses of ill repute" to use lower class whores for sexual pleasures.

The male half of the population was given under-the-table social license to find pleasures in sex because the great majority of the female half was assigned sex, child-rearing, and related hard work as social duty to reproduce and increase the integers of population, preferably without indulging in too much pleasure.

For ends of maintaining and increasing population, the great social beast siphoned off a small percentage of women to be utilized to gratify male sexual pleasures, in itself a reward for males supporting and defending the social order.

At the same time, it created its own social definitions of male sexual pleasures and promoted notions of the sexually bizarre to encourage and enhance them. This seldom spoken but widely recognized "perverse" sexual activity served to increase the defined degradation of the defined-as-defiled female whore and thus all the more instilled those fears that kept lower class women "proper" and in their child-bearing, child-rearing, and hard-drudgery places.

Over eons it became finely tuned. Our own liberal democracy was founded on the principle that "all men are created equal," probably

originally intended as such and not a gender-overlooking sense sometimes attributed. It was an ethical step up from notions of the times that
some men are created kings, some dukes, some earls, some barons, etc.
But women were denied the right to vote or hold office. But the great
amorphous social beast allowed male liberal democracy. Fine-tuned in
allocating social relationships and functions, it feared lethal disruptions
that might grow out of freeing women from procreative and child nurturing servitude.

But the new liberal democracy limited to male participation had
opened a Pandora's box—if I may borrow the misogynic metaphor
from ancient mythology—and created opportunity and demand for
invention. The resulting overwhelming of old orders by new technologies interrupted eons of fine-tuning created unanticipated snags.

As the republic evolved and slave labor of the south was seen as being
in unfair competition with paid labor of the industrial north, a great
and bloody war was fought so that black men could be included in the
"all men are created equal" founding liberal principle.

The military surrender of the slavery-cause at Appomattox brought
legislation that gave black men legal equality with white men, but did
nothing for either black or white women.

Theoretical liberalism, though, cannot tolerate any fully functioning
adult human beings being excluded from the equality model. If its
equality model is to be stated correctly, it must be the updated paraphrase of the Jeffersonian assertion: "all people are created equal."

This inspired and inspiring liberal ideal, as Frances Ferguson[7] points
out, has inherent pitfalls and limits in that "it may seem to see its work
as complete at the outset when it affirms the priority of virtually uni-
versal human faculties over particular circumstances."

In other words, the trap into which liberals may sometimes fall is the
one that fails to see circumstances and experiences creating inequalities
among individual people. For instance, an inner city child from a
poverty-stricken single-parent home is certainly not going to mature

into an adulthood where he or she is equal to someone who had grown up amid the care and attentions of wealth, the education of a private school with the best and best-paid teachers, the enriching experiences of travel, and the future prospects in higher education and employment that the powers and accesses of wealth can provide.

"All people are created equal" may be a generous ideal on which to base a democratic legal system, but it eventually comes into conflict with biological, geographical, and social realities.

Nevertheless, even while gender experience and circumstance continued to confine women to lower status, the liberal model insisted that they be granted legal equality. And after several more generations of long hard struggle it was finally fully legislated.

Eventually tort law was put to work to define hidden social devaluations of women. A tort is a breach of civil duty by a party or parties which some other party becomes entitled to sue for damages. Resolution of sexual harassment and equal employment opportunity torts now appropriate "damages," something not likely to have been imagined when Jefferson penned his "all men are created equal."

As Ferguson points out, however, the tort law paradigm eventually comes into conflict with the liberal democratic paradigm. While we see these two functions of our legalistic society operating to abolish slavery and then grant women equality, they essentially exist at cross-purposes.

Under tort law a person files a lawsuit because he or she claims to have been devalued by a willful act, by an accident, by a slanderous statement, etc. He or she seeks to be compensated for the lost value, as Ferguson so nicely puts it, "for the value that an unblemished reputation, undamaged property, or uninjured limbs would have had for him or her." A right to "damages" is invariably present when a tort is committed.

Libel and slander are torts. Under the law, every person has a right to have his or her reputation unassailed by false and defamatory imputations. To defame is to devalue. Reputation derives from the Latin *reputare*, the *putare* of which means "to reckon." In the word "reckon" we see terms denoting and connoting value: count, compute, and estimate. Tort law thus assigns value to individuals.

By assigning values to people, tort law implies the obvious—that all people are not equal. Some have more value. To put it another way, some have more valuable reputations, some have more valuable property, some have invested in their persons more valuable education or experience, and some may have more value in the appearances of their facial identities and features—so that a person named Madonna might claim devaluation by so many millions of dollars because someone had used an intrinsically copyrighted photograph of her face in an advertisement without paying her, something most readers might not be able to claim.

In our democracy, and indeed in the global legalistic business culture, we find ourselves weaving in and out of the equality-under-the-law notion and the tort-law notion of each individual person's status-economic value. The conspicuous cross-purposes of the legal system merely reflect a wider reality. We are daily compelled to conceive of ourselves as equals among our fellow human beings, especially in equal-under-the-law society, but simultaneously we are coerced to accept a personal ranking in the socioeconomic scale of individual values.

Ranking, more than equality, defines interpersonal relationships, and by its nature constructs dualisms and dichotomies, boss-employee, foreman-worker, buyer-seller, doctor-patient, landlord-tenant, clerk-customer, and, as always throughout the history of civilization, client-whore.

As civilization progressed, perplexity increased in this last relationship dualism and social-ranking dichotomy. *De jure* and *de facto* equality cannot exist where prostitution is still criminalized, but outside the direct client-whore relationship women must now acknowledge themselves *de jure*—and to a large extent *de facto*—equal, and yet as whores they must submit to being of low value, as reflected, for instance, in tort-law value for recovering any damage to "reputation."

Even where prostitution is legal, to call a whore's client a whore might be lawsuit costly, but to call a whore a whore is a statement of fact and therefore not a tort. If a clever lawyer might find an angle and make it a tort, damage to the "reputation" of a whore generally still would not bring much, if any, restoring recovery in terms of money.

But with some humor, and not without noting a glimmer of hope for change, one may note that 1996 San Francisco County Supervisor candidate Margo St. James actively and blatantly campaigned as a former prostitute. In doing so she was forced to repeatedly speak out to counter opposition campaign claims that she had never actually had been a prostitute and was only claiming to have been one to get elected in that ultra-liberal city that loves to embrace the bizarre. Having been a prostitute had given her a higher tort-value than not having been one. I remember reading *San Francisco Chronicle* columnist Herb Cain[8], albeit jokingly, conveying a suggestion that St. James might file lawsuits against those who had attempted to lower her personal value and reputation by falsely alleging that she had never been a prostitute.

St. James, who ran a low budget campaign, got 72,003 votes, coming in a close seventh in an "elect six" field of twenty-eight candidates for the position of Member of the Board of County Supervisors. Like three of the six who were elected, she received eight percent of the total vote. None of the six got more than ten percent. In other words, this woman who blatantly ran as a former whore was considered a serious candidate for a serious elected office and undoubtedly was qualified for the job.

What we may be seeing in this unique San Francisco election is the effect of an extension of the invention of photography—the TV camera and the TV set—on social concerns and political candidates, as well as increasing values and powers of one or two generations of genuinely liberated liberal-paradigm-equal women at the ballot box.

The general rule, however, is that under the tort-law paradigm, the client-whore relationship is initiated and then consummated between a person of higher value and a person of lower value, while at the same time, perhaps titillatingly, under the liberal paradigm the two persons meet as equal individuals making free choices, and the whore then submits to being devalued and used for sexual gratification while accepting money in compensation for loss of equality during the use.

If one reflects, this is not unlike what happens daily in the modern workplace and has happened in workplaces throughout the history of civilization. The differences in values between employers and their employees are obvious, and workers submit to being made temporarily unequal for use in manufacturing products or offering services and are compensated.

But unlike the boss-employee relationship, inherent in the client-whore relationship is the history of prostitution itself—the ancient social necessity to label women who engage in sexual prostitution as "whores" at the rock bottom on the social scale to keep "respectable" women in their "proper" places. If the liberal paradigm promotes equality among all women as well as between men and women, the tort-law paradigm gives value to "respectable" women's "reputations" and serves the great amorphous social beast to further subjugate "whores."

Additionally, there is the debaucher-debauchee relationship. The whore accepts commercial payment for sexual gratification services, but included in it is compensation for being debauched, not only in the agreed assignation, but for accepting a permanent debauched and thus degraded status in society. But even within the "pay for sexual gratification services" resides a titillation allowed by the liberal equality paradigm, a psychological "identification" of the whore as a "girl next door," or "looked a lot like the lady across the street," in other words a person equal to those but at the same time usable as a degraded whore and for sexual gratification.

The real girls next door and ladies across the street, of course, had their "reputations" enhanced and their "proper" places in social rankings protected by the relegation of other women to degraded categories of "whores."

Not solely by coincidence, increasing legal equality of women paralleled the development of laborsaving technologies. At the same time, those technologies permitted an increase in the value of individual women from the wealth created by them, from the training and education necessary to use them, and from undercutting genuinely menial "women's work" and thus forcing women a notch upward on social scales.

Inventions of all kinds contributed, but photography did so uniquely and tangentially.

The invention of photography disrupted ancient categorizations and in doing so slowly created avenues for social change.

A century after the invention of photography, pornography was just beginning to show its liberating influences.

Even in its earliest days, the new invention of photography quickly added a new type of "whore" to the ancient social niche, a nonexistent illusive virtual-reality whore, the photographed naked woman, and, possibly more to the point, the photograph of the naked woman.

Virtually a hundred percent of the male or female readers of adult magazines featuring naked women have never knowingly met and never would knowingly meet the pictured undressed women themselves. For all intents and purposes they are simply fantasy images made all the more interesting because photography had captured the authentic undressed appearances of some anonymous real women somewhere out there somewhere.

As authentic images derived from reality, the naked women pictures nevertheless fill the same social function of real whores who are examples of socially defined humiliation, and thus the "fallen women" women who posed for them are quite plainly regarded as such and socially speaking, only worthy of attitudes reserved for whores.

Until pornography was decriminalized and widely distributed in public, a large number of young women who posed in the nude for photographers could expect to socially get away with it. Some of their nude posing might, for instance, genuinely be considered posing for art—although no upper class respectable woman would be likely to pose naked for a photographer, art of not.

In cases of sexually suggestive and explicitly revealing poses that might not pass for art, by and large the only viewers who would see them would be secret ogling men who would have obtained the illegal pictures from underground sources and therefore not be likely to reveal them to many, if any.

It served to keep the pool of viewers confined and small, and unless the nude women were prostitutes who posed naked for pictures in a whorehouse context or catalogue intended to deliberately excite clientele and create business, they were far more anonymous than the present-day ones who appear in *Penthouse*.

As time went on, girly magazines went public on newsstand and drugstore racks. The first girly-magazine girls kept their panties on and their tits titillatingly covered.

Then magazines published completely nude women, but airbrushed out identifiable female sex organs and pubic hair.

Through the mid-1960's more and more was revealed—not to the camera, which captured all just as it appeared, but to the public viewer.

Magazines, girly movie theaters, and peep-show booths were revealing female genitalia, female anuses, female pubic hair, breasts and tits, and clear images of the facial expressions and identities of the women who had posed naked for national publication by the time pornography became decriminalized and public.

But even so, by and large only a handful of people knew who they were and had actually met them. As cases in point, a young woman who performed in soft-core pornography as well as posing in the nude for magazines and M-PEGS on the Internet, and another photographic model who regularly posed in the nude, were near neighbors for years before I found out. Every now and then a female celebrity would pose nude and reveal all for *Playboy* or *Penthouse*, but while the ogling magazine viewers might know her identity, virtually none would ever actually meet her.

By and large, the women who posed naked for girly movies or magazines could change their hairstyles, their facial and eye makeup, and put on clothes so few readers would recognize them with any degree of certainty.

There would be some social stigma if they were recognized. Some jobs would become closed to them. But in those days there were not many higher echelon positions for women where reputation mattered, especially for those without expensive college educations or lacking upper-class family connections. There was virtually no pool of female corporate attorneys to draw from for nude photos or movies, for example, so no female corporate attorney did it on-camera, and we have only guesswork insight now into what might have happened.

Arguably the largest paid occupation of women in the mid-to-late 1960's was waitressing. A waitress found to have posed naked for a girly flick in those times might have to laugh it off, but she might still keep her job if she could take the ribbing and accept the customers knowing what all of her looked like.

On the other hand, a sexy attractive lower class girl who posed naked might secretly reveal it to a lower class boyfriend and land a husband as a result, more or less an upper limit on female career aspirations at the time.

Subsequent years of kids, cleaning, cooking, husband-satisfying and most likely extra-income-job grunt-work drudgery to make ends meet would allow her little time to reflect on this little tidbit hidden away in a corner of her mind.

If she had, she might have weighed those hours or days of comparatively easy work of wiggling her twat and bare fanny in front of a camera to the subsequent years of being used for hard menial work for little or no pay.

Society had defined whoring as degrading and shameful to keep women like her bearing children and subjected to the hard menial tasks involved in child raising, related housekeeping, and other grungy work required to keep the social structure moving and permit women in the upper echelons to have time for study, reflection, and frivolity derived from wealth. And when photography and later motion pictures captured images of women who undressed and cavorted in front of lenses, these naked lower class women were characterized as degraded whores for the same social example reasons.

As the decade of the 1960's entered its last years, the nude-girly magazines and the bare female peep-shows found themselves offering something more to attract customers. The next step in sexually explicit publications and movies was hardcore pornography, at tenuous first sex acts involving lesbian women.

But they were just slightly more explicit photographs and motion pictures of naked females, young women engaging in erotic oral breast arousal, cunnilingus, sometimes in anilingus, and occasionally in dildo vaginal sex—in other words, more of the same authentically photographed and published degraded female "whores."

In the new liberalism and radicalism of this era, feminist activism turned on the increasingly explicit and public pornography phenomenon that used only females.

Perhaps women were more aware of the degraded whore stigma that the great amorphous social beast had created, largely for them.

In addition, no social mechanisms other than cost and criminal law had emerged to handle the new and increasingly inexpensive and easy-to-use technologies of photography and motion pictures, and old criminal law had been overturned by case-law decisions.

After public pornography in Scandinavia had been shown to reduce sex crimes, restraints were removed in the United States. A huge legal public pornography industry grew to meet the new demands.

Moreover, new inexpensive visual image technologies were making it impossible to control with criminal law. The courts saw it and gradually abolished old and largely inappropriate legislation.

Ancient socially fed appetites remained even as criminal control faded, and explicit sexually suggestive girly magazine photos and peep-show movies grew rapidly into hugely profitable legal businesses.

In exploring out into the unknowns, the new feminist rebellion against ancient second-fiddle status—that had existed before the Neanderthals—struck out at pornography.

It was an easy and obvious target. On the face of it there was female degradation. Almost exclusively at that time, the naked porno models were women, and public nudity and sex were socially defined as degrading.

But it was a shot fired at a virtual decoy. Society had created definitions of whores and defined these new published images of naked women as degradation and slipped them into the whore niche. The enemy was deeply ingrained definitions going back to pre-verbal and thus nonverbal beginnings and feelings.

The feminist protest was insistent, however, and it elicited another change. They pointed correctly to the fact that all the publicly exhibited images of naked porno models showed females.

The response of the new and growing pornography industry was to insert fairness and procure male porno models to strip naked and engage in sex with naked females. The motivation was hardly altruism. At very first it sprang from human nature's incurable willingness to experiment, but the experiment instantly showed a profit potential—and, as it turned out, a huge profit potential.

It rapidly expanded. There was a great demand to see naked males and females engaging in sex.

Sex magazines, peep-show booths, and porno movie theaters sprang up to fill the demand and show naked males and females engaging in sex, heavily weighted to coital sex at first, but quickly including fellatio and cunnilingus and then anilingus as suppliers acted to fill demand.

More bizarre sex acts had their limited followings, and when visual image technologies became less expensive, pornography suppliers acted to fill smaller demands of these followings. But these demands never grew.

The great majority of commercially sold pornography images viewed over the last quarter century have been and continue to be reasonably normal images of male and female coital sex, fellatio, cunnilingus, with some titillations of oral female breast stimulation and male and female performances of anilingus on the opposite sex.

Perhaps an irony is that the feminist protest against perceived and socially defined degradation of women in pornography led directly to the present huge male-female sex-act pornography industry.

But it is not a genuine irony. The feminist cause was actually aided by having men strip naked and have their bare behinds and sex-organs examined and associated with their facial identities while engaging in coital and oral sex-acts on-camera for public viewing.

Myths about male superiority melted. Lower class men who appeared naked in sex films were also classified into the "degraded whore" niche in the new sexual equality, and increasing numbers of liberated women, largely in upper classes, snickeringly viewed these men's prostituted bare behinds, male sex organs, and identifiable facial features as they allowed themselves to be debauched by engaging in sex-acts for adult public sport and entertainment. These were the same pleasures once limited to men viewing naked women.

Once having scrutinized a naked male porno "whore's" genitalia and examined his facial expressions and identity while he performed cunnilingus and anilingus on his female costar in a commercial adult movie, a liberated upper class female could hardly stand in the same obedient awe of strutting self-important power-structure males dressed in expensive suits.

And a more realistic perspective on relationships between the sexes and pornography in general emerged from male-female sex acts on camera for public entertainment.

Equally applied stigmas of shame, disgrace, and degradation invited inspection of concepts of power, dignity, respectability, and reputation.

The social niche filled by these images of naked people engaging in sex remained that of the whore, and indeed, many of the naked females who performed these heterosexual sex acts on-camera had indeed already acquired "reputations" and tort-law values as prostitutes.

Identified lower-class males now newly included into the whore niche found they could laugh it off in the same way identified female whores had always done, but it was also the same self-deprecating laugh that admitted acceptance of low status and "whore" stigma and value.

And it is interesting that while a certain social stigma stuck to both male and female hardcore porn performers, the female niche and stigma was still understood as the prime social example of degradation and humiliation.

Males, especially lower class males with minimal education, may have been equally branded, but it less vehemently. By and large they appear to have felt fewer compunctions about stripping naked and engaging in sex on-camera.

In working-class contexts, a few of the male porno models I talked asserted a degree of pride or at least pseudo-pride about their scandalous appearances. It might be difficult for them to run for political office, but few had even vaguely aspired to that anyway.

A few females asserted the same pride. One I talked to while writing this—who has a stable executive husband and kids now—continues to perform in M-PEGs on the Internet and mentioned being mildly unsettled from once-in-a-while seeing for sale the packaged porno movies that she had appeared in for the going rate of $250 each in the early 1980s. But even so, she was generally pleased at what she had done and was doing. But females seem to have had to fight a more uphill battle against confining social definitions of proper female behavior and resulting reputation and status growing out of the degraded whore niche in which they found themselves after deliberate or accidental recognition from performing in hardcore pornography.

And they have had to do so amid liberations and liberating influences that went along with legal public pornography when females were pressing into the male power and money apparatus.

Those lower-class females who performed sex-acts naked in commercial pornography seem to have helped pave the way for educated and upper class female entry into the male power and money structure, but in doing so they denied it to themselves.

Females became military generals, but no female porno whore ever became one. Females became corporate attorneys for major old law firms and power corporations, but no woman who appeared naked sucking male genitalia in a commercial porno movie did. And none would ever be considered for chief executive officer of a giant military-industrial corporation.

On the other hand, since the great female protest, males have widely been able to strip naked and effectively prostitute their bare bodies for pay in commercial pornography, something not possible in the in the naked girly photo era prior to it.

As a result, no male porno whore ever became a military general either. Nor has any male who appeared naked licking female genitalia in a commercial porno movie become a corporate attorney for a major old law firm or been considered for chief executive officer of a major military-industrial corporation.

Public hardcore pornography has leveled the playing field. We now have equal opportunity disrepute and stigma.

In fact, the pendulum seems to have swung the other way. Noted feminist author Susan Faludi[9] visited and interviewed several male porno models, some auditioning, some naked on the set, and some in more everyday circumstances.

She found that even beginning attractive women can get comparatively good compensation in the thousands of dollars—as opposed to beginning men who get a hundred to a hundred-fifty dollars per porn scene—for appearing in porno movies, sex magazine spreads, and porn videos. Women can additionally command amounts like $2500 per week for subsequently showing themselves off as porno models on the nationwide nude-dancer circuit, and it has become an incentive in itself for women to appear in a porno movies and porn videos.

Moreover, a number of women have become porno movie and porn video directors, and Faludi examines one of them, a young woman called Tyffany Million, an "example of a new kind of woman in porn—one who is moving behind the camera." Similar to Candida Royalle's Femme Productions in New York, where porno movies and porn videos are directed and produced by her and other women, Tyffany Million operates a porn video concern called Immaculate Video Conceptions in southern California.

At the same time that women are becoming non-performer successes in the porn business, the men who strip naked and engage in sex on-camera for them are, if one is to accept Faludi's article, a sorry lot—underpaid, largely unsung, and prior to the invention of Viagra, at least, were under great physical and psychological pressures that female porno models do not experience to have both penile erections and to ejaculate on-camera, and without access to the lucrative post-production incomes from the nude dance circuit.

Much of her article revolves around the suicide of one of them, Cal Jammer (stage name for Randy Potes), a male porno model for, among others, female porn producer Tyffany Million. Jammer seems to have accepted the pressures of performance and the life-limitations resulting from categorization as this new pornographic "male whore" and appears to have been comfortable with them. But like so many heavily involved in offshoots of rock and heavy-metal music, troubled romantic situations, and one may suspect dope consumption, he tragically took this way out, interestingly one of very few male or female porno models known to have committed suicide.

The new male porn-performer pseudo-whore was always lower on the internal pornography social scale than the female porno-whore, but possibly now he has slipped lower than the female whore in the general social scale.

By the mid-1990s there had evolved a new dimension to the debaucher-debauchee relationship with a debauched naked male porno model being directed to perform sex-acts on-camera by a respectably attired female film or video director while being recorded by a female camera person in a female-produced porn video or porno movie. Even if the historically weighted female-derisive term "whore" might not apply precisely to the low paid naked male sex-act performer, his tort-law reputation value is certainly far less than that of his female director, his female cameraperson, or his female producer, and probably less than that of any given female whore. Even the lowest ten-dollar-per-trick New York "fast food" massage parlor whore can get a thousand dollars a week, not counting tips[10]. In addition, his pay for stripping and performing sex-acts on-camera is far less than his female costar's.

A little over a century and a half after Daguerre invented photography, its effects on social change have come, among other things, to this.

CHAPTER FIVE

Facsimile and Reality

A female porno star who sprang into international prominence as a result of her paid hardcore film performances at roughly the same time as Linda Lovelace was a college-educated young woman, Fifi Watson, stage-named Mona Watson. Her large blue eyes and all-American-girl look captivated the new and growing feature-length porno movie audiences nationwide and worldwide.

Rumor has it that she had been drawn into porn-performing as a college lark. The prank became a porn epic, the world-famous *Mona* [11] porn film classic, released in 1970 and subtitled *The Virgin Nymph*. The subtitle may have been derived from the story line: Mona will only perform fellatio until her wedding night. Thus Mona is given dramatic license to perform fellatio on-camera for the audience, which in its production year of 1970 had "stag film" shock value as public explicit-sex pornography was still emerging.

If this recollection may not be precisely correct, or may even be wrong in "Mona" Watson's particular case, that scenario is certainly true for a reasonably large number of lesser pornographic performers who appeared unclothed while engaging in sex-acts on-camera. Many, of college age and often touted as "college girls," got into it, knowingly or unknowingly, in something that began in prankish frivolity and then became one of those countless less famous porno movies and porn videos over the last few decades.

I had the good fortune of meeting Fifi "Mona" Watson and talking to her for not much more than a minute once several years after the release of her world-famous hardcore porno film, *Mona.*

But it was only weeks or months after the nationwide release of the last of her feature-length porno films, one that the billing claimed she had also had directed, and apparently did, at least in part.

Porn-film director or not, in this last one, as in her two or three other phenomenally successful X-rated films, Mona outrageously stripped and made public her private parts while she and her several female costars performed fellatio and coitus in a variety different poses and positions and from a variety of camera angles.

Recollection of history leading to the stuffy context of the mid-1960's may assist in grasping the attitudes in which Mona effectively—consciously intentional or not—struck out against with this monumental social protest of performing in the new public pornography. Later regretted or not, it virtually became the main statement of her life.

As the decade of the 60's ended, what were regarded as "stag films" had just come out of the closet to become the bases for the new commercial porn industry.

Stag films were ten-to-twenty-minute black and white hardcore porno movies of adequate clarity and quality for the times to show facial identities and expressions and the naked bodies and sex organs that went with them and unambiguously show the sex acts that were performed. They could be shown with home or classroom 16-mm projectors on folding screens.

Stag films had been, prior to decriminalization in the late 1960's, secretly and illegally shown at snickering, cackling privileged-class, and largely all-male, gatherings since the beginnings of motion pictures at the turn of the century.

Even here, technology had made possible a filtering down the social status ladder of amusement at prostituted nakedness and scandalous public sex exhibits of lower class individuals.

Before the invention of photography, and especially prior to the invention of motion pictures, more jaundiced members of the very upper classes, as we find hinted in DeSade's writings, procured low-class individuals for live sex entertainment, purchasing not only exhibits of their bare flesh and private parts for entertainment, but buying their performance of sex acts in front of audiences dressed in the best high-class styles and fabrics.

And these shows of naked peasants, to put it in terms of the entertainment, literally fucking in front of party audiences would not only have been for the party givers' and partygoers' giggling and tittering amusement but to enhance a certain personal party satiety standing with their fellow upper-class party-givers and allow amused jeering and contempt about the low-class and immorality and juicy gossip about scandal.

Here in the United States these jaundiced upper-class amusements may have been rare in the puritanical north of the pre-Civil War USA, but they must have been widespread in the south where black slavery was the law of the land. One can reasonably presume that over and above the usual and widely known use of slaves for sexual gratifications there must have been merrymaking pastime sessions or "breeding" excuses where naked male and female black slaves were compelled to engage in coital and other sex acts in front of groups of white masters and mistresses and their guests for their snickering amusement.

If the new invention of photography was utilized to record any of this, it is apparently lost now. But early photographs, between the very first experimental ones in the United States as the 1840's dawned and the last days of legal slavery a quarter century later, took a great deal of care to set up, and people posing for them had to remain very still. Photography of an actual sex act would have had to have been contrived and carefully staged, and the somewhat terrorized and deliberately uneducated naked black men and women may not have been able to understand this, or were otherwise unable to remain perfectly still enough in that sexual context.

One can only guess now that still hardcore pornography photographs of black slaves were attempted and that these were not satisfactory enough and later too culturally intolerable to be saved.

A few carefully posed pre-Civil War photographs of naked black slave women and a few naked black slave men were saved and still exist to suggest that slave-owner photographers may have attempted to exploit their human properties in hardcore pornography but found the technical problems too challenging.

And even if they may have had some minimal blurry successes, they were probably hidden away for private viewing pleasures during photographers' lifetimes and deemed too scandalous to family "reputations" and hastily destroyed after their deaths.

Published as *Storyville Portraits*[12], E. J. Bellocq's charming set of historical photographs of nude and seminude female prostitutes taken a generation after the Civil War in the turn-of-the-century southern city of New Orleans still exists to remind us that uses of the new art and technology extended to nudity and sexuality in the deep south. But cameras had improved and photographic techniques had allowed for faster pictures and easier developing and printing by then.

If the New Orleans prostitutes, whose very business was engaging in varieties of sex acts with varieties of different men, would so carefully, pleasantly, and willingly pose naked, one could easily assume that some of them, like prostitutes continue to do, performed in live sex shows with lower class males for selected affluent customers. And if so, attempts must have been made to photograph these sex-acts, or even, on request, male client and prostitute sex acts, and probably female prostitute with female prostitute sex-acts. It is difficult to imagine it not having been tried. But it could not have passed for "art" under the wildest stretches of Victorian-era imagination, and heirs to estates would have seen scandal and would have been blinded to even momentarily conceiving of their historical value, and thus, sadly, destroyed them.

Similarly, post-slavery oppressed poor blacks in the south would probably have continued sporadically to be live sex-act entertainments in antebellum southern manor houses. During these, or more private sessions, they must have been subjects for pornographic photography as the nineteenth century drew to a close—although after legal slavery ended less spectacularly public. But again it is only reasonable conjecture. No photographs seem to have survived.

At this juncture motion pictures were invented. The first public showing of a motion picture was by one of its inventors, Thomas A. Edison, on April 14, 1894, but it was not until 1903 that a credible motion picture with a reel-length storyline was produced by Edwin S. Porter, an Edison cameraman, titled "The Life of an American Fireman." It was followed by the more famous "The Great Train Robbery." The first motion picture theater was opened, for whatever reasons, in Pittsburgh, Pennsylvania, in 1905.

Kenneth Turan and Stephen F. Zito point out in *Sinema; American Pornographic Films and the People Who Make Them* [13] that the first use of the new medium as "pornography" may have been to show a female dancer named Fatima recreating her 1893 World's Fair nude dance on-camera.

They go on to point out that the law took some time to take notice of these uses of the new invention. If we did not yet have motion picture theaters as such, arcades had already acquired peep-show motion pictures utilizing flipping cards (the direct descendants of which are the present ubiquitous adult bookstore video peep show arcades).

"There was no societal control over motion pictures during the first decade of their existence, and early films, especially those designed for peep-show viewing, were often relatively risqué."

Turan and Zito continue on to inform us that the first film censorship, then on a municipal level, came into being in 1908, undoubtedly responding to a growing social awareness and problem.

With or without censorship, motion picture "whore graphs" or "whore stories" had come into being. With a small but still considerable outlay, an entrepreneur could acquire a motion picture camera, spotlights, and film-developing equipment. He could procure males and females willing to strip and perform sex-acts on-camera, invariably prostitutes and low-class males, and shoot a roll or two of black-and-white porno film.

Linda Williams, in *Hardcore; Power, Pleasure, and the "Frenzy of the Visible"* [14], apprises us amateur pornography researchers that The Kinsey Institute for Sex Research has a few of the early explicit sex porno movies. Their earliest accurately dated one is "Am Abend," made in Germany in 1910. Another, "El Satario," was made, according to Kinsey Institute dating, in Argentina between 1907 and 1912. The first American one was "Free Ride" (also known as "A Grass Sandwich") is dated by the Kinsey Institute at between 1917 and 1919, but San Francisco porno movie pioneer and entrepreneur Alex de Renzy, who produced "The History of the Blue Movie" (1970) dates it at 1915.

Whether earlier porno movies may have been produced and lost, dates for surviving projected celluloid motion picture pornography ranging from 1907 to 1919 betray an early enthusiasm. As time went on, porno movies would be produced, numbers of prints copied, and then the films would be sold for on the underground market, probably for considerable more than the going rates at present adult bookstores.

With a roll of less than professionally produced black-and-white pornographic movie film, a less influential member of society than the upper levels of the old aristocracy could show images of bare low-class individuals engaging in sex. As technology continued to improve, costs came down even more, and technical movie-making personnel proliferated, more and more illegal porno movies were produced.

Even though they were illegal, coaches got hold of folding home movie screens and rattling home movie projectors and showed these stag films to professional team members on the highly speculative theory that hormone levels might induce athletic achievement.

Male lodges secretly showed these poorly produced porno movies in jeering sessions, which sometimes included female guests, in which chiding snickers, taunting titter, and ridiculing catcalls communicating aspects of disrespect were exchanged while images of naked porn performers engaged in various sex-acts on-screen.

And middle-class whorehouses used "blue movies" as both added attractions and enhancers of business, even while upper-class whorehouses may have continued to sometimes exhibit live sex-performances by the whorehouse whores and their lower class male associates.

But at the same time, a radio and motion picture censorship apparatus was in place that forbade even remote sexual inferences and sexually loaded words, let alone naked genitalia displays and explicit sex acts.

In this atmosphere the prevailing view was that even photographs simply showing unclothed human bodies were "dirty pictures."

Sexually explicit porno movies, if they were even guessed at, were regarded as "filth." Indeed, even those in the know who sneaked into those secret stag movie screenings regarded them as scurrilously entertaining but still "filthy pictures." In the prevailing attitudes of those times, the laughingstock contemptible whores and counterpart male trash who appeared naked and engaged in sex acts in these photographed "nasty lewd movies" were regarded with amused scorn.

But a decision in the New York Court of Appeals in 1957 concerning a nudist film *The Garden of Eden* (1955) held that nudity *per se* was not indecent, and therefore showing it was not illegal. There followed what some call exploitation films, some call nudie-cutie films, some call girlie pictures where generally limited female nudity was shown.

A new quasi-legal porno movie industry toyed with new limits of both public acceptance and case-law legality, nudity movies retained nomenclature of "dirty movies" in the public mind, and the naked people who performed in them were seen as having risqué reputations.

Limited audience "art" theaters showed these. An early and successful one was *The Immortal Mr. Teas* (Russ Meyer, 1959)

Then, through a series of successful court challenges, a number of increasingly risqué feature films began to be shown in downtown movie theaters. Some were represented as travelogues concerned with the new sexual freedom in Scandinavia, as was *I Am Curious—Yellow,* produced by Vilgot Sjoman at Sandrews Film Studios, Stockholm, 1968. This was followed by Alex de Renzy's *Censorship in Denmark*, and his *History of the Blue Movie* (1970), not only represented as history to mollify the censorship mentality, but a genuine document in itself.

Perhaps motion picture sexuality had been suppressed too much. The sudden penetration of the artificial barrier of censorship of not only public nudity and verbal sexual text but frank explicit sex seems to have burst the bubble, almost as a great national protest demonstration by both porn producers and porn audiences.

A series of unabashed pornographic feature-length movies publicly portraying explicit nakedness and sex, culminating in the classic *Deep Throat* starring Linda Lovelace (summer, 1972) and The Mitchell Brothers classic *Behind the Green Door* starring Marilyn Chamber's (1972), were released in downtown theaters in New York, San Francisco, and Los Angeles, then in major cities.

A year earlier, as mentioned above, another classic feature-length porno movie titled *Mona; the Virgin Nymph* (1970-71) was released in downtown theaters across the country. It was legal, or at least quasi-legal and tolerated. But only a year or two earlier it would have had to be shown illegally in secret snickering "stag movie" situations if it were to be shown at all, and the attitudes surrounding this context were still quite prevalent.

Even so, and even though these three feature-length porno movies quickly became literal genre classics and were at some level intentional satires of prevailing Hollywood and Hollywoodisms, their porno movie appeal clearly lingered in old "stag film" shock value. Mona, Lovelace, and Marilyn Chambers not only publicly exhibited their bare bodies in living color larger-than-life on the silver screen in downtown movie theaters, they all widely performed fellatio, one of the graphic and outrageous "stag film" sex acts.

Mona Watson appeared in at least another major feature-length nationally distributed porno movie not long after her first one, and then she made her last one two or three years later.

This apparently final one was, like the others, professionally and even creatively filmed, and it was sexually explicit. For close to two hours Mona and her bare male and female costars were variously captured performing coital sex, fellatio, and cunnilingus.

Mona's naked male costars performed cunnilingus on her. A viewer can only imagine she enjoyed both directing them to do it and enjoyed the erotic feelings it generated.

But unlike Mona Watson's other porno films—as best I can recall—in this last feature-length skin flick, which she also directed, she amusingly had several of her naked male porno models put their faces in her bare behind and other girls' bare behinds and perform anilingus on-camera in a variety of poses, sex-positions, and camera angles. One can only speculate on prerogatives of this director and the entertaining entanglements of these complex master-servant, buyer-seller, debaucher-debauchee relationships.

But directing herself and others in a pornographic feature film seems not to have been any more adequately lucrative than simply stripping nude and performing sex acts in a porno movie.

Watson was, on that day of our brief meeting, adding to her income on the nude dance circuit, her "porno star" billing being utilized as a box-office enhancement for her striptease act, the showing of images in one or another of her porno movies enlivened by her real bare flesh on stage.

In the early 1970's the great old striptease-dance burlesque houses, complete with live bands and live stand-up comics, were still in operation. Big name striptease artists who made the national burlesque rounds with their fancy gowns and sequined "pasties" and G-strings were still the main attractions.

But by then they were competing with, and losing customers to, the new porno films showing nationally in movie theaters. Theater owners had just found the new explicit sex films more profitable than cowboy pics and musicals.

Movie houses showing sexually explicit porno films had a great economic edge over the complex "money-and-labor-intensive" burlesque-circuit business. Everything was on film, which only had to be shown. There were no personnel problems with performers, no scrambling to replace performers who did not show or became ill, no hotel room costs, no costume problems, no dressing-room requirements, and all the other aspects of live theater production.

As a result, within a decade of the advent of public explicitly filmed pornography, the great old baroque burlesque houses folded. The nationwide support network of performer agents, managers, and theatrical booking machinery either went into peripheral business lines or smaller low-maintenance storefront-size strip joints—that sometimes included sexually explicit live acts or showed filmed and videotaped hardcore pornography—or they retired.

The burlesque theaters are all gone now. Strippers on the small stages of strip-joint bars no longer come out on stage in lavish gowns and costumes and slowly and erotically peel to the ooompah-beat of a live band.

Now they simply wear scanty T-bars or G-strings around the establishments all evening and from time-to-time go up onto a small stage and wiggle their flesh as erotically as possible to ultra-loud canned music for several numbers and then return to the floor to mingle with, and extract "tips" and drink-money from, the customers.

In the early 1970's the Follies Theater on Sixteenth Street in San Francisco, still had a live band, and genuinely talented strippers came out on the great old theater stage in gaudy gowns designed with brightly colored feathers and sparkling sequins.

Like most burlesque theaters, the Follies had long-unused film projection booths and screens and had latched onto a mix of showing X-rated feature films and presenting striptease dancers in order to stay abreast of the times and thus financially afloat.

On that day in the early 1970's when I had my one and only ever-so-brief verbal exchange with her, Mona Watson was stripping at the Follies burlesque theater. The added box office attraction was the showing of—as I recall now—this last of her X-rated films and her latest addition to the rapidly growing worldwide 35 mm pornographic feature-film library, one of three or four porno movies featuring her bare flesh with "Mona" in the title.

There was a bar next to the Follies burlesque theater where strippers went to cool off. Mostly male bar patrons slipped in, often from the burlesque house next door, to mingle and chat with them.

On opening day for the weekly big-name striptease-artist attraction the bar was where the strippers met media people to garner some publicity.

Mona Watson was not only the striptease-artist attraction of that week, she had years earlier gained worldwide fame as a porno star. And the most recent porno movie she had appeared in was showing at the burlesque house in conjunction with her striptease act. As a result, she had talked to a number of media people in the bar the first day of her performance-schedule.

The hardened and jaundiced entertainment newsies had amused themselves with talking to the woman they had seen live and naked on stage as well as naked and performing sex acts on film, with a few of them writing brief titillating risqué articles for entertainment sections.

When I ambled into the bar around midweek of her striptease billing, the news people had done their thing and gone. Around the bar were scattered male customers who, like me, had watched her striptease performance and seen her most recent porno movie.

We had just watched the flickering silver screen showing her naked and engaging in oral and coital sex larger than life—as well as those amusing acts of anilingus she toutedly directed the bare male porno actors to perform with their faces and tongues in her behind.

Then we had been entertained by her teasingly stripping naked and baring it all for us on the stage of that great old baroque theater in her burlesque dance routine.

Mona sat at the bar decently dressed, as I recall in street clothes, but possibly in the costume gown she wore at the outset of her striptease act.

She was sitting for a second alone with her drink. I think the gentleman or other stripper she was with had gone to the bathroom.

I don't recall the precise conversation now, only a gist of it, so I must paraphrase for the flavor.

She sat there with a faint cynical smile that seemed to betray a kind of resentment, the resentment that any legitimate factory employee might feel at having to do sometimes slightly undignified things for a meager living.

But she sat there after having been, in the eyes of most of her beholders, paid to disgrace herself on stage and on film. She was a bright, sophisticated, and sensitive woman. While she sipped her drink, she had to be aware of her employment position as a professional sex object, an educated woman who had eaten from the biblical tree of knowledge of shame and degradation and had made herself into a sex-industry amusement-character.

I glanced around the sleazy and dingy bar.

Female strippers who had not performed in X-rated movies, a few other women of unknown occupation, and male patrons mostly there from the burlesque theater sat on the barstools nursing drinks. All had their own secret ideas about her, and I can only try now to vaguely remember mine.

To convey a feeling for her perceptions and emotions as well as mine as representative of audience, I have to emphasize that virtually all of us at the bar had seen her at one time or another on the big movie screen, larger than life, "debauched" (in the sense of this treatise) and naked. Moreover, to utilize terms of pornography and offer a flavor of the general ambiance, we had all watched her fucking, sucking cock, getting her twat sucked, and getting her anus licked in a porno movie. She sat there knowing that.

Then, following our viewing of her porno movie, we had been amused with her dancing out on stage in the great old theater and peeling off her gaudy striptease costume to publicly expose her bare body and private parts for the inspection of a largely male, fifty-to-a-hundred member, audience.

Then she had further entertained us with several postures that flaunted her immodesty, such as that in which she further advertised her debauchedness by kneeling naked on stage with her legs spread apart and her bare ass toward the audience. Such a pose could only have been cooked up to call attention to her ass, anus, and twat with slow sensual movements of her shapely bare behind in the spotlights while several in the audience snickered, cackled, and guffawed. A few of them let out catcalls, at her artful display of effective self-degradation.

And she sat at the bar knowing we had seen her doing that, too. There was, of course, nothing that she could do to change it. As with a variety of people, from nude models to reputed prostitutes to porno stars, disrepute resulting from her socially-defined "disreputable" activities had, of mental-emotional necessity, become of less importance to her than to others who engaged in exchanges, dealings, or relationships with her. It had become, as with all who had participated in so-called "disreputable" activities, just something else to integrate into her personality and live her life around.

I remember looking over this young pretty blue-eyed all-American girl as she sat there decently dressed. Unlike most of the other American girls high on a pedestal, she had just finished flauntingly exhibiting her bare boobs, her twat, her anus, her buttocks to me and the others in the burlesque audience.

Moreover—and I must utilize the terminology of pornography to convey the ambiance and its subpsyche shock intentions in many anecdotes—I had watched her and her female costars very publicly naked in porno movies shown there and in downtown theaters sucking guys' cocks and getting fucked by them. I had watched her writhe in erotic pleasure while different guys ate her pussy.

I had just come from watching some of those guys, as I recall now—decades later, and to put it in the shock-term of pornography—lick her asshole on-screen while she lustily yelled at them to keep licking it and stick their tongues into it. If memory of specific porno models fails it is because the porno movie did contain similar scenes of anilingus, which she purportedly directed. But I do vaguely recall this scene of her, and at any rate she had been naked in other scenes in that movie equally pornographic.

She took a sip of her drink and shot me a thin sheepish smile.

I returned a slight smile and looked her over with a mixture of admiration and condescension.

She was, on one hand, a world-famous figure who had voluntarily and courageously participated in a project she knew would break down social barriers to make way for the new, and I was a nothing-nobody with a part-time job afraid to do much more in life than observe.

On the other hand, she had just exposed her naked body to me and a theater full of others for our entertainment and had, among other things, purposefully displayed her bare behind, her asshole, and her twat to me and the others in an erotic striptease routine.

In addition, I had just come from watching her and her female porno movie costars naked and fucking, sucking cock, getting their pussies eaten, and getting their anal orifices licked, bigger than life on the silver screen.

In the prevailing subtext attitudes of the times, she was thus the latest slut of a smut movie who had additionally just stripped naked on stage to offer erotic views of her boobs, twat, buttocks, and even focus attention on her asshole and further advertise her scandalous reputation. Almost three decades later, in the present Internet-porn era, these attitudes may have changed slightly, but the terminology used to express the attitudes is still commercially useful. Literally millions of porn images are now accessed with mouse-clicks from almost endless lists with terminology like slut, smut-slut, whore, fucking whore, bitch cocksucking bitch and other uses of the language of pornography to describe sex-acts that they had performed on-camera for viewer amusement.

What she was commercially selling and being sold as still sells. Back then, of course, attitudes were emerging from dark ages, and Mona did not have the scandal-diluting benefit of sharing company with millions of different naked human beings who had performed sex-acts on-camera for commercial publication. Nor had humdrum and ho-hum of billions of distributed images of their facial identities, bare flesh, sex-organs, and sex-acts sapped shame and scandal of their significance. Public porn was new, and she was still one of the very few, and far more scandalous and singled out for it.

I had seen a couple other people in the bar, including, as I now recall, a well-dressed woman, pat her on the shoulder and tauntingly, and in mocking voices, tell her, "Saw your show. You were pretty good."

It was, of course, to tease her that they knew she was that porno star and that they had their fun with the appearance of her publicly exhibited private parts in the strip show. But there was showmanship in her show. She was a creative stripper and nude performer and put on good libidinous and sensuous performances on and off camera. And she had a rare, charming, and communicative personality. Her fame came as much as or more from those attributes than the mere public images of her shapely bare physical attributes.

"Thanks," she had said several times in a tone of voice that let them know she understood the intent was something less than a compliment.

I did something like looking at my half-full glass of beer and glancing at her nearly finished drink as if to assess the amount of time she might continue sitting at the bar one stool away from me.

"Pretty good strip-act," I told her, as best I can remember now a couple decades later.

"Thanks," she replied with a cynical knowing bland voice.

"I enjoyed your porno movie," I said.

"Glad you liked it," she returned.

"Fun making it?" I ventured.

She looked me over to size it up. "No," she said somewhat sourly. As I vaguely recall, A faint hint of bitterness glared from her eye.

I was not sure whether it was from weariness with repeated inquiries into her stripping and porno movie performances with their inclinations toward teasing, or whether she was reflecting back with a touch of fury at those moments when she was naked and engaging in sex-acts on-camera—and its resulting world-famous very public, in the sense of this essay, debauchery.

"No?" I asked.

She shot me a look of resentment.

"You going to make more porno movies anyway?" I asked with a genuine interest in knowing, but also a teensy bit to tease.

She scowled slightly. She apparently did not care much for the direction of my inquiry was taking or its intrusion into her plans and life. But she was a sex-industry performer, and I was a customer. She flashed a quick perfunctory smile before looking at me with a serious glare.

"No more movies," she told me in the most definite of tones.

"Why?" I asked her.

She looked away thoughtfully for a second, then looked back with a sigh.

"You know what it's like to have it frozen in celluloid for eternity?" she asked.

"It's done," I replied. "What's the harm in making another?"

"No more!" she emphatically told me.

Her companion came back and ended it.

"Ready to go?" Mona asked him.

"Yeah," the companion told her. "Let's go."

She slid her now decently covered famous fanny off of the barstool.

"Show time. Got to be going," she told me nicely. And they wandered toward the door while I contemplated the movement of her fine public fanny and pictured it as I had seen on stage and in her porno movies, bare. They went out and toward the Follies Theater for her next striptease performance.

Contrasting with her wanton stage and screen performances and public porno mega-star image, she struck me as a well educated, kind, and refined woman, a quiet person with a good mind and great capacity for philosophically reflecting on meanings in life.

Her somewhat irritated response may have been to my unintended mocking tone when I had asked her if she would ever make another porno movie. But I don't think so.

Damage to her "reputation" and the tort-law value of the "property of her person and its images" had already been done. When I pried, she hinted that beyond a resigned resentment of her porno star reputation, the processes of major 35 mm porno movie production had made her too uncomfortable to make another. That may be reading a lot into a few words, but thoughts were also communicated by tone of voice and body language.

And later another minor porno model confirmed my suspicions. It was less fun that it seemed. In those days a feature-length major porno-movie-filming situation in a professional studio was very public in itself.

Unlike modern video productions, the 16-mm or 35-mm color film feature-length porn epics of the early 1970's required full male and female staffs. There were grips, gaffers, directors, full camera crews, lighting technicians, sound boom operators, sound technicians, electricians, secretaries, script supervisors, and even if they may have doubled at jobs, there were others such as janitorial staff people, receptionists, and investors looking in on during the filming.

The motion picture equipment itself was imposing. Thirty-five and even sixteen-millimeter cameras were much larger than even modern professional video cameras. Cameras had to be mounted on vehicles. This, in turn, required filming to be done on sets constructed in large drafty echoing warehouse-like studios under banks of professionally arranged large spotlights.

Lighting technicians had to take constant sets of readings to readjust lens settings at changes of focus, distance, and angles. Sound technicians had to constantly rearrange sound booms. Other personnel had to keep track of high-power electrical systems and wires needed to operate equipment, and thick black electrical cables were strewn like spaghetti all over the set floor and required more personnel to move, plug and unplug, and rearrange. It was enough to make hardened decently dressed actors experience tinges of timidity, let alone a naked young woman engaging in sex-acts on-camera amid it all.

In addition, since major porn productions were still a novelty, there were invited and even uninvited male and female guests, sometimes minor news people, mostly out of curiosity, and other mixed-gender onlookers.

On a porn set in a studio there could on rare occasions be, I venture to guess from hazily remembered sources of input, as many as fifty people looking on in one capacity or another.

At very least there were always a dozen-or-so core male and female film production people necessary to the enterprise.

Thus all three or four of her feature-length porn acting gigs had required Mona to be naked and performing sex acts not only in front of a camera but in front of dozens of decently dressed and ogling onlookers.

And it was not for just an hour or two and then wrap it up as it is now in porn video productions. She had to be with all of these people on the movie set daily for weeks, even months, in these 35-mm feature-length color motion picture productions.

So virtually every production day that she would go to her "lewd" work and take off all her clothes, sometimes on-camera, off-and-on for hours she would be naked and engaging in sex acts in spotlights on-camera in front of a crowd of ogling onlookers. Then at other times like lunch breaks or when crews were shooting other sequences, she would get decently dressed, or at least draped, and quite naturally socialize and chat with these production coworkers and onlookers.

Even all the fawning "star attention" that was showered on her could not have altered the daily dishonor of stripping naked and fucking or performing other sex-acts on-camera, followed by dressing for lunch or breaks or whatever and mingling and talking with any number of the dozens people who had ogled her nakedness and public degradation, and then stripping naked in the spotlights in front of them and performing sex acts like, to use the vocabulary of pornography to convey ambiance, sucking cocks, getting her cunt sucked, or fucking on-camera while they snickeringly watched her humiliating antics again.

If after a while it may have lost its shame and embarrassment, it still must have been awkward. But I can only guess.

She could have been quite serious about retiring from hardcore porno movie performing when she briefly chatted with me. Whatever her reasons, as far as I know Mona Watson never made another feature-length porno movie after that.

I heard that she may have made some "loops," after her last feature-length porno move. A loop is porn industry terminology for a short (ten or fifteen minute) 8-mm or 16-mm porno movie consisting solely of nude sex acts and without even a contrived perfunctory story line. They were generally more graphically and continuously "obscene" because they were largely meant, in those days before videotape and VCRs, for showing in peep-show booths for a quarter per one-minute play, and only continuous and graphic "obscenity" and degradation kept the quarters dropping into the coin boxes.

But the "loops" may have been shot prior to her last feature-length porno movie or printed from "outtakes" filmed during feature-length productions and not used in them. At any rate, Mona Watson retired from performing in porno movies around that time and never made another "Mona" series feature-length porno movie.

She continued for a considerable time after her last skin flick, however, to strip on the burlesque circuit, even long after her very pretty and attractive bare young body had grown older and increasingly flabby. And now, approaching her old age, there she is—with a touch of irony considering our brief conversation—eternally pretty, young, and girlishly attractive frozen in celluloid and copied that way onto modern videocassettes.

CHAPTER SIX

Chastened and Exhibited

As best I can now recall, I last saw her naked-and-no-longer-all-American-girlish body dancing in the late 1970s the upstairs combined porno movie theater and strip-show stage of the Sutter Street Theater in downtown San Francisco, where Arlene Elster and Lowell Pickett had helped break the explicit-sex-act-movie taboo almost a decade earlier by producing and showing the first explicit "X-rated" movies in the early 1970s.

Less than a decade later the rebellious social protest of those early heady days of explicit-sex public pornography was largely gone and the Sutter Street Theater had slipped into strip-joint routines and even something close to sleaze.

Like the others in its stable of a half-dozen to a dozen daily female strippers, Mona went through an obligatory routine strip act, including those strip-joint postures of getting on all fours with, to put it in its own terms, her bare ass presented toward the audience and thus calling the generally male, but sometimes mixed male and female, audience's attention to her bare buttocks, shown-off cunt, and displayed asshole as she slowly wriggled and writhed her naked body to the beat of canned music. Her decade-older age was beginning to show. On paid live exhibition was her no-longer-flat tummy and mature slightly sagging breasts. Her world-famous bare behind and the renowned shapely thighs supporting it were showing early signs of the curse of cellulite. May be good that we do what we do when we do it?

She was still a sexy, shapely, and attractive woman, but the star attraction was her internationally famous X-rated movie-star name. And it drew a larger audience than the Sutter's regular shows, and at least the couple times I was there, a mixed male-and-female one. Some of these must have been either her many movie fans or the curious who had to see her famous bare flesh live.

I also recall, that evening, being amused at seeing a wad of fresh sperm and semen clinging to the pubic hair by one of the strippers' cunts as she exhibited her ass on all fours to the audience as part of her act. As I try to think back decades later, I am fairly certain that it was one of the other strippers and not Mona.

But Mona and all the strippers made the same down-on-all-fours or lying-on-their-tummies exhibition of their behinds to the audience as part of their acts, so it might have been.

At any rate, the naked stripper with the wad of cum had clearly—to use terminology suitable for the ambiance of happening—been fucked just prior to coming on stage.

Strippers in these new small clubs could earn bonuses as prostitutes, even between strip acts, and the semen still on this woman's sex organs and pubic hair in that context certainly hinted at a quick trick, but she may have just fucked her husband or boyfriend. She either wanted to show it off or was unaware.

As the bump and grind strip routines wound down to the end, the movie projectionist arrived at the booth in the back.

Mona had emerged from back stage decently dressed in, as best my memory can now dredge up, her tight-fitting shimmering satin striptease gown. If it was not the gown, then it was street clothes with a tight-fitting skirt or tight jeans.

She was standing by the strip joint door to the stairs that went one flight down to the street. The strippers were all leaving for their hour break during the porno movie showing.

The lights dimmed and the feature-length skin flick came on-screen to entertain the audience, not, this time, one of Mona's. She had evidently lost control over copyrighted showings of porn she was in.

I knew she could not possibly remember me from two-minute chat almost a decade earlier, but I was curious to follow it up.

I got up and went to the turnstile by the door. I remember saying something to her, a "hello" or something like that.

She snapped back something and gave me a cold shoulder. So I shrugged it off and went to the counter and got myself a snack or popcorn. Everyone has a bad day.

I recall glancing back at her, at her pretty face and cute coquettish mouth, the same mouth and tongue that had so mellowly stimulated male sex organs in porno movies some years earlier. I vaguely remember a clipped retort and remarking to myself that her mouth and tongue now had a sharpness.

My memories are fuzzy. I recall an expensively dressed gentleman who had apparently been in the audience escorting one of the strippers out of the strip joint with a sexually suggestive disrespectful feeling around her behind through the sleek shimmering striptease-act gown fabric in a blatant public nonverbal mocking taunt.

I had gone to the joint that afternoon or evening solely to see Mona, so Mona was one of the strippers. But I only have a vague quarter-century-old impression that the stripper whose fanny was being felt was Mona. Whether it was or not really does not matter for my argument here. It was hardly a unique experience for strippers and their male escorts, and it is difficult to imagine that Mona did not experience it a number of times.

Whoever the stripper was, she non-verbally replied submission to it and advertised acceptance by pretending to ignore it. She felt his hand feeling her behind and probably saw others winking and smirking, so her pretending made its own statement about role-playing.

The middle-age gentleman shot the young woman a grin at her surrender and contemptuously grabbed and squeezed one of her buttocks.

She returned a scowl but said nothing about his hand feeling her ass and made no effort to move her rear end away from it while looking straight ahead with a blank stare.

And scowling stripper and grinning gentleman departed the lounge area that way, with his hand insolently pawing and squeezing one of her buttocks.

It probably was not Mona but one of the other strippers. Only a vague impression that it might have been Mona now lingers after something like two decades.

And whether that stripper was moonlighting as a whore or not, strippers did. And the cute little episode illustrates the whore image coming into play. One can easily imagine, true or not, that all of the strippers, including Mona, daily dealt with prostitution propositions and accepted like or similar assertions of disrespect.

So it occurred to me that the stripper and the well-dressed middle-age gentleman might have been heading somewhere to lighten his wallet so he might deposit a wad of semen on or in her, or so my strip-act stimulated imagination thought.

Again, it could just as easily have been the stripper's husband or boyfriend and they enjoyed sharing something special with the blatant public ass-feeling. But I did not see it that way. Perhaps she gave him a scowl. Something she did seemed to non-verbally communicate that while she had surrendered to being regarded as a whore and had acquiesced to being led off to be used as one, more or less with everyone's knowledge, she accepted the insult as part of a package of whoring degradation for something of value in return and was playing out that part.

The flagrant ass-feeling intended to non-verbally express mockery, scorn, and degradation was culturally defined. Had it been between team members on a playing field, it would have said something quite the opposite. Verbal and nonverbal expressions require contexts.

The male half of male-dominated society may or may not be more responsible for culturally defining the degraded whore, but the designation requires both genders to participate in maintaining the social order.

The well-to-do gentleman publicly feeling the stripper's buttocks to intentionally degrade her was only doing his deeply ingrained social duty to keep the focus on a fallen woman's degradation, and I would say, all in all, he was doing it in a kindly way with his hand tenderly sliding around the stripper's behind and teasingly giving one of her buttocks some gentle squeezes.

To say it was his male prerogative misses the point. It was his power-and-wealth class-status prerogative. Having the wealth and power to acquire a whore for use in sexual gratification was included in the package of his upper-class-male rewards for promoting and supporting the social order.

Lower-class males might occasionally receive the same reward, but they function to keep the rudimentary social machinery going rather than promoting and guarding the social order, and they thus live on survival incomes without frills for excesses. For most lower class men society keeps the cost of acquiring "fallen women" high enough to be an infrequent reward rather than a regular amusement pastime.

And the "fallen women" available to lower class men are those socially defined as whores. Males higher in the social strata can get "mistresses," who are themselves, largely as a result, a bit higher up from rock bottom in the female strata.

A "mistress" is for sexual gratification rather than procreation, so they are still "fallen women." But a lower class mistress receives a certain amount of respect and creature comfort from her upper class male procurers. And the arrangement has a degree of permanence where genuine long-term affection is exchanged.

Down at the bottom, whores are temporarily procured to be used, psychologically as well as physically, for sexual gratification, including the whole gamut of Freudian sexual gratifications, and then released to be used for sexual gratification by another customer.

As civilization progressed and upper class and then middle class women gained degrees of independence and sequestered small social niches of wealth and power for themselves, a lower class male counterpart to "fallen women" emerged, the gigolo.

But in the male-female social dichotomy, the female analogy to a gigolo is closer to a mistress. There are and have been successful male whorehouses where females temporarily procured males for use in sexual gratification, but these are rare, partly due to the differences in male and female sexuality and limited temporary male sexual capacity.

The "fallen man" stigma is applied with far less vehemence and even winked at in the case of gigolos because males have traditionally been permitted under-the-table promiscuity, and males have only peripheral parts to play in bearing and nurturing children.

Gigolos, therefore, rank above culturally defined-as-degraded female whores, who are classified at the bottom. And while the new heterosexual male porno models had been tenuously classified along with naked women who posed for cameras into the social "pseudo-whore" niche and could thus be socially scorned as whores for the first time in history, there still seems to be slightly less of a stigma.

And yet in reality, as we have seen, female whores can live better and more comfortable lives than lower class respectable women and even sometimes enjoy those brief periods during their employment where the stimulation of sexual-pleasure nerve endings come into play.

To keep its respectable women doing hard mean dull respectable things, any given society has to attach shame, disgrace, and degradation definitions to whores, rock bottom "fallen women" social strata classifications to them. And when those do not wholly suffice, the social control that goes with criminal penalties and criminal records and reputations.

Degraded female whores are, as we have seen, social inventions, examples to keep lower class women in line. And thus society insists on male as well as female duty to advertise and call attention to this socially defined disgrace and degradation of whores.

So the well-healed upper-strata gentleman feeling and squeezing the lower class stripper's buttocks was only fulfilling his social obligation to call attention to degradation. And the stripper, for her part, behaved like a perfect whore and accepted it while pretending to ignore it.

If this particular stripper was not Mona, it was this kind of attitude and behavior that she would have had to face daily during her striptease gig.

I fuzzily recall hearing from others that Mona had become unhappy with and down on them, too. One can see why. If the incident above happened to a stripper other than her, it still illustrates realities peripheral to the stripping and porno modeling professions and what she daily had to put up with and the opportunities for prostitution always open to her.

Her strip-act in the new small-scale and by then sleazy strip joint betrayed what seemed to me to be an unfortunate turn in Mona's life. It never appeared to improve for her beyond those heady days as one of the world's most famous and best loved young beautiful porno stars.

If she had made another porno movie, might she have made more money? Her bare image would have been permanently preserved in celluloid again, but probably life would not have been any worse for her.

If a good manager had gotten her a book deal, a talk-show and speaking circuit tour, several more porno movies to appear in for better pay, a better cut of the box office from her world-famous porno movies that she had already appeared in, and any number of other things an entertainment manager might be able to get, Mona Watson could possibly have been happier.

But who knows. And I certainly have no way of second-guessing a history that has already happened. She did it her way, and that's all that really counts.

Mona may have fought the amorphous social beast and won some change. But she seemed at that time to have lost a personal battle to find meaning and comfort in it.

The ancient amorphous virtual beast that had evolved from proto-human into human society had defined shame, and she appears to have experienced some of that anciently defined and perhaps no longer appropriate shame and to have reacted with a touch of bitterness.

Long after the first proto-human woman as symbolized by Eve had covered her twat and bare behind in some real Pliocene Garden of Eden, Mona had removed her clothing and publicly exposed her twat and bare ass while flauntingly engaging in varieties of sex acts on camera, and people all around the tiny Spaceship Earth zooming through space had been entertained by seeing it on movie screens in the early 1970's. And some continue to be entertained by her defiant naked antics on videotapes even today, as time marches on and technology and society have considerably changed.

As I left that makeshift upstairs strip joint and porno movie house where she was striptease dancing that evening in the mid-1970's, rightly or wrongly I carried away an image of an unhappy naked middle-age woman exhibiting her slightly bulgy bare body for the snickering entertainment of mostly men, but some couples, who may or may not have remembered her for her defiance of the great amorphous social beast and maybe appreciated the changes in it that she had so courageously, as it were, helped to initiate.

Even if she had grown bitter about being used, about growing old, and about having become one of the first famous globally debauched porno movie women the world had ever known, with nowhere to really hide from it, she still had done it and changed the social structure.

Being, like Linda Lovelace, one of the first world-famous porno queens, Mona Watson had to wiggle her way through a hostile social climate. There was no real supportive structure in place and no tradition to fall back on to offer help and guidance for either of these famous early women of professional feature-length pornography whose bare bodies and sexual antics had been viewed larger than life on silver screens all over the world.

Hollywood, which pornography parodied and mimicked, had agents and managers for its stars. But legitimate considerations of "reputation" and fallout consequences kept them away from porno stars, who were thus left to drift or be represented and managed by charlatans or incompetents.

So they drifted in a hostile social sea which had sharks of "shame" and "disrepute" and "disgrace" and "embarrassment" swimming around. They seem to have become disillusioned with themselves even though it was not constructive. If so, disillusionment may have led to bitterness.

They had been loosely categorized as "whores" in an etymological sense used here because slow-reacting word-based society behaving like a great social beast had not yet assimilated a category for nude models and sex-performers captured by lenses of all-too-recently invented cameras and they thus had to suffer with the "whore" stigma while the beast gradually adapted over lifetimes.

CHAPTER SEVEN

Shame Shame Shame

If Watson and Lovelace felt shame and this resulted in some expression of rejection of what they did, it is quite understandable. Certainly for a time they had become bigger stars than Hollywood's contemporary offerings. As movie stars, rather than as a result of being porno models, they lost their private lives.

A male porno star of roughly the same historically brief period of big-name Hollywood-aping stars was John C. Holmes. Holmes's character was borrowed for the 1998 Academy Award-winning mainstream movie *Boogie Nights*, which may illustrate a growing acceptance of pornography and its performers and personnel by mainstream America. Possibly to his regret, Holmes became a big-name porno star. Like all movie stars, mainstream and pornographic, fame brought on fans, fandom, a glare of constant publicity, and a reduction of personal private life to nil.

He is quoted in *Sinema; American Pornographic Films and the People Who Make Them* [15] as responding to a question about his private life, "Private-life-wise, I can't have a private life. Very difficult, very difficult."

The media frenzy eventually died out as the novelty wore off, and the "star" system, which had been part of an industry and media satire on Hollywoodisms and their reflections of American values and the American Dream, shrank to an internal industry value and rating arrangement. But in that span of maybe only five or six years in the early 1970s, worldwide pornographic mega-stars had been created. The few porno movie performers who were spotlighted this way not only had to deal with the problems and lack of privacy from being public figures but the ever-present scurrilous innuendo resulting from, to borrow the famous newspaper typo, being internationally known pubic figures.

Lovelace, set adrift without support, later fell in with groups of well-intentioned people who nevertheless had never shared her experience and as a result could not understand her needs.

These people were deeply immersed in the old order where social values such as shame, respect, dignity, degradation, and disgrace manipulated their lives. In falling in with them, Lovelace had to accept their values and when she did, struck out at those she felt had embarrassed, disgraced, and shamed her.

In socially conservative traditional terms, her manager and the porn industry had, of course. So it became a truism.

Linda Lovelace, born Linda Marchiano, daughter of a New Jersey cop, wrote an autobiographical book titled *Ordeal* in which she claimed that she had been forced into performing in hard core pornography by her husband, Chuck Traynor. It was immediately seized upon as a weapon against pornography in general by feminist forces with old-time concepts of decency and their conservative Christian allies.

Lovelace had every right to counterattack. But her counterattack was sometimes dishonest and left false impressions.

Embarrassed or not, one impression Ms Lovelace sought late in her sadly short life to create was false, and she had to know it.

Even, as ACLU president Nadine Strossen points out in her book *Defending Pornography*, if Lovelace had been forced to participate in hard core pornography, it was not by pornographers themselves but by her husband, Chuck Traynor, who had no other connection to pornography or the porn industry other than through his wife Linda. If Lovelace's claims are true, Traynor was simply one of an unfortunately very large number of brutal wife-beating husbands, and Lovelace was simply one of an unfortunately very large number of domestic violence victims. There are far far more of those than actresses who have, voluntarily or involuntarily, appeared in camera-based pornography.

Strossen points out that in her book *Ordeal*, Lovelace tells of finding a temporary refuge from her husband's brutalities on the pornography sets where she stripped and engaged in sex-acts on-camera—and with the pornography people who treated her well while she was there.

Linda—understandably if her claims are true—eventually divorced Chuck Traynor, and Traynor, a gun shop owner in Las Vegas, went on to marry another (by then) world famous mega-porno-star, Marilyn Chambers, star of, among other porno smash hits, the Mitchell Brothers epic "Behind the Green Door."

If Lovelace had been forced to strip and perform in hard core pornography, she is by far an exception rather than the rule.

Hardcore porn models and performers—however embarrassed or not embarrassed they may be on-camera or afterward—strip and engage in sex acts in front of cameras voluntarily, and in most cases for pay. Many, if not most, do it with exhibitionistic enthusiasm and delicious defiance, reveling in their parts in the great gossipy social game of debaucher-debauchee that came with civilization. Others need or want the money and do it for the pay and thus may have complex qualms and subsequent regrets. And some may be cajoled into it, but anticipating sexual pleasures and being centers of attention, strip and engage in sex-acts on-camera without being terribly disinclined. Virtually none are actually forced.

The huge global pornography industry would dry up, or be quickly dried up, if forced naked porn performances were the rule—indeed, if even a tiny fraction of porno models were found to have been forced to strip and perform sex acts.

Lovelace, like most porno models, financially benefited only minimally from her performances, as opposed to the producers, distributors, theaters, and others in the porn industry who as a whole made millions of dollars from the amusement of porn customers at Lovelace's flesh and fellatio. She certainly had a legitimate gripe. Gerald Damiano, who had produced Linda Lovelace's porn epic "Deep Throat" for about $25,000 in 1972, reaped millions from it. Lovelace got nothing more than close to minimum wage for stripping naked and performing sex-acts on-camera for literally all the world to see.

But in retrospect one has to wonder whether her financial embarrassment and anger over such minimal shares of eventual huge worldwide box office receipts was caused by poor entertainment representation and management.

If so, it was sadly one of those hindsight things that often accompanies new commerce and industry and not her fault.

Putting aside the possibility that Lovelace may, indeed, have been coerced into stripping and performing lewd acts on-camera, she certainly entered into a fledgling industry that was making its own rules and precedents as it went along.

Stag films and blue movies had been around since the invention of motion pictures. But suddenly in the late 1960's the lid came off. American pornographers began producing sexually explicit movies for adult public screening.

The leading edge of these American explicit sex movie enterprises was in San Francisco, California, in the late 1960's. The peace-and-love hippie movement had hit its peak with the 1967 Summer of Love in the

Haight-Ashbury and Golden Gate Park and was fading. Local pornographers had indeed capitalized on the free-sex aspect of the young people's movement and had garnered a number of rebellious attractive middle class young women to strip for nudie "beaver loops."

But by 1969 the ongoing brutal war in Vietnam and the US government's illegal covert activities against any shape or manner of war objection had radicalized the protest movement and turned it toward counter-violence.

The Mitchell brothers, Artie and Jim, opened a nudie "beaver loop" theater on O'Farrell Street in San Francisco on, Friday, July 4, 1969. For years other theaters like the Peerless on Third Street (about where Love Bakery, the spark for Mark Twain's short story "Aurelia's Unfortunate Young Man" had been located a hundred years earlier, now itself torn down and part of the Convention Center park) and the Paris (also torn down, and now the only park specifically for drunks in the world) on Sixth Street showing short films of scantily clad, and later completely nude, women cavorting sensually and suggestively on-camera.

When they began showing "full vaginal nudity" the law bore down with all its force. On Friday, July 25, 1969, precisely three weeks after opening, the Mitchell Brothers Theater was raided. Three weeks after that the Peerless Theater was raided.

The resulting eventual court defeats of the authorities paved the way for explicit sex to be shown.

At first this, too, was illegal.

But the emerging "Big Three" of San Francisco's porn industry, The Mitchell Brothers of the O'Farrell Theater, Alex de Renzy of the Screening Room Theater on Jones Street, and Arlene Elster and Lowell Pickett of the Sutter Street Theater, went ahead in spite of current interpretation of the law.

They were raided. The authorities eventually lost court cases. And the quasi-legal public showing of explicit sex films became a reality in 1970.

Experiments in Europe, especially Denmark, which had legalized written pornography in 1967 and further legalized obscene pictures in 1969—allowing for the only large-scale national study ever done to evaluate the effects of pornography on criminal behavior prior to legalization and post-legalization—had found a drop in crime following legalization of pornography. Influenced by this, as well as a growing realization that new and increasingly less expensive and untraceable photographic and videographic hardware made enforcement of obscenity laws concerning pornography impossible to enforce, a new American film rating system was put into effect that allowed publicly shown and sold "adult" X-rated movies showing full nudity and explicit sexual acts as long as children were excluded from audiences.

As this was still in the early stages and in fact still being tested and protested both in the industry and in the courts, Lovelace was given a part in late 1971 in a third-rate sexually explicit movie, "Deep Throat," released in New York in the presidential election year, 1972.

No one could have known then that the film would become—in terms of audience and box-office receipts—a towering success, and for decades afterward a porn classic and an erotic epic widely shown in downtown adult theaters and even in college auditorium weekend movie specials.

Lovelace could not have dreamed, during those moments on-camera, of the huge worldwide audiences who would eventually see her "doing her thing" and who would, as it were, continue to do so long after her death on videocassettes, the technology of which had yet to be developed when she was on-camera.

She was cheated, of course. The hugely profitable porn industry could have siphoned off something to her.

But the entertainment industry as a whole, which has to include pornography, is a field where agents, managers, lawyers, and financial backers create employment and corporations around written contracts, rights, and residuals. And in the early days of X-rated movies, few, if any, thought to include porn performers and producers into the accepted scheme of things.

Mere possession or showing of pornography was still in a criminal justice twilight zone. It had been a crime. In those days participation in production of pornography on either side of the camera was anxiously regarded by participants as still latently criminalized. It mattered less to them that criminal contracts are not legal contracts than that they might need criminal lawyers if they got caught by the long arm of the ambiguous law.

Both established and freshly innovating movie and show business agents, managers, corporate lawyers, producers, and financial backers—who had backgrounds, training, and contacts to create wealth, employment for themselves, and corporations to enrich stockholders around written contracts, rights, and residuals—were waiting in the wings as the criminal Berlin Wall against pornography was being brought down. But as Linda Lovelace was going on-camera, there were many uncertainties.

Production, distribution, and corporate anonymity had been, virtually right up until then, effectively governed by the assortment of criminal codes. By necessity, production and distribution were by underground networks defined by anti-pornography laws as criminal. Corporate and legal contracts were thus null and void. Payments to directors, photographers, motion picture camera operators, models, and the occasional gaffers and other technical personnel were strictly in under-the-table cash or illicit barter.

And even today, whether growing out of this or for some other reason, most porno models are almost always paid a flat amount per performance on-camera. That is to say, porno models rarely receive percentages of productions, called points. If a porno movie, porn video, or even a published porn magazine is an outstanding financial success, the porno models who appeared in it get only whatever they had been initially paid, and no more. These are now accepted payment conventions of a now established corporate porn industry.

Additionally revealing about the nature of the pornography phe-nomenon is the now socially accepted legal fact that porno models do not have quite the same intrinsic contract rights and copyrights to uses of their naked images as do "legitimate" actors, actresses, and models of images of their recognizable features.

Like porno models, legitimate non-pornography photography mod-els such as fashion and advertising models, and in general their legiti-mate stage and screen acting colleagues, are required to sign "model releases" as a condition of their employment as living visual objects for art, advertising, and entertainment created by people using cameras and related photographic and imaging equipment. These model releases give the photographic artists, their publishers, producers, broadcasters, and artistic and corporate associates permission to copy-right and use the photographs or other images of them in which they appear and absolve them from any liability to the model associated with presentation or publication of the model's likeness and give the photo-graphic artists rights to copyright the images they create of the model. As a result, once having been photographed, filmed, videotaped, or computer-imaged after having signed one of these, the legitimate model loses control over the images of himself or herself.

But models in the legitimate modeling industry have agents, man-agers, and additional written and signed contracts that place limits on the model releases and provide additional compensation for additional uses. Major porno models may also have agents, but seldom of the same caliber. And these are the big name porno models. A majority of porno models, and virtually all of the so-called "amateur" commercial porno models, have no agents and get little more than a pittance for the initial performance and nothing for publication, broadcast, and exhibition reuses.

The continuing subsurface nature of pornography places virtually no limits on publication, broadcast, and exhibit of a porno model's image. The porno models' manifestly voluntary public defamation, defilement, disgrace, and resultant tort-law devaluation of themselves severely limits compensation to them for reuse of their images and of course disallows compensation for slander and libel damages. In short, while both legitimate models and porno models sign vaguely similar model releases, original remuneration, remuneration for reuse, recourse to compensation for copyright infringement, libel, and slander damages are significantly different.

Let me illustrate this with two model releases. Before giving these slightly reworded model releases to illustrate the contractual legal standings of legitimate and pornographic models, I have to caution anyone who might want to use either of the two following ones that I have slightly altered some words and phrases to make them more comprehensible, and therefore neither should be used verbatim as a model release. If a reader may have need for either a straight or pornographic model release, it would be advisable to consult a model agency or lawyer.

SLIGHTLY RECAST LEGITIMATE MODEL RELEASE
BETWEEN_____
AND _____ DATE_____
I hereby give _____ the right to copyright as well as to use, reuse, broadcast, publish or otherwise utilize, for profit or not, any photograph, videotape, or film recordings of myself, along with any printed matter in conjunction with said videotapes, films, or photographs, moving or still.

I hereby agree to release from harm the above named photographer, videographer or filmmaker, including the photographer/videographer/filmmaker's agents or publishers, for any liability resulting from these photographs and/or this production or any alteration or distortion of any likeness of myself which has been recorded on film or video material, no matter what the consequences of any release of said material may be.

I hereby disallow any right to inspect the finished product or production, whether on film or video material or both, or any portion of the completion of its soundtrack, as well as advertising material, photographed, printed, videotaped or filmed, that may be used in conjunction with the material's release, publication, or marketing. The only exceptions are if an additional contract has been signed voiding this portion of this release between myself and the above-named photographer, videographer or filmmaker.

I hereby attest that I am over eighteen (18) years of age, able and competent to contract in my own name. I also hereby attest that I will not hold the above-named photographer/videographer/filmmaker responsible for consequences due to any false statements made by myself, particularly concerning my age.

Having read the above and in full and complete understanding of its terms and conditions, I hereby sign in understanding.

SIGNATURE_____

NAME(print)_____

ADDRESS_____

WITNESS_____

In these legitimate photography/videography/filmmaking model situations, there is general agreement and tacit understanding between the model and his or her interests and the photographer and his or her interests—for understandable good business reasons—that the photographs and images will have a more or less favorable aura. Nevertheless, Jenni Bidner, editor of *Petersen's Photography Magazine* has commented, "If you are saying to yourself, 'Who in the world would sign this?' you're not alone."[16]

Bidner's observation is meditative. The reasons for signing are obvious. No commercial photographer/videographer/filmmaker could copyright, sell, display, publish, broadcast, or otherwise use the photographs, videos, films, or computer-images of a model's likeness without having from him or her a signed release. They will, accordingly, only use models who sign them. Therefore the reason models sign model releases is to get jobs, gigs, or whatever they may be called. Don't sign, don't get! That's why. That's who-in-the-world.

The same, of course, goes for porno models signing pornography model releases. If they want to go on-camera for pay or any other incentive, they have to sign a slightly more binding and tort-damage-relinquishing model release form.

Pornography model releases—and nude model releases—naturally grant pornographic photographers, videographers, filmmakers, and computer-imagers more rights to the photographs, videos, films, and computer-images of a signed porno model's clothed or nude body. These releases also thoroughly—and of course calculatedly and of necessity—disallow signed models any recourse to sue for damages for the flagrantly slanderous, libelous, defamatory, and sullying exhibited, published, and/or broadcast photographs, videos, motion pictures, magazine prints, computer-images they volunteer to have made of themselves.

Consider this in that light. Models' faces and facial identities are at least as important as models' bodies. Mere promotion of stylish clothing, for instance, could be done by draping it on a mannequin. Users of dressed advertising and fashion models purchase images of models' facial identities, features, and expressions to promote their products. People are interested in faces, the stories faces tell, and the persons and personalities that go with them. In using model releases, advertisers and fashion designers literally buy rights to models' faces and identities. And in contrast, an image of a body or body part like a hand, leg, or shoulder published without an identifying face might belong to anyone and therefore in some infrequent cases may not need a model release.

Model releases required for people using cameras to record and publish images of nude art models, nude softcore models, and nude hardcore pornographic models are all similar, sometimes identical. As with fashion and advertising uses of models, these model releases are at least as much for images of the facial identities of the nude models as for images of their nude bodies.

Most model releases for nude models, whether for art or hardcore pornography, contain phrases or clauses absolving camerapersons, their employers, agents, and future publishers and exhibitors of liability for slander, defamation, and/or invasion of privacy resulting from exhibit and publication of nude images of the model.

Model releases for specifically nude models—porno or art—have a twofold purpose. One is to preemptively deter the nude model from later returning to even gripe about, let alone take legal action over, his or her embarrassment, defamation, degradation, or invasion of his or her privacy resulting from exhibit or publication of the contractually released nude images. The other purpose is, as with advertising and fashion model releases, to have a signed contract from the model intended expressly for eventual buyers and publishers of his or her images to create a salable commodity. If camera-based art or pornography is to become an exhibited or published commercial property, persons intentionally modeling nude for it must voluntarily surrender their rights to the property in a model release.

Model releases are only required for camera-based modeling. Artists may draw, paint, and sculpt nude models without needing any kind of model release. For these, the nude models are regarded as having consented to being used in the creation of art. Even if renderings of their facial features and expressions may be very accurate and identifiable in association with explicit renderings of their bare bodies, genitals, and associated private parts, nude models have no claim on exhibition or publication of these subjective works of art. Only camera-based art or pornography, which is objective and factual in depiction, requires model releases.

All of these signed model releases simply cover images of the models. They do not cover activities of the model while on-camera. The fact of being on-camera for the creation images that may invade the model's privacy requires this release contract. This enables production of physical commodities with no outstanding liens. Basically it is the invasion of privacy and the exhibit and publication of images of that invasion of privacy that the model consents to and releases the cameraperson and his or her associates from. What the model consents to do on-camera while his or her privacy is thus being invaded to one degree or another is of little or no legal concern.

Model releases signed by nude hardcore porno models virtually never mention sex-acts as such. They only address the release of images of the nude model, that person and that person's effectively naked body.

Porno models, almost by definition, will be effectively naked. Public sex-acts are simply an extension of the on-camera invasion of the privacy of their private parts and a further volunteered indignity. The initial indignity results from consent to publicly expose certain private parts in conjunction with their facial identities. Porno models may or may not be erotically costumed, but any costuming intentionally subjects them to views of their bare buttocks, bare female breasts, genitals, and anuses. To be pornography—rather than anatomical illustration—views must not conceal facial features and expressions of the models so that the identities of those submitting to these widely presumed defamations can be exhibited and published.

Rights to having privacy-invading accurate, authentic, factual, and truthful images of their genitals, buttocks, anuses, and/or female breasts and nipples and facial identities exhibited and published indefinitely for no further compensation or claims to defamation damages are what porno models and other nude models knowledgeably relinquish by signing model releases. While this releases camerapersons and all their associates from libel and slander, these camerapersons and their associates would seem to plainly get a certain malicious delight and amusement from permanently defiling, degrading, and defaming their nude models this way.

And these images of identifiable persons voluntarily submitting to wide public exhibit of their private parts are, of course, what pornography buyers would seem to take a certain malicious delight in buying. And their perverse delights may become all the more juicier, of course, when these identifiable persons who are degradingly exhibiting their genitals, female breasts, bare buttocks, and anuses are also submitting to debasingly being publicly and commercially shown engaging in sex-acts.

Consider this 1970's-era pornography model consent, authorization, and release contract. It represents the tone and quality of a variety of porno model release forms in present use. One reason that it is very slightly modified by drawing from other model release forms is because there was a hint of using "legalese" to slightly obfuscate, to the signing porno models, precisely who was signing away what and for how long, and who was the beneficiary. This may be clearer.

MODEL CONSENT, AUTHORIZATION, AND RELEASE
Name of Company_____
Address of Company _____
Billing Name:_____

I, the undersigned, for myself, my personal and legal representatives, do hereby irrevocably grant to _____, its successors, affiliates, subsidiaries, assigns and licensees, the right to license to copyright and to renew and extend any copyright, use, reuse, in perpetuity, reproduce, publish, distribute and exhibit my name, picture, portrait, likeness, voice, or musical rendition on any instrument, or any or all of them, or in connection with any sound or silent motion picture, still picture, sound-track recording, disc recording, tape recording, filmstrip, and musical interpretation, or otherwise howsoever, without limitations as to time, place, manner, or extent.

I also consent to the use of any printed matter and to giving me, or not giving me, a credit, in sole discretion of any of the aforementioned parties to whom this authorization and release is given, in conjunction therewith.

The rights herein granted include and relate to all rights of every kind (whether now known or hereafter known) in and to and for motion-picture purposes and all rights of every kind (whether now known or hereafter known) for radio and television and any other use whatsoever, at any time in any part of the world. The rights herein granted in addition to being for the benefit of the _____, shall be for the benefit also of any successor, or assign thereof, and any licensee or sublicensee thereof, including television broadcasters and exhibitors and motion-picture distributors and exhibitors and any affiliates and subsidiaries of the

_____.

I hereby waive any right that I may have to inspect and/or approve the finished product or the advertising copy, printed matter, or record jacket that may be used in connection therewith, or the use to which it may be applied.

I hereby release the _____ and any person, firm, corporation, or association deriving any rights or license therefrom or thereunder from any and all claims or liability for damage, for libel, slander, invasion of the right of privacy, or any other claims or liability whatsoever arising out of the exercise of any of the rights and licenses granted hereby, including without limitation upon the generality of the foregoing any claims or liabilities under sections 50 and 51 of the Civil Rights Law of the State of New York or any law amendatory of, or supplemental thereto, and similar laws of any state of any other country.

In the event of any dispute or controversy with respect to the rights granted hereunder, the same shall not constitute any basis for any withdrawal or revocation of the consent and release, and I hereby agree that this consent and release is irrevocable and that the only remedy in the event of any dispute or controversy which I may invoke is for arbitration, in accordance with the rules and regulations of the American Arbitration Association. I am over 18 years of age, and I have read the above authorization and release in full and complete understanding of its terms and conditions prior to its execution and have received a copy thereof.

Date:_____ Model:_____
Witness:_____ Address:_____

(Composite from several nude and porno model releases, but mainly derived from a 1977 form.[17])

You may repeat, "Who in the world would sign this?"

Virtually no commercial porno model has ever failed to sign one of these or something very similar because signing one is the only ticket to get on-camera, for pay or whatever. No commercial pornographer is going to create and produce salable pornography from porno models who do not sign all-inclusive and all-waiving model release forms like this—that I call "porno model release forms." For legal and business reasons, camera-based pornographers must require their models to sign them, and models who want to be on-camera in pornography must submit to signing them. The key word is "must." Behind it, though, one can detect a voluntary debaucher-debauchee alliance for commercial production, exhibition, and publication of porn, a contractor-signer relationship.

These consent, authorization, and "porno model release contracts" have stood the test of case-law challenges for over a quarter of a century.

Effectively since the practical decriminalization of pornography, no porno model has ever appeared in commercially distributed and exhibited pornography without having signed one of these model release contracts, all of them fairly similar. So all porno models since the late 1960s have legally signed away all rights and copyrights to their names, likenesses, pictures, portraits, and voices—and most of these contracts are excruciatingly inclusive of everything. The pornography producers and distributors can use these likenesses, pictures, portraits, and voices, etc., in movies, printed pictures as in magazines, and in any new technological way that may come along—as video cassettes later came along and as computer-related images are now coming into being.

In the fifth paragraph of the "porno model release" we see that all commercial porno models additionally sign away their rights to sue for libel, slander, invasion of right of privacy, or any other claims of liability whatsoever arising out of the rights that they have signed over to the pornographers—and anyone the pornographers may deal with—to use these names, likenesses, pictures, portraits, and voices, etc. And if the porno model does not like it, all he or she can do is ask for arbitration, effectively by someone of the pornographer's choosing.

Moreover, early in the era of quasi-legal pornography—in the late 1960's and early 1970's—an explicit-sex porno model sued a person who had taken a photograph of his naked body in a locker room without his permission. He lost the case and lost the appeal—and to my knowledge it was never overturned. The apparently still standing decision basically said that any porno model having voluntarily engaged in nude explicit sex on-camera, and having thus signed one of these release contracts, effectively acknowledged anyone's and everyone's right to film, photograph, or otherwise capture images of his or her clothed or naked body, and/or facial identity, and/or sex organs, and/or sexual activities and to publish and exhibit those images. Porno models have no rights to sue anyone for damages resulting from any use of those images or from their publication and/or exhibit.

So we see that porno models, by a combination of deeds of their own doing and the forces of legal and social coercion, are made to live among the others in society with diminished civil rights and relegated to lowered legal and social statuses. The social and legal structure would thus appear to need and demand that whores—and in our era of photography, surrogate male and female "porno-whores"—be treated like whores.

Contrast a porno model's diminished civil rights to sue and denial of additional compensation for uses of his or her image with the rights, copyrights, and even trade mark protections given non-pornographic mainstream entertainers and sports figures. It is literally just the opposite. Anyone who wants to use a copyrighted image of the singer-actress Madonna—even those images that appear to border on soft-core pornographic—had better be willing to write a check with a significant number of numerals. Even non-news uses of most publicly taken photographs, film, and video images of her and other big-name entertainers and sports figures require their or their agents' personal authorization, usually for an amount that includes many numerals after a number.

Clearly a deeply imbedded social need engendered this enormous legally enforced divergence in evaluation and estimation of people involved in entertainment.

While porno models are paid—sometimes well, considering a paucity of acting talent and minimal work-effort—all but a very few of them are simply not within the loop of producers, agents, managers, lawyers, corporate executives, and financial backers who have created high-paid employment for themselves and high-value corporations around written contracts, rights, and residuals, especially the above model authorization and release contracts.

So porno models are literally the meat of a now established huge corporate porn industry. As such, they are legally, economically, and socially treated as debauched carnality to be recorded by cameras and used for debaucher profits. But the treatment and attitude extends beyond the inner workings of the porn industry.

After all, what is the social niche and purpose of a whore unless she or he can actually be physically, sexually, emotionally, and socially used as a whore? And what would be the purpose of the new post-photography pseudo-whore—the porno model—unless he or she could be psychologically and socially used as a debauched virtual-sexual whore? So the porn industry additionally adds to the entertainment of its customer-spectators by economic and social debauchery of its porno whores.

At the dawn of quasi-legal pornography, and in continuity from the underground blue-movie and stag-film productions, the debauched carnality of porno models was known to debauchers, debauchees, and porn spectators alike. But the potential for a huge span between naked debauched model and licensee assigned the lucre had not been grasped by any of the participants. Linda Lovelace signed a model release, did her nude sex thing on-camera—embarrassed or not—for a smidgen of pay. She would reasonably have expected, as with stag-films, for comparatively few to see it, and would have anticipated an escape route, aided by time, into anonymity.

Instead, a few months later she suddenly became a nationally and even globally known celebrity. As it turned out, in the next thirty years of virtually global public and quasi-legal pornography, no other porno model ever attained her peculiar kind of fame and notoriety. She was, and remains, *sui generis* in the world of pornography.

Linda Marchiano Traynor was transformed into the never equaled and world famous Linda Lovelace virtually overnight and literally could be "recognized" by millions of people who had seen her bare flesh, facial identity, and sexual proclivities—even while in a kindly way nationally and globally admired for her blatant antics—she could only have been deeply shocked.

And in the context of those times, it is difficult to imagine that at some level she was not deeply embarrassed.

And she had a right. Her embarrassment was, in fact, part of the entertainment. And she had a right to feel that not been adequately compensated for either her virtual worldwide—at least at some level—disgrace, or even for her actual porn acting performance work.

In short, in the swirling accumulation of enormous national audiences who recognized her, slick publicity stunts that put her features and identity in the general worldwide media—like her run for president and huge box office receipts it helped promote—low paid, lewd, and nude Linda Lovelace could only have begun to be greatly embarrassed, even if she had not been on-camera.

Nixon, who was president at the time, never appeared to be particularly embarrassed by his political acts even if his virtual ouster from office may have been embarrassing where his political acts were not. The embarrassment was in the loss of power, the loss of status.

On the other hand, Lovelace (and others) have expressed degrees of after-the-fact embarrassment at their undressed images engaging in sex acts being widely published.

But if porno models may understandably suffer temporary or permanent and large or small after-the-fact embarrassment and shame in addition to tort-law social and economic devaluation, porn customers who view these pornographic motion pictures—as well as during-the-fact live sex show audiences—are not themselves greatly "embarrassed" by porn performers' and live-sex performers' naked appearances or lewd acts in the same way as voters may be "embarrassed" by subsequent political performances and decisions of their choices of candidates.

The political candidate named Linda Lovelace showed neither shame nor embarrassment when she was playfully running for president in the early 1970's. Her epic X-rated film *Deep Throat* had been released in every major American city and widely released overseas. To most observers she seemed to revel in being nationally and world famous, or perhaps infamous.

She certainly had no trouble with "name recognition," but her candidacy, if there were even a smidgen of seriousness in it, was in trouble from the start.

She had become a woman with a "reputation" on a grand scale, massively and genuinely devalued in tort-law recovery standing and yet running for president by right of being born into equality among fellow human beings. The candidacy was from its inception a publicity stunt revolving around a parody of our sometimes silly simplistic liberal notions of democratic equality among presidential candidates.

In the more puritanical American political climate of the early 1970's—as opposed to the more tolerant Italian one of the mid-1980s—and with her whimsical run for the highest office in the land in the nuclear-armed world, Lovelace's problem was both "reputation" and credibility. These were certainly issues Staller had to face down, but in a more tolerant atmosphere and for a more realistic public office.

Even if Lovelace had run for a more realistic minor office in the 1970's, such as an American city council seat, she would have faced, as did Staller, the problem of "reputation."

And what is tort-value "reputation" that its sexual connotations are so bound up with credentials for political leadership and teaching?

The answer may lay in the fact that virtually two enormously capital-intensive decades go into child raising, inculcation of dynamic technological society values, education for earning (and as a result breeding) position and comprehension of the growing complexities. These two decades represent almost twice as much time as the physical processes leading to biological puberty.

The artificially high value on sex that human society created through ritualizing sexual relationships and placing social and legal limitations on them remains. It rears its ugly head in many ways.

Across the cultural and national board one can see a high value placed on sexually attractive, youthful, and virile appearances. The strategy worked all too well, making us the largest number of any higher species on our small and limited planet.

Whether linked to this or not, the illegalization of pornography served to give it a higher value. It was obviously done out of fear of social disorder and possible chaos.

Prior to the invention of the printing press there were handwritten pornographic stories. No one cared. They were the private matters of some in the upper class.

Prior to the invention of the camera there were pornographic drawings, paintings, and sculptures. Costs of making these forbade popular distribution.

The printing press and the camera changed that. Societies, responding to the transformations brought about by these new devices, first defined pornography, then made it illegal.

But it did not stop the creation, production, and wide distribution of pornography. For one thing, as time went on and technologies developed and refined, it became easier and easier to create, produce, publish, and distribute pornographic images, still and in motion.

Now, with xerox reproductions and video camcorders available to virtually everyone and elaborated by FAX and Internet dissemination, it is literally impossible for governing authorities to contain erotic visual or text material. Even acceded as deleterious and therefore widely outlawed "kiddiporn" has effectively escaped legislative and law-enforcement containment. "Kiddiporn" not only continues to be widely produced, it has been and continues to be so extensively published and disseminated that it would be functionally impossible to recall and destroy all images of suggestively naked children and their sexual activities—even if "kiddiporn" production were miraculously brought to a complete halt tomorrow afternoon.

Outlawed pornography differs from other outlawed substances. Outlawed drugs are consumed and must be replaced from agricultural or manufacturing sources. Stolen jewels have a one-time resale value to the thief.

But pornography can be easily produced, copied, and mass-reproduced, legally or illegally. In addition, in our age of the Internet as well as FAX and phone dissemination, it can be widely and instantaneously published. Like anything, making it illegal only boosts prices and values and creates a criminal subculture, generally more harmful to social order and culture than the product itself.

Human society has dealt with psychoactive and intoxicant drugs for eons, probably back to the beginnings of the Stone Age itself. It socialized drug uses, ceremonialized celebrations with them, and restricted the more powerful mind-altering drugs to priestly and ruling classes.

Similarly, theft of property has been dealt with for as long as a proto-human initially made and "owned" a sharp stone tool or shred of proto-clothing and had created rudimentary words to define clothing, tools, and possession.

Mass-distributed pornographic entertainment has sprung suddenly new on the eons-long human social scene, but it appears to have arrived at a timely juncture.

It is, indeed, subversive. But this may turn out to be its good point.

The old human cultural values concerning sex, procreation, and as a result, family, clearly need changing if our species and our planet's biodiversity are to survive. There are too many of us.

Additionally, the high cultural value on sexually attractive, youthful, and virile appearance is the very meat of pornography, almost literally.

If hyper-evolving technological society is to contend with the destructive forces revolving around these anciently rooted values—seen in everything from multi-million-market television advertising to selection for corporate executive leadership—a freer legal and cultural rein must be given to sexual expression and its recorded aspect, pornography.

CHAPTER EIGHT

Pornography Confronting Racism and Social Stagnation

One merely need go into an adult bookstore or a porno movie theater to see a wide variety of interracial pornography that covers the whole spectrum of the human species. Naked black men engage in sex with naked white women. Bare white men engage in sex acts with bare black women. Undressed Orientals do it with undressed Orientals, whites, blacks, and Hispanics. Stripped Hispanics do it with nudes of all other racial backgrounds.

The common denominator is that they are all naked porno models. There is a leveling and implied equality in bare bodies. Appearing naked like the day that they were born and literally divested of those symbols of rank, ethnicity, wealth, and power that clothes betray, the porno models would seem the very essence of religion-based injunctions of equality among human beings.

Beyond equality implied by their nakedness, porno models further offer themselves as pseudo-whores relegated to the bottom of the social scale as a consequence of their intentional and voluntary porno modeling, all of them sharing this additional alikeness at the bottom. There they satisfy perceptions closer to reality inherent in the tort-law model of differentiated value in human beings. Some of us are always going to be less equal than others, to invert George Orwell, and if we are democratically "equal under the law," porno models are among the least.

The reality of inequalities between human beings, "equal in the eyes of God" or not, is manifest. While Church and State pander to ideals of human equality, the stark reality all around is that human beings are neither born into an equal playing field of life nor should expect to find any more than hypothetical human equality in their journeys through life.

While offering up naked human beings as stripped not only of clothing but human pretensions of rank, office, wealth, power, and birthright as depicted in attire and abode—representing and symbolizing adult idealizations of their being "created equal"—pornography at the same time blatantly exposes and makes more "self-evident" obvious physical differences, sexual male and female, muscular and weak, fat and thin, tall and short, dark-skinned and light-skinned, and if one reads the bare bodies' interactions with even a modicum of care, smart and stupid, or at least mentally sharp and dull. We see on one hand the great similarity of bare human bodies and their interactions and reactions that require equality in social prescriptions and on the other hand the realities of birthright, physical, and mental differences that lead to differentiations of social and economic rank-valuing.

"Equality" is an ideal so vital to modern technological civilization that it must constantly strive to foster "equality" even amid all the obvious inequalities. The more opportunities that exist in a society and resulting greater mingling and melting of manifestly similar but unequal human beings, the more military-economic power that civilization will have. The thus-created social cohesion passing through levels of social rankings allows a greater the illusion of "equality" and generates those increases in personal "freedom" that propel progress. The melting and mingling of many minds, backgrounds, goals, and outlooks promotes both social and technological progress.

In modern complex post-industrial societies, the opportunities open to individuals are enormous and result in a wide range of "equalities of opportunity" based on merit to that society. But, paradoxically, merit creates new tort-law ranking of personal value, and new inequality. Vitality drains from a society when new merit-rankings become calcified and fluidity of opportunity polymerizes into new solid strata of human powers and pretensions. Only a prevailing liberal ideal of equality—legislated, religiously held, or social-incentive promoted—may keep society open and permit the marvelous mingling and melting of minds that fuels progress.

Among other things, pornography offers glimpses of social change and economic and social mobility in both directions.

Decriminalized publicly sold and shown pornography, the present quasi-legal gigantic billion-dollar pornography industry, was born in one of the most socially fluid times in human history, the late 1960s and early 1970s.

The Civil Rights struggle had just finished abolishing the "separate-but-equal" *de jure* racism of the Deep South. Forced school integration had merged big city education in the north. Voting rights legislation had reasserted equality at the voting booth. And most importantly, the philosophy of racism began to be attacked.

"Equal opportunity" employment legislation attempted to level the playing field. For the first time since Reconstruction black people were elected to both houses of congress, appointed to federal judgeships, appointed to high positions in government bureaucracies, and given leadership positions in the private sector. Women, and other ethnic minorities, quickly followed.

In the pre-decriminalization "stag film" days, there appears to have been little, if any, interracial pornography. The naked porno models who engaged in sex acts in monochrome black-and-white home movies were average-American white people.

As case law granted more and more freedom of expression, there was still very little interracial pornography.

Even in the "girly loop" days of the mid-to-late 1960s, when marginal downtown theaters began to show "anatomically correct" naked females suggestively squirming on beds and rugs, these "soft-core" porno movies were almost invariably bare white women and a few bare European-background Hispanic women.

As the decade of the 1960s came to an end, the first hardcore "loops" publicly shown in peep show booths almost always used naked white porno models, again the exception being European-looking Hispanics. Even the first feature-length porno movies of the early 1970s used white porn actors and actresses.

But most of the rebellious young men and women, behind and in front of the pornographic cameras, were part of the larger protest of the 1960s, the protest against the senseless Vietnam War as well as its related rebellion against rampant institutionalized racism and economic injustice.

The early all-white porno movies seem to have been in part the result of limiting protests to one at a time. Inherent in camera-based pornography when it was still illegal was a great daring to flaunt the prevailing puritanical attitudes and prudish law. Additionally flaunting predominant racism mixed the protest metaphor and added unnecessary risks. So pornographers used naked porno models representative of the great white majority—where the underground market was and with whom they did not want quarrels that could lead to arrest and prosecution.

In subsequent gray-area years, as pornography was emerging from blatantly criminal to quasi-legal, producers and distributors still felt the old dread and continued to limit their expressions of protest in the same way.

In a mix of voiced and unvoiced intention, protest-generated intended and unintended case-law interaction, and historical accident, publicly sold and shown explicit pornography sprang into North American and European society simultaneous with the late-1960s and early 1970s protest movement against war and racism.

In centers of the "flower-power and free-sex" hippie movement that evolved into the great anti-War and anti-racism protest, largely New York City and San Francisco, most of the courageous young pornography producers and many of their daring young naked porno models were deeply involved in the Great Protest Movement.

Moreover, it was a time of protest, a time when protest had become acceptable, a time when protesters were expected to share others' protests. And at the very heart of pornography there always lurks protest against social norms and values.

So very rapidly the all-white pornography producers, camerapersons, porno models, and even audiences were brought into participating in the Great Protest.

In San Francisco, in the depth of the Great Protest and while the FBI was devoting virtually all of its energies against Great Protest factions such as the Black Panther party and the Weather Underground, the Mitchell Brothers produced the now classic and blatantly interracial porno movie *Behind the Green Door* starring a white woman, Marilyn Chambers, and a black man, Johnny Keyes.

Even before this monumentally successful porn classic, however, small porn producers of color film "loops" for both the porno movie theaters and the peep-show establishments, virtually all of them white males, began to use interracial porno models.

Not only did a protest against camera-based interracial pornography fail to emerge, the apprehensive producers of it found that there was a genuine demand for interracial porn, especially black males engaging in sex acts with white females—in fact, the blacker the black males and the whiter the white females the better. Using and accenting stereotype, as in literature and theater, a whole category of "Blacks and Blonds" super-eight color film porno movies of naked white women engaging in sex acts, including obligatory fellatio, with bare black men went on sale in adult bookstores—all the more interesting because in those days purchasers had to have home movie projectors, home movie screens, home movie speaker systems, and the knowledge and patience to thread eight millimeter film into projectors.

The only protest, in fact, was from the emerging female liberation movements who targeted not interracial pornography but all pornography, which in their emerging sensitivities they felt was specifically demeaning to women. Much of this protest targeted at heterosexual explicit and hardcore pornography has now died down, if not died out, as a result of discussion and examination from within female liberation movements. But there never was a genuine protest against interracial pornography, as such, and one has to wonder why it never materialized.

There are two aspects to interracial story material and its expression in pornography, dominant-culture females in sexual relationships with minority or servant-culture males and the reverse, dominant-culture males in sexual relationships with minority or servant-culture females. The most commercially successful interracial pornography in North America has been naked white women engaging in sex acts with naked black men. Its opposite, naked black women engaging in sex acts with naked white men continues to be less successful but is clearly not a box-office flop.

This reflects the historical growth of story material concerning inter-racial sexual relationships. In our European-based and therefore "white-oriented" literature most of the surviving—and therefore interesting enough to survive—stories concern sexual relationships of white women and black men. In other words, nothing new to our culture is reflected in the greater success of the interracial pornography of white women engaging in sex acts with black men over its gender opposite.

In his book *A Completely New Look At Interracial Sexuality; Public Opinion and Select Commentaries,*[18] Lawrence R. Tenzer shows that there had been fascination with interracial sexuality long before the European discovery of America. He points out that the earliest extant literary work after Gutenberg's invention of movable type, a collection of short stories titled *The Novellino* by Guardato Massuchio, published in 1476, dealt with interracial sexual relations. Two of the short stories are concerned with interracial sexual relations between white women and black men.

It was written at a time when slavery was legal in Italy, and it was written by someone in that white-dominant society for readers in the white-dominant society of Europe as it was poised to become the dominant world society. That is to say, there were probably similar inverse gossipy written or oral stories about interracial sexual relations between black women and white men circulating in African societies. But what has been preserved in the historical record, largely due to the success of European world domination, is one-sided—gossipy sexual innuendo stories like these two of Masuccio's, white women and black men.

Shakespeare utilized similar themes in both *Othelo* and *Titus Andronicus.* Thomas Southern's *Oroonoko,* and William Walker's *Victorious Love,* stage plays of close to the same time period, also dwell on themes of interracial sexual relations between white women and black men. Whenever we find fictional story material about interracial sexual relationships, it almost always concerns white females and what we would call minority males.

Gossipy interracial sexual relationships turning up in historical fact betray a different reality. White John Smith did indeed marry Native American Pocohantas. White Hernán Cortés, while politically unable to marry did indeed openly have children with his Aztec slave woman we generally know as Doña Maria and decently established a plantation for her and cut their children into his will. The reality is that far more white men had sexual relationships with "minority" women than the gender-opposite case.

As we find suggested in the Cortés case, the white men faced a certain cultural censure, but it was less than white women faced for interracial sexual relationships.

In those days just prior to massive black slavery in North America and subjugation, dehumanization, and even effective genocide of Native American people, fictional European stories about white women and black men were gossip about the legally permissible but socially rejected—similar to interracial pornography today.

The white female and black male story interest derives in part from the unlikelihood and unusualness of the sexual relationship. Real sexual relationships between white males and black females were far more common and in the historical male-dominated racist societies just one of the unspoken realities. The historical, though not well documented, romantic and sexual relationship between Thomas Jefferson and his black slave woman lover Sally Hemings,[19] and later the motion picture *Jefferson in Paris,*[20] only found itself into our general literature in these more race and gender liberated times, two centuries after the fact, due to unwritten social censorship of these unspoken realities.

But if literature was quiet about sexual relationships between white males and black females in order not to rock a status quo, gossipy fictional stories, especially those with innuendo about impropriety, exploring outcomes and consequences of white females having sexual relationships with black males may have served social purposes of keeping "proper" white females in their childbearing and child-rearing social strata places as part of The Great Social Beast's restrictions against female sexual pleasure.

Nevertheless, all art contains minute future orientation if not prediction, and intrinsic in these stories are inklings that a time may come when female love and sex need not be solely for baby manufacture and subsequent life-energy devotion to child care, that white women may one day have a sexual relationships with no more unrealistically difficult consequences with black men than with white men, but may enjoy sexual pleasures for their own sake.

But those few women of that time with adequate educations to read these stories or social status enough to go to the theater could only dream, if indeed they could allow themselves to sexually fantasize. These stories were not pornography offering sexual fantasy, but texts and dramas offering social caution and prudence—even when condoning interracial sexual relationships—to a limited literate management-class audience.

The very fact of published story material and dramatized stage material on the subject offered hidden censure and warned of unending gossip for those women foolish enough to try it. Even from the ancient beginnings of civilization the personal evaluations reflected in later tort law were present, just not spelled out. Higher valued white women might hesitate to risk losing personal standing and value even against powerful forces of sex and love.

Othelo and the other stories offer a glimpse into what might have been if specifically black slavery had not become such a powerful economic institution. But interracial sexual relationships were to undergo even more censure and stigma.

As slavery became economically institutionalized when Europeans colonized the New World, interracial marriage became itself illegal, or was otherwise legally punished, out in the colonies where production required massive black slave labor.

In 1662 the colonial legislature of Virginia passed legislation clarifying the slave or free status of children born out of interracial sexual relations. The children of white men and black slaves would have the slave status of their mothers, and the children from sexual relationships between black men and white woman would also suffer because the white woman was heavily fined.

Seventeenth century legislation passed in neighboring Maryland made white women who married black slaves the legal property of the owners of their husbands. This led to fraud that allowed white slave owners a loophole obtain white women as their legal property, presumably for, among other things, sexual purposes—as if access to black slave women for sexual gratification were not enough. So the law was later modified.

It illustrates that use of legally enslaved women for—undoubtedly— sexual pleasures was not in itself, even in North America, a racial manifestation. Stories of sexual relations with slave women (and slave men) go back through all human history.

But in the British North American colonies and later in their political reorganization into the United States of America, legislation concerning interracial sexual relations was primarily aimed at those between white women and black men. Mulatto children of slave owners abounded, so much so that Abraham Lincoln had to comment on their numbers (in the hundreds of thousands) in a speech in 1860. But what little legislation had been passed concerning interracial sexual relations between white men and black women was totally ignored by both law enforcement and society in general.

Still, white women did have sexual relations with black slave men, and even married white women had these taboo sexual relationships. Laws abolishing sex or aspects of it are always doomed to failure. Tenzer includes some accounts from Maryland newspapers where white men declare that they have divorced their white wives and will no longer be responsible for their debts because they had children by specifically their own black slave men. In spite of the law, white women "ran around with" black men.

Over two hundred fifty years of legal slavery in what is now the United States, and during the century that followed legal abolition of it where nothing was done to abolish the deeply ingrained social and economic aftermath, some fifteen generations of black men and women had between zero and very low tort-law value—the one exception being value to others as slave property. At the same time white men (and to some extent their women) amassed fortunes, acquired educations and social standings, built "reputations," and gained sometimes great tort-law value.

By the 1960s and after fifteen generations, the gap of markedly different personal value between black people and white people had become so deeply and so unconsciously part of the culture that it went largely unnoticed. That was just the way things were, and protest against it was deemed un-American and antisocial.

During this same fifteen-generation time period, European civilization came to dominate the planet, something no other civilization in history had done. European values were imposed first in their colonies, then as Europeans came to politically, economically, and culturally dominate the planet, their values were mimicked and absorbed virtually everywhere else.

European standards came to guide all art, music, literature, drama, philosophy, values, and even law. Even European ideals of physical and facial attractiveness and beauty prevailed.

In the United States, in addition, black people, long removed from their own art, music, literature, drama, philosophy, values, and law, were socially coerced into absurdities of trying to look and be white while culturally and economically being relegated as a class to lower personal value.

Thus while case law was decriminalizing pornography and redefining everyone's equality-under-the-law rights and responsibilities in regard to it, it was doing it in a European-based white dominated and racist structure. The resulting publicly shown and sold pornography not only had to reflect it, but by the nature of protest inherent in it was bound to experimentally offer and induce social changes. Unlike the coy falsities of sexuality in advertising or cute sexual innuendo in mainstream journalism, pornography projects an objectivity and candor

about sexual activity and even a pitiless honesty about social consequences of publicly stripping and engaging in sex acts. Camera-based
pornography blandly showed interracial sexual activity "as is," devoid of
layers of obscuring pretensions and censorships.

Most, but not all, of the new interracial porn producers were white
men, the classic example being the Mitchell brothers, Artie and Jim.
These white male pornographic film producers were just, as a result of
the nature of capital and their own experience and track record to latch
onto it, the better capitalized.

As camera-based explicit-sex pornography edged toward decriminalization and the handwriting on the wall became clear, a few black
men formed small cooperative associations, and at comparatively small
outlay and expense—but not trivial due to 16-mm color filmmaking
costs—began producing their own ethnic-black and interracial porno
movies with local Afro-American and white American porno models.

In San Francisco one of these associations constructed its own small
porno movie theater out of a storefront on the ground floor of the
seedy cheap-rent Anglo Hotel. The Anglo Hotel was one of several run-
down old hotels where prostitution was endemic on then seedy Sixth
Street, and it was a block down the street from one of the initiatory
hardcore pornographic movie theaters, the Paris Theater. That part of
Sixth Street was in an area where a large racially black area merged with
a poor white and Hispanic district in the inner city at the periphery of
the downtown area.

The dumpy little porno movie theater on the ground floor of the
Anglo Hotel building was named, apparently as a lark and parody of
Hollywood-type film festivals, the "Film Festival Theater." Especially in
those early days, this kind of touted parody played on intrinsic social
protest in all pornography and especially inherent in the new blatant
public and decriminalized pornography.

In 1968 the small group of black producers, including a filmmaker
named "George" (I vaguely and phonetically recall "George Hurd," or

similar-sounding) a bona fide filmmaking and pornography talent, and the effective proprietor of a grocery store next door to the storefront porno movie theater, started making their own films. George lived, at least for a while, in Anglo Hotel and often doubled as projectionist.

The group of black porno movie producers used various bedroom, living room, and other locations around the San Francisco Bay Area. A few of the porno movies were shot in rooms in the seedy Anglo Hotel above the porn theater, and one of them appeared to have been shot on location in the projection room itself.

The black porn-making cooperative obviously had no other outlet other than their own small porno movie theater. America had a considerably more racist climate than now, and these black porn producers had to have in their lives deeply felt the racism they had been born into and grew up in. The only way to break through the porn-production racial-economic barrier was to both make their own ethnic-black and interracial porno movies and to show them in their own theater, and that is exactly what they did.

In this considerable effort one can see motivations reaching beyond pure business and profit. The cost of acquiring or constructing and then maintaining the small porno movie theater, including movie projection and sound equipment, had to have been substantial.

Filmmaking was and is a rich person's art. Even a used sixteen millimeter movie projector and related used sound and basic lighting equipment did not come cheap. The additional costs of undeveloped color film stock (which had to be kept in a refrigerator it was heat-sensitive), the costs of developing it, the costs of printing it (usually several times in "work" prints, "answer" prints, and final prints), and the costs of professional editing equipment, even if rented by the hour, were considerable. So we're talking up to thousands of dollars in outlay for each porno movie.

A comparatively very small amount had to be reserved to pay the porno models. Males, if they got paid, got as little as thirty-five dollars for appearing in a porno movie that took up to three hours to shoot. Females usually did not get much more. Naked porno models were cheap in ever sense of the word, the last and least cost consideration, approaching one-percent of the total.

The real costs were the thousands of dollars that went into the theater, the film equipment, and the film developing and printing that went into each twenty-minute porno movie. At two and later three dollars per ticket, the small size of the theater—never filled to capacity—made it impossible to recover the costs until after at least a week of steady showing. Until a library of at least three of the Film Festival Theater's about half-hour-each porno movies had been accumulated, the management had to fill out at least an hour of showing time by renting or otherwise acquiring outside feature-length commercial porno movies.

Given the cost, then, an enterprising soul could have invested the same amounts in less risky, less day-to-day bothersome, and far more profitable moneymaking schemes. One is led to conclude that the Film Festival Theater team produced hardcore explicit pornographic movies and then showed them in their own porno movie theater for more than just the money.

They never came out and said it, but after talking with a couple of them I came away with a clear impression that they relished debauching—"making a fool out of" was one term used—the porno models. They left no doubt in my mind that they got much amusement and pleasure from cajoling their acquired porno models into stripping naked and engaging in sex acts in front of them and their movie camera for a very small amount of money. I recall that more than one from the production team insinuated how they all greatly enjoyed the public scandal and unrecoverable defamation inflicted on their local San Francisco Area porno models as a result of locally advertising and publicly showing half-hour films of their *de facto* defilement ten times a day for three-week runs, and additional reruns, to thousands of local people. And the public debauchery of these naked local people engaging in this characterized "smut" was blatantly shown in their own flagrant porn theater.

Other porno movie and porn video producers over the years have made it fairly clear that they all shared similar feelings about what they do to their porno models. Some were almost proud of it, much as these early minor ethnic-black and interracial porn producers had been.

Considering the cost of the theater and the large expenses in film production, the first several porno movies were made effectively at a great financial loss with only vague hopes of breaking even. The real motivation would seem to have been that the Film Festival cameraman and his associates got a great deal of enjoyment out of hiring people to appear in their porno movies. If the subtle record in their films is any indication, they would seem to have gotten gratification out of putting these people in spotlights on-camera and making them literally and figuratively squirm as they anticipated consequential stigma and social devaluation. They would seem to have gotten entertainment jollies out of requiring these people to then strip on-camera as part of that and then out of watching them naked and publicly engaging in sex-acts on-camera to bring about that. And some of them seem to have gotten satisfaction out of mischievously projecting them doing it onto the smut-theater screen as paid and *de facto* degraded "porno whores" in camera-based "whore stories" to their fellow San Francisco area residents to make that binding. Several of them to whom I talked briefly either clearly gave that impression or sometimes flatly said as much about this or that aspect of their motivations.

Their amusement at pressing the porno models to undress on-camera specifically for obscene public entertainment and all that accompanies urging people to strip naked seems clearly implied in the Film Festival porno movies. The cameraman left little doubt—by his creative input of angles, takes, and conversations with the porno models before and after they stripped—that he was amused by the never-completely-without-shame discomposure that they betrayed, indeed that anyone would betray as he or she strips in front of properly clothed others and from the additional misgivings that those peeling porno models betrayed because they were intentionally stripping on-camera for publicly shown "smut."

They undoubtedly got more amusement out of over-and-over exhorting the naked porno models to degradingly engage in this or that sex act or exhibit their bare flesh in a different sex-act pose in the spotlights on-camera with a small audience watching, and quite often to ask white women to suck black guys' cocks on-camera while they looked on amused and then out of filming them from maximally degrading angles to make publicly noteworthy their scandalous disgrace. Anyone could see it in the porno movies that were shown, and I got additional clear impressions from talking to the cameraman and another producer associate.

At least in some cases the black cameraman and associated producers of the group of black men got additional direct sexual pleasures from, especially, the naked white women after these women had finished tortlaw devaluing themselves on-camera.

And then there was the additional insinuated amusement and satisfaction of knowing that the local people they had paid to strip and perform sex-acts could be seen by the local paying public in their small theater and would have to endure lasting debauchery, disrepute, and social and economic devaluation as a result of appearing in the Film Festival Theater's widely touted raunchy productions.

That the whole Film Festival Theater enterprise eventually broke even and then turned enough of a profit to keep it going for some years may have only been an accident. There were clearly basic motivations other than business success.

Similar motivations would seem to have driven other more mainstream camera-based pornography productions. Whatever the motivations, the resulting effect of the Film Festival Theater's raunchy productions was the early promotion of interracial pornography.

A few Film Festival Theater prints seem to have found their way into other San Francisco area theaters showing hardcore porno loops. Some may have been pirated. By and large the Film Festival group recouped the large filmmaking costs by showing and re-showing their amateurish and "real-time" raunchy porno movies in their own small, sleazy, fifty-seat theater at about two dollars a ticket.

While George, the cameraman, was skilled, the equipment he had to use was less than professional. The porno models he had to film were very much amateurs with no acting skills, no experience in front of cameras, and no previous exposure—in either sense of the word—in still or motion-picture pornography.

This was well before the days of inexpensive home video cameras. The Film Festival Theater porno models were first-timers in front of any motion picture camera let alone movie cameras intended solely to record their nude bodies and facial identities for explicit-sex pornography. And even when a few of them appeared in second and third Film Festival porno movies, they still only had the experience of their previous porno movie or movies.

There had to have been some on-the-set tension because these were not inexpensive videotaping sessions. The film could not be erased and re-shot. The developing and printing had to be done quasi-clandestinely, and the cost of color film and its developing and printing was, as now, quite high even when done out in the open.

As a consequence, the Film Festival Theater showed whatever the camera captured the first time around. Its porno movies thus varied in quality and were sometimes optically too dark, too light, fuzzy, or otherwise visually poor. Additionally, due to printing and developing costs, the Film Festival group was forced to project at least some of its original footage onto the movie screen, something a well capitalized professional producer would absolutely never do. The originals were tape-spliced, and sometimes in the middle of a showing a splice would break and the audience would have to sit waiting in the small dark roughly fifty-seat theater until it was re-spliced, re-threaded, and then shown again.

And yet for all these drawbacks the pornographic content was creative and insightful—"the dirtiest porno movies in San Francisco" one of my acquaintances once told me.

They were not, in our present-day more seasoned and liberated view, "dirty" as such. What they were is fascinating amateur ethnic-black and interracial pornography at the onset of the era of publicly shown pornography, effectively amateur porn videos years before videocassettes were even developed for marketing.

Over time the Film Festival Theater acquired a small stable of its own porno models, both black and white. The sad fact is that they never made a great number of porno movies, undoubtedly due to the high cost and low return from the single porno movie theater. But they did produce somewhere around fifty separate twenty-minute to half-hour porno movie "loops," and several of the women and men appeared in from three to five of these Film Festival Theater movies.

My first trip to the Film Festival Theater was in late 1972. They already had a small library of their own porno films, but not enough to re-show at every new weekly billing without risking loss of regular audience. So they were obliged to show old mainstream feature-length porno movies from New York and Los Angeles to fill out time. They were, however, making a new amateurish 20-to-30-minute "loop" porno movie every two or three weeks in that time period around early 1973. As their own porno-movie library grew, it no longer became necessary to show the old commercial porn features.

By early 1974, the Film Festival Theater was showing three or four of its own 20-to-30-minute color-film porn productions, generally a new porno-movie of the latest two-week period and two or three old ones, for a circa two-dollar ticket.

The accumulating library of black and interracial porno films were shown over and over for almost a decade, but the neighborhood got seedier and the mainstream pornography industry eventually grasped the appeal that made the seedy little Film Festival Theater with its poor quality and constantly fracturing films attractive enough to venture there and bother sitting through them.

As the average box office gradually diminished, the economic incentive for producing new interracial porno movies kept slipping. Declining box office receipts seem to have led to an internal fracas, and "George," the cameraman, gave up on making new porno films around 1976. His successor lacked both his filmmaking talent and his pornographic imagination and made less appealing and poorer quality films. "George" apparently briefly relented and came back to the Film Festival Theater group and made a couple more, but that was it.

Due to lack of script or contrived story content, and arriving on the newly decriminalized porno movie scene as some of the first interracial motion picture pornography, the Film Festival Theater porno movies had offered both insights and historical perspective.

Two of their repeat porn performers were a tall mid-thirties black man stage-named Pharaoh Amos and a thirtyish brown-haired white woman with a southern accent whose name I can no longer remember. I talked to Pharaoh Amos briefly as the theater was on its way out of business. He seemed quite happy and proud of his pornographic performances. In the world of tort-law rankings and values he had begun near the bottom anyway. Fucking white women in films could well have raised his ranking and increased his relative personal value even if it may have simultaneously lowered the several white women's down to his, if not lower. Shortly after our conversation he headed for Los Angeles where porn producers paid considerably more for known-quantity male porno models, and I think I saw him in a feature-length porn production originating there a year or so later.

One of the standardized formats of the Film Festival theater was to always begin filming the porno models fully dressed and chatting among themselves. I think the one exception was a film, outlined below, in which one female and two male porno models began in their under-clothes on a bed. But even these porno models began with at least their underclothes on.

In a few of the other films, they began the porno movie outdoors in parks with the decently dressed or at least adequately attired porno models engaging in small talk. Usually, though, "George" began each porno movie by filming his porno models fully dressed inside kitchens, living rooms, restaurants, massage rooms, bedrooms, or other indoor locations.

Before I relate my feelings and descriptions of a couple of these unique old porno movies, I have to say that it has been a about quarter of a century since I last saw one of the Film Festival Theater's films, and at best memory is hazy.

The outstanding thing about them is that they were generally "real-time" and predominantly full-shots of the porno models. In this respect they anticipated the format of the amateur porn video by decades.

I have to guess that the Film Festival Group did not have expensive ultra close-up lens systems and wanted to avoid costly and labor-inten-sive cutting and editing. But the unintended results created the good "dirty" and effectively more "voyeuristic" porn of seeing complete naked figures men and women engaging in sex-acts in unedited, unspliced real time that my acquaintance raved about. Perhaps better financed pornographers became too engrossed in the capabilities of their equipment. Seeing full bare bodies engaging in sex acts would seem to hold its own considerable fascination, and close-up shots may best be used briefly for accent and clarification, anyway.

Seeing the real drama of the audiovisual "whore stories" of paid aver-age pornographic pseudo-whores unfold, uncut and unedited in real time, including all the blunders, faux pas, careless oversights, and expressions of real emotion, would seem to come closer to genuine pornography than contrived "stories," cute camera angles, slick cutting and editing, and extremely well endowed models.

In real time, unintended story interest is told by the naked body language, the hints of balking, the exchanges of emotion and nonverbal communication, the real feelings of pleasure or sometimes even the pleasures of sexual discomfort, the unintended nonverbal disclosures of momentary shame or awareness of stigma and disgrace, genuine unrehearsed lust, betrayal of comprehensions of being "used" and debauched in verbal and nonverbal communications with directors and camera persons, and many other subtleties.

Equipment limits and cost demands had advantages. The Film Festival Theater porno movies had refreshingly interesting unedited, uncut, and unspliced real-time foibles and imperfections. Like a modern amateur porn video maker, the cameraman turned on his sixteen-millimeter camera and began filming. The pornographic subtexts that the cameraman and on-set directors were attempting to convey and the many little sub-stories that were unintentionally acted out were not removed or obscured as in carefully cut and edited high quality porno movies.

There would be the obligatory introductory shot of the porno models sitting around in street clothes talking small talk for several minutes. Their voices were usually, but not always, recorded. Even when the porno movie was made without sound, the format of beginning the movie with the porno models dressed and exchanging the appearance of talk was adhered to.

Most of the porno movies began with sound, and generally the voices were intelligible. The porno models exchanged trite talk between themselves and sometimes they responded to the voice of an off-screen director, cameraman, or spectator. To the untaught observer the scene would be of an interracial couple exchanging banal everyday banter between themselves or with someone just off-screen.

But even to the untaught observer there would be minor blunders. Lighting cords for the spotlights running along the rug could often be seen. Sometimes accidental shots of the spotlights themselves could be seen on-screen. They served as effective reminders that these average and average-attired people were on-camera and aware of it.

The on-camera banter between decently dressed people established them as your normal everyday fellow human beings, the kind of people you might meet on the street. And all of the porno models were clearly the kind of people you might meet on the street. None were statuesque beauties or even remarkably good looking. None were, though, unattractive. The low budget Film Festival Theater porn producers took what they could get in the form of low paid or voluntary porno models. But the blatantly average people they got as porno models spoke slightly different sentences with their bodies than the more carefully selected standards of physical beauty did in the offerings of big business commercial porn. They by and large had never been on-camera let alone naked on-camera and engaging in sex acts for public amusement.

Moreover, all of these porno models were opening their performances in front of George's movie camera in the early days of decriminalized pornography when expectations of consequences would seem to have weighed more heavily. Many of the women seem to have been local prostitutes who might naturally have worried about police consequences. None had conscious or unconscious knowledge, as with present porno models, of a vast population of hundreds of thousands of past and present porno models who had done it, more or less had gotten away with it, and existed out there as a potential support group. So they had, whether they showed them or not, more anxieties than the present generation of porno models.

In launching the porno models into explicit-sex pornographic films in street clothes and exchanging small talk, the Film Festival producers outwardly, and probably with some reasonable production intentions, appear to have attempted to relax some of those anxieties.

But the other side of the coin is that they seem to have delighted in recording their porno models' anticipations as they manipulated them into a gossipy little lewd news story of degradingly stripping naked and engaging in sex-acts on-camera for public viewing by any adult who bought a two-dollar ticket.

A pertinent commentary should be made here. If the reader may feel that the Film Festival producers were a bit callous in their treatment of porno models, compare their behavior with a the commonly accepted and apparently acceptable behavior of a half-dozen-or-so news-camera people poking their news cameras into the face of, say, a crying distraught mother whose child has just been killed and is in a state of shock and utter despair—solely because that kind of "good footage" is claimed to be exciting "news" (and making profits far beyond those of small porn productions). Now that's Obscene (with a capital "O")! The Film Festival Theater porno models were always voluntarily on-camera, and, unlike the above lady who became "newsworthy," usually paid.

While these hired interracial porno models were on-camera still dressed, the manipulative exchanges of their small talk were contrived and nervous. Anyone on-camera is nervous, and especially when it is the first time, and these porno models knew that they were on-camera to literally degrade themselves for public amusement—more so then than now—and would, at least for years into the future, if not all their lives, have decreased social and economic value and lowered self-regard as a result of it. The Film Festival Theater producers and directors seem to have had a flair for this and other entertainment attractions inherent in pornography.

In those first minutes on-camera—which simultaneously were last minutes of their old respectability and their old higher tort-law personal value—the first-time Film Festival porno models sat amusingly straining to act "normal" in the uniquely, and permanently, debasing situation.

The second-or-third-time porno models were less strained, but also appeared not entirely indifferent to their situation and a little uneasy. For them, their tort-law personal value previously reduced and personal respectability already undermined, their uneasiness would appear to have been from facing having to strip naked and perform sex-acts in front of a small and not entirely uncontemptuous audience of production person-nel, as well as the unique demands of having to do it on-camera. But they also would have had an awareness that inherent in being in a second or third porno movie was the taint of professionalism.

That is, when they had appeared in their first porno movie, they might claim excuses of perhaps being unthinking, unsuspecting, and maybe a little unintentional. But this second or even third time that they were being paid to strip naked and engage in sex-acts on-camera for public showing, they could only be regarded as consciously consent-ing to effectively prostitute. So at some level of consciousness they expected to have that additional stigma shackled to their reduction in tort-law personal value and new disrepute.

Whether on-camera for the first-time and anticipating being seen and forever known as smut models, or doing it for the second time with no excuses of innocence, the Film Festival producers grasped the enter-tainment value of showing pre-public-nudity and pre-public-sex-per-formance misgivings and even embarrassments. They let the camera roll for some minutes on the self-consciously waiting-to-be-used, decently clothed models.

As these porno models exchanged nervous banter between them-selves, and sometimes with the camera person—or live spectators whom they knew were looking forward to inspecting their bare flesh and sex organs—they were anticipating both sexual pleasure and a last-ing kind of social discredit containing ingredients of disgrace and scan-dal. On-camera they betrayed understandable and entertaining anxieties in stress in their voices, in unintended glances at the camera recording them, in an unease in posture and body language. There were elements of a news story in it.

Audience could read the gamut of faint-to-conspicuous misgivings about their consent to strip on-camera and engage in sex-acts, and aftermath disgrace, coupled with usual vanity anxieties about how they might appear when the film was processed and shown. And they could see that the events had ensnared the porno models were propelling them along to publicly stripping and "doing it on-camera," misgivings of not. Like divers on a diving board, they were ready to take the plunge, but a plunge they knew for certain would make at least some embarrassing and discomforting changes in their lives.

They thus knew at some level that they were being debauched by the debaucher-cameraperson and the debaucher-producers. The cameraman and associated producers clearly took a devilish delight in debauching them and projecting their debauchery to the audience.

Of course the white females who stripped naked and engaged in sex acts with black men began their on-camera performances unarguably higher in the social rankings of the time than their black male partners. Even those white women who were prostitutes began as higher in the racist society's rankings because as prostitutes prior to porno modeling they could have slipped back into mainstream society of white women with prostituted pasts generally unnoticed. Thus audience—the mostly lower and middle class black and white males of the audience, but also the occasional middle class women accompanying them—enjoyed the white women's obviously greater debauchery.

Following the introduction of affected banal everyday banter between decently dressed interracial porno models—possibly a threesome of a black woman and a white man and a black man, or a white woman and two black men—the Film Festival Theater films would cut to the same still decently dressed two or three people in the location where the explicit-sex porn shooting would take place, sometimes a bedroom, sometimes a couch, sometimes a floor area. Sometimes the camera was not turned off and a "cut" made, and the decently dressed porno models would instead walk on-camera to that site.

Once there, it was—known to viewers as well as porno models—get down and dirty "show time." It had become time for that scandalous on-newscamera revelation-confession of their real naked bodies caught in acts of sexual indulgence, and in the eyes of the beholders, public sexual indignities. The porno models might sometimes speak a few more uneasy strained words to the cameraperson, the person directing, or a spectator. Most of the time they appeared to just sexually go at it—less it seemed out of real and understandable sexual desire than both to get it over with and fulfill their effective porno modeling contracts, and to escape from the pressures of realizing what they had become and anticipating what would become by physically doing something that would allow them temporarily to forget.

The fully garbed porno models began combinations of fondling and undressing ceremonies. You knew, of course, that they were porno models and that they were going to amuse you by stripping naked and publicly engaging in varieties of sex acts.

The cameraperson recorded their voluntary subjugation into sex-objects for public amusement while they submissively stripped. He made sure Film Festival Theater viewers would see their sex organs and bare behinds. When they were naked, they may sometimes have talked about the specific sex acts they would engage in. Most of the time they simply did it.

In its small stable of female porno models, the Film Festival Theater had a medium-size-and-weight and average-appearing thirty-something white woman with reddish-brown head and pubic hair who spoke with the southern accent.

She was a narcissistic expert at making her public fellatio acts look degradingly lewd and clearly enjoyed showing off her oral-sex talents to the camera and the audience. She always appeared, in the three to five Film Festival Theater films that she performed sex-acts in, with black men, usually different ones.

With her age and southern accent clearly implying at least a comparatively privileged white girl's upbringing in the racist South of the 1940s and 1950s, her sex acts with black men, especially fellatio, implied and projected a leveling in tort-value ranking.

On-screen naked, the white race's pedestalled and protected naked white female was sucking the naked black former-slave race's long stiff dong. The late 1960s and early 1970s audiences knew that in the Deep South when the white woman was a girl, black men had been literally lynched for looking crooked at white women. So the obviously designed depiction by the porn producers of this black porn production cooperative, and the clearly intentional portrayal by the porno models themselves, was both defiance of inoculated values and promotion of social change. But it was also a portrayal of the debaucher-debauchee relationship at several depiction levels.

The first and most obvious was the lower tort-valued black male debauching the obviously higher tort-valued white female. Then there was the cameraman relishing debauching them both, but especially the white female, who offered herself to both cameraman and audience as agreeing to be debauched and permanently lowered in value and social standing to a naked whore who engaged in sex-acts on-camera. Then there was a veiled debauchery of the racist system, with a black male engaging in sex acts not only unambiguously engaging in these sex-acts on-camera with a white female and insisting that they publicly perform the more degrading sex-acts, but being filmed by a black cameraman intent on maximizing her social plummet and disgrace through camera angles, close-up focuses, poses and positions he required of her, and even banter about their sex acts before, during, and after their naked sex-act performances.

The thirtyish white woman performed sex-acts with several different black men in several different Film Festival movies, so there should be no dispute about her intentions. In all those films she appeared to genuinely enjoy stripping and engaging in sex on-camera, most notably in those decently dressed introductory minutes in the second and third (and I vaguely recall fourth and fifth) porno movies where she knew what the film location procedure was and knew what was coming and yet was still comfortably dressed rather than that slight unease of subsequent public on camera nudity.

In those fully clothed introductory scenes of her second and later porno movies, she coyly toyed with her male partners with less anxiousness about the camera, the small audience present to watch the porno movie filming, the future porno movie theater audiences and what they would see. She had already done it, and the expectations of what she would be doing and how her acquaintances would regard her after having stripped and engaged in sex-acts in a publicly shown porno movie were now known history. If they had laughed it off with her, they had laughed it off. If they had insinuated she was now a slut and a publicly exhibited piece-of-ass, they had done it. She was what she was, and more fellatio on-screen would hardly do anything to her reputation, one way or the other.

But on-screen it was a white woman coyly toying with black men waiting to fuck her—fuck her on-camera and have her publicly suck their cocks. And both she and the audience clearly knew it. Thus the preview interaction had some elements of classical farce and made the resultant porno movie all the more enjoyable.

In what may have been the last of her porno movies with the Film Festival Theater group, the cameraman and director seemed to feel that she needed little introduction.

In that one, as in the others, she began respectably clothed in a full green dress. In less than a minute running time, however, she was lying on top of her fully dressed black male partner with her legs spread as far as her dress would allow to straddle his. She was talking with him and glanced back while he reached down her behind and legs and mockingly pulled up her dress to reveal her bare buttocks, an act that apprised the viewers that the lady in the green dress had gone on-camera prepared to strip. That the cameraperson's angle had been set-up from behind to capture this obvious depiction of her immorality and public degradation was clearly no accident. And the cameraman made it quite plain by bringing in her bare behind in a close-up to exhibit—to put it in terms used by pornography—her bare ass, asshole, and split bulge of her cunt so it would publicly show larger than life across the silver screen of the off-downtown porno movie theater.

The two porno models continued to converse between themselves and, I believe, exchange some banter with the cameraman while the general focus of the take was on her degradingly exposed bare ass, either in close-up or in a full-body shot from behind as the two of them lay on the couch.

The bare-assed white woman with the southern accent was, by then, well known to the Film Festival Theater regulars. There was certainly no need to introduce her to them as "your average white lady next door." Regular audience knew as soon as they recognized her facial identity that she was already a disgraced "porno whore" and for purposes of that kind of entertainment nothing more. The cameraman and director did not want to waste color film with evaluations of her as an everyday white woman at the moment she was poised to voluntarily disgrace herself stripping and engaging in sex acts on camera for public amusement—with a black man, or black men, in those more racist days.

In this movie she was an already known "porno whore" to the small porn theater's regulars. "George" launched right into her known debauchery and lewdness as portrayed by the black man exposing her bare ass, anus, and female sex-organs to a porno movie audience—with her obvious consent. Her wanton shamelessness was intentionally represented to the audience by the unseen cameraman with his camera angle and focus on her bare behind as her dress was being slipped-up to expose it, and into banter with her black male porn partner and the unseen cameraman while she conspicuously portrayed herself as a bare-assed smut-movie whore. The audience viewed her voluntary public debauchery and whatever additional humiliation it may have been.

The porno movie then progressed to her usual expertise at fellatio in several acts and sex-act positions and to her publicly enjoying cunnilingus, and to her several coital sex-acts. These were in themselves hardly much different than her four previous porno movies.

In one scene of an earlier porno movie made prior to the above, she lay naked on a living room straw-mat rug engaging in sex-acts with two large black men. She had by then gone through the usual fully dressed introduction, had stripped on-camera, and had engaged in at least one act of fellatio.

As she lay on the floor half on her side, one large black man was fucking her. The other black man, as I try to recall, was lying on his back. She seems to have been sucking the other's cock in her characteristic lewdly slurping way when he rolled over and presented his bare black buttocks in front of her face. In this era of exact quotes, I may be ever so slightly paraphrasing dialogue due to memory from a quarter of a century ago. But if not an exact quote, the following must be almost exact.

She looked toward the lens of the capturing camera and presumably at the director and/or cameraperson. "Do you want me to lick his asshole?" the microphone picked her up asking the cameraman or director. Although one of the people either directing of filming may have given her a nod that was quickly overridden, I got the impression apparently that she went ahead without waiting for an answer.

On-screen she pressed her white face between his black buttocks and quite obviously got her mouth and tongue on his anal flesh.

But for whatever reasons the "take" abruptly stopped at that point. Clearly the woman had no qualms about performing anilingus on-camera. I can only guess that the black porn producers had qualms about showing a white woman licking a black man's anus in their porno movie theater. They were, at that point in the early 1970s, still testing the waters and with considerable daring.

My memories are vague after a couple decades, but if the sequence is a little off, the pornographic actions is correct. As the porno movie took up the action again, the other black man was again fucking the white woman in about the same pose and position. But the other black man now sat on her chest and fucked her in her mouth, deep down her throat, while the sound boom picked up her gaggling and grunts, while the camera person focused on her facial expressions of a mixture of gaggling discomfort and sexual pleasure. All the while, another black man fucked her.

The scene of anilingus had obviously been deliberately cut out, but the scene of a large black man sitting on a white woman's chest aggressively fucking a long meaty black penis in her in her mouth and thrusting it down her throat while she audibly and visibly gaggled with choking grunts was deemed to suffice.

To put it in perspective, in another of the Film Festival Theater's porno movies titled "Amazing Grace," evidently an irreverent poke at hypocrisies in conservative black religion but also recalling Rubins' voluptuous female nudes in "The Three Graces," a tall shapely young black woman, presumably the character named Grace, a muscular young white man, and a large heavy black man began in a bed talking not only among themselves but clearly to the camera person.

They removed the bed covers and then stripped off their underclothes and engaged in cunnilingus, fellatio, and coital sex.

The highlight of the film, and perhaps that which made Grace amazing, was her long and aggressive performance of anilingus with her pretty black face between the white man's buttocks. In this case she did not ask to perform this sex-act on-camera, but simply positioned herself behind the white male porno model, pressed her face between his buttocks, and performed the defiling act of anilingus for repeated public showings over a number of years in the Film Festival Theater. The same black porn producers apparently felt quite safe in showing a black woman performing anilingus on a white man in their small San Francisco porno movie theater.

For some minutes they held the camera on her at different angles while she licked around his anal flesh, forced her tongue into his anal orifice, and looked from time to time proudly and cutely into the lens of the capturing camera.

What "Amazing Grace" was thinking and feeling while licking anal flesh on-camera for public amusement can only be known to her. But in his 1993 book *Bottom Feeders; From Free Love To Hard Core; the Rise and Fall of Counterculture Heroes Jim and Artie Mitchell,* [21] John Hubner offers a glimpse of porno star Marilyn Chambers' feelings while naked on-camera in her interracial epic *Behind the Green Door*, made about fifteen blocks away at almost exactly the same time. Hubner quite clearly had talked with Chambers and was not simply offering hearsay.

Naked on-camera with a small supporting cast and in front of a number of production people and invited onlookers, first-time porno star Marilyn Chambers was portraying a character named Gloria. Hubner says on page 191:

"She took the penis of the man on the trapeze in front of her in her mouth and, for a moment, was once again utterly amazed at what she was doing. I wonder how this is going to look on film? Marilyn asked herself."

One can only guess what "Grace" might have been thinking, but the look on her face while her tongue slipped around her male porn partner's anal flesh seemed to have an "I wonder what this is going to look like in the smut theater" expression.

To go back to Hubner's study of Marilyn Chambers on-camera, walking distance from there, on page 189 he says of her personal feelings while she was posed naked on-camera and in front of everyone in a sex scene:

"It was the fact that she was the star of the show, the center of attention...Everyone was waiting to see what would happen next, and Marilyn found that especially exciting..."

One may read similar thoughts and feelings into Grace's on camera act of anilingus. She clearly was enjoying being the center of attention even while the cameraman was enjoying debauching her with angles on her tongue—to put the image in words that describe the pornographic act in its own terms—slipping around the guy's anus and additionally moving to debauching angles from behind that included her bare ass and twat while she publicly licked his anus.

After several minutes of anilingus, she and the young muscular white man scrambled around to a new porn position, and—to use the descriptive word—he fucked her on-camera.

I talked to the cameraperson once in his dual capacity as projectionist in the projection booth. I cannot exactly remember the conversation now. But the drift of it remains. He said, in effect, that he enjoyed "making a fool" out of her and the other porno models. In other words, he enjoyed debauching and permanently defiling them.

And he was the ultimate porno movie cameraman-producer debaucher. He himself never appeared in any of the Film Festival Theater porno movies, but a couple of the black men in the cooperative group did.

He made one porno movie in the upstairs hotel. The movie was apparently fully filmed in one of the hotel rooms while its door to the corridor open. A few onlookers who were apparently other hotel residents were accidentally or deliberately caught by his panning camera and viewed. It would seem that the cameraperson, presumably "George" had his fun implying that the naked debauched "fools" engaging in sex acts in public and on-camera for everyone to see in the hotel and everyone to see in the theater downstairs for years to come.

Toward the end, the Film Festival Theater closed down its upstairs projection booth and the ticket-taker doubled as projectionist with the clattering sixteen-millimeter projector showing through a slot cut in the first-floor ticket booth. By then, circa late 1977, they were clearly no longer making new porno movies and simply re-showing the old library to drunks sleeping it off and a few of the old audiences returning for the "dirtiest porno movies in town." One could go next door in the same hotel building to the grocery store—run by one of the black men loosely associated with the Film Festival Theater—and buy a beer, smuggle it into the porno movie theater, and sip brew while watching the naked porno models on-screen.

The Anglo Hotel, in which the small porn theater and grocery store were located, became part of San Francisco city-run housing for the poor in the 1980s. The grocery store remained open, but the historic interracial porno movie was closed down and remained vacant and unused with a padlocked iron-grill gate across the entrance. The hotel building was severely damaged in the 1989 San Francisco earthquake and had to be demolished. "George," the cameraman had by then moved across San Francisco Bay to Oakland.

But by then the videocassette had been perfected. Home video cameras were selling for five hundred dollars and up. VCRs cost a mere one hundred fifty dollars. And there were no great color film costs, developing costs, and printing and editing costs. "Dirty" amateur porno movies like those could be made by amateurs videotaping naked "fool" porno-model amateurs almost anywhere at any time. Story material inherent in interracial porn evolved as attitudes changed, social and economic opportunities became more equal, and black men and women began to achieve strata of tort-law personal values slowly approaching those of white men and women.

But the pioneer "amateur" interracial porno movies made by the Film Festival Theater clearly broke new ground. Human similarities had their racial and cultural differences. Tort-law higher value of white females could be leveled to the lower value of black males not only when they both stripped and engaged in sex-acts on-camera but as a lasting consequence afterward. The naked black female shown enjoying degradingly licking the anal flesh of the white male lost little or nothing in tort-law personal value, nor, probably, did the working class white man who stripped to become level and engage in cunnilingus with her for public amusement lose much.

Some of the interest had to be how these racially different people sexually and otherwise interacted while naked on-camera. The different tort-law personal value and the altering of tort-law personal value as a result of signing away rights to images in model releases and then appearing naked and engaging in sex acts for public amusement had to be part of that amusement.

Heterosexual pornography is a constant stream of generally larger males engage in sex acts with generally smaller females and as a result may project impressions that males are dominant. In all pornography there are dominant and submissive roles at any given time, and they may alternate in the progress of live or on-camera sexual activities.

Word-based communication is by its nature conservative of social values, but these values extend beyond word-based concepts. Social values of male and female beauty in face and form, sexual attractiveness, and their opposites of ugliness and repulsiveness require no words.

As signs of masculine beauty, Aztec warriors wore lip-plugs, jade and stone objects pierced through lower lips. When Cortés and his Europeans saw them they found them ugly and repulsive, and after the Conquest of Mexico, European standards of manly beauty quickly replaced Native American ones.

Visual facial and bodily beauty is both learned and socially standardized and undergoes only very slow alterations within cultural artistic constraints. People exposed only to Western art must study Asian, African, and Native American art and only slowly learn to appreciate different standards of beauty both in nature and depicted human form.

As our overpopulated multi-ethnic and multi-racial world merges and clashes, and especially as it merges and clashes in multi-ethnic and multi-racial societies like those of North America, civil strife may be alleviated by creating new common grounds of learned standards of beauty. Inherent in pornography, with its base-level of sexually interacting varieties of living human bodies divested of attire and pretensions, is growth of new more widely acceptable standards of beauty out of this common ground.

The invention of photography, and its subsequent modifications in motion pictures, video, and now Internet-connected computer images, certainly brought all the world's different cultures, ethnicities, and races into instant contact and began assimilation and redefinition of standards of beauty.

With the invention of photography came camera-based pornography and eventually hardcore pornography that not only leveled the naked human participants but also made blatantly manifest the universality of human sexuality. Race-based attitudes toward sexual partnership, cohabitation, and marriage began to melt away.

Through pornography we get tangential looks at social transitions in the master-servant, higher servant-lower servant, buyer-seller, servant-slave relationships in society and in debaucher-debauchee, artist-model, boss-employee created by pornography, and how they may interact to foster and promote social change.

The leveling and additional liberating effects of pornography may work to establish new attitudes in relationships between men and women. Countering root psychologies of racism would seem to be happening with interracial pornography.

We see in it European whites of the dominant culture with its dominant standards of physical beauty and facial attractiveness. But they are naked and stripped of attire and pretensions that give them an edge in interactions with other races. At the same time we see nude blacks, Hispanics, and Asians brought to the same level as the whites in their nakedness. And on this level playing field of a pornographic set or location we see the equalized bare porno models consensually and knowingly engaging in sex acts that lead to their subsequent defamation and thus lower tort-law personal value.

The gossipy story of interracial sexual relationship in camera-based explicit sex pornography is no longer the consequences of interracial children but the consequences of signing away rights to damages for loss of reputation and status and the resultant permanent lowering to a class of whores and pseudo-whores at the bottom of the social scale.

Through ages of human history sexual relations between young men and young women meant children, loss of personal worth to feed and care for them, loss of degrees of personal freedom involved in years of raising them, and only pat-on-the-back social approval as a reward. These are great losses, but the sexual urge is powerful and the pressure of social conformity excruciating.

Upper class women of the dominant culture had the most to lose in this regard, and yet pursued pleasures of the sex drives, acknowledged the nebulous rewards of social conformity, and sought and accepted subsequent personal losses knowingly.

Pornography depicts people pursuing the same sexual pleasures but accepting a different category of economic and personal freedom losses. Interracial pornography depicts, among other things, white women as consenting to loss of potential worth and loss of future personal freedom of social movement, but it depicts black men as defined lower class and less to lose in engaging in sex on-camera with them. White men engaging in sex-acts on-camera with black women may not hold the same interest partly because black women do not represent the same world-culture dominant white European standards of beauty and protected status and partly because it is the male volunteering to be stigmatized as a whore or pseudo-whore, something males are not enculturated to feel as much pain or anxiety about.

But in any case, the gossipy story is of a leveling, democracy in action, and a debaucher-debauchee voluntary defamation projecting suppressed fears of the spectators of the real world of consequences and potential downward social mobility, and the sport of watching others than oneself losing, and by inference, then, winning.

CHAPTER NINE

Seeing Porn For What It Is Not

British writer Laurie Taylor[22] recalls a visit years earlier to sexually liberated Sweden and viewing pornography there. She comments: "Perhaps, as the American sociologist Harold Garfinkle believed when he dispatched his students to porn shops with the instruction to see how quickly they could clear the premises by talking loudly about what they saw, it is the juxtaposition of pornography's explicitness and the restraint of other public conventions which is so much more intriguing than its actual content."

The attraction of pornography may indeed stem more from its juxtaposition with, and therefore protest against, social conventions than with sexual and other interest in the bare bodies, sex organs, and explicit sex acts themselves. After having seen a pair of boobs, a cock and balls, a cunt, and a bare fanny, one might expect a viewer to drift into boredom at seeing repeats if that were all the interest. Even if it were the attraction of the hidden and forbidden suddenly revealed, interest would probably rapidly decline after initial exposures.

But for over a quarter of a century publicly sold and shown commercial pornography has been a remarkable business success and shows no sign of not continuing to be. Consumers do not seem to be losing interest. Adult bookstores selling both pornographic novels and camera-based pornography and adult theaters showing porno movies continue to draw customers and viewers, the majority of them repeat customers and viewers. Internet porn is now a multibillion-dollar industry and shows not the slightest sign of waning. So there would seem to be considerably more attraction to pornography than views of bare bodies, sex organs, and sex acts.

There would seem to be elements of recreation, both in the etymological sense (to re-create oneself) and the entertainment sense. These are probably the same elements that one finds in other entertainment like sports, parlor games, books, mainstream movies, and legitimate theater—amusement at antics, identification with mental risk-calculations and resulting physical actions, storyline gossip about character, needling of decision-based consequences and failings, portrayal of alternative selves and personalities, and identification with bodily and mental activity pleasures.

The juxtaposition, then, may be a segment of the recreation. But there is obviously more to the recreation of pornography than that. In reading works of fiction and as audience for dramatic productions we are asked to suspend our disbelief, but never at the cost of our natural human skepticism.

In participating as readers we are engaging the authors, and in participating as audience we are engaging dramatists, screenwriters, directors, actors, and cinematographers, at every step of the unfolding story. One element that makes a good work of fiction or drama great is its carefully crafted ability to sustain itself against our natural skepticism. And when works lapse into failure against reader or audience skepticism, we have words like "melodramatic" or "shallow" to describe the breakdowns.

Readers of news and history and audience for documentaries also engage the journalists, historians, and documentary producers with the same skepticism at every step of their unfolding stories. Here, though, the facts govern the stories and we do not so much suspend our disbelief as critically question the factual material and the storytelling and editing processes that went into retelling it.

Similar processes take place in spectators of sporting events. As the facts unfold themselves on the playing fields and courts, spectators participate at every step of the play by critically examining the action for skill, decisions, tactics, errors, false steps, and adherence to the rules. Every now and then sports spectators find themselves betrayed by fraud. A boxer "takes a dive." A basketball player or team "shaves points." A runner enhances skill with drugs. As keen spectators they watched the play but were denied all the facts, therefore fraudulently denied their honest engagement and participation.

How can it be any different, then, in pornography? It has elements of fiction, dramatic production, gossipy news, history (as that which has been recorded in time), and sports. Even still photographs of pornography engage natural discerning processes of viewers, but motion picture, videotape, and live-sex-show pornography make the participations by audience abundantly clear.

Porn spectators engage the porno models, porn producers, and camerapersons with the same critical skepticism. To the extent that most pornography is largely ad lib, porn spectators participate by critically examining interactions between the porno models themselves, interactions with the environment of the set or location, and many if not all of the same elements that interest sports spectators.

To the extent that all pornography is gossipy history and news, viewers participate by skeptically examining the unfolding material for its authenticity, its factual detail, its journalistic and historical record of porno model interactions and responses, and the producers' editing and storytelling processes.

To the extent that all pornography is a staged performance, audience participates by mentally engaging the developing depiction and created whore-story material at every step, weighing performer and producer artistic license for composed and ad lib story creation against the candor and realities of personal and social protest, debauchee sex-performer capitulation and debaucher cameraperson-producer subjugation of them, and sex-performer acceptances of social reputation and personal value consequences.

As with all entertainment, pornographic audiences actively engage the entertainment material. Bare bodies, sexual body parts, and sex-acts are the medium more than the message. But in pornography the active mental engagement interplays with the life-force of sexuality and the devices of culture and society that both promote and restrain it. Both in the presentation of the pornographic material and in the audience mental-process engagement with it, the medium, by its very nature, treads on thin ice.

Early "blue movie" and "stag film" pornography shown in atmospheres of subterfuge may have struck largely inexperienced pornography viewers with social-defiance shock value. The same bias toward shock value would seem to have been present in the early tenuously decriminalized pornography, and some of the protest against it may have derived from this shock and resulting rushed consideration.

As an industry grew to fill a demand, feature-length porno movie productions, which additionally entertained by parodying Hollywoodisms, literally overwhelmed this rushed and not carefully pondered protest. As decriminalized adult-public pornography proliferated, it merged into mainstream entertainment. If a lingering subculture of much maligned "dirty old men" (who are certainly entitled to their harmless enjoyments and are no more obsessed than the huge female audiences of soap operas) still slithers into porno movie theaters, the larger share of pornographic entertainment money now comes from rented or purchased video cassettes shown on living room or bedroom television sets and magazines delivered to homes. It engages viewer minds and audience participates as in any other accepted form of entertainment.

Like uniformed athletes and costumed actors, naked porno models perform on "playing fields, courts, sets, and stages" where the rules of activity are different from those of the real world, idealized, and more narrowly defined.

Their audiences, spectators, and viewers, in placing themselves in the midst of the juxtaposition of a fictional or quasi-fictional world of bodily and character abandon and convention defiance on one side, and the surrounding real world of social restraints and consequence considerations on the other, may experience simultaneous liberation and tension similar, if not identical, to that experienced in spectator sports and mainstream arts.

It is not clear in reading Taylor's article whether she had seen much photographed, filmed, or videotaped pornography in Britain or anywhere else prior to her eye-opening trip to less puritanical Sweden. A reader gets the impression that it was limited, but the commentary seems to have been motivated more by Taylor's viewing live naked male and female human beings publicly performing sex acts for audience amusement in one or more of those famous Swedish "live sex shows" than by Swedish camera-based pornography.

Live sex performances and camera-based pornography have been separated by critics from other forms of entertainment and portrayal because they seem to merge the distinction between actors/actresses and the acts they depict on stage or on-camera. In traditional theater and motion pictures, actors/actresses represent emotions and sensations that are not necessarily the actual sensations and emotions felt by them at the time of the performance.

In pornography and public sex-performances one might say, as does Frances Ferguson in "Pornography: the Theory," that there is a "representational collapse, in which the representation of action involves the action," which may strike some as a pornography paraphrase of Heisenberg's uncertainty principle.

Ferguson goes on to cite the Committee on Obscenity and Film Censorship's justifying a prohibition of live sex acts by arguing a distinction between them and camera-recorded pornography. As the Committee put it: "the situation is changed completely when the spectator is confronted with, where that involves *being* in the same space as, people actually engaging in sexual activity," and continues about the shared space to point out that "the ground of relation between performer and audience which is not present with, for example, a film of such activity."

The Committee rightly notes an important distinction between live sex performances and camera-based recorded pornography. There is a genuine and always present low level interaction between naked live sex-act performer and decently dressed audience that cannot be present in a recorded pornographic image—except by intentional representation with other decently dressed performers, or even unseen camera persons and directors, acting out parts of being audience.

But the Committee then uses this difference between recorded and live presented-on-stage sexual activity to call for prohibition of all live sex shows, appearing to summarily denounce live sex performance rather than dispassionately consider its intentions, statements, and effects.

That aside, the distinction can serve to create a perspective on claims of "representational collapse" in pornography, and Ferguson utilizes it to show the Committee's reasoning in differentiating recorded camera-based pornography from live sex shows and to advance a perspective, the distinction being "distance between an action and a spectator observing it." Distance here means a distance in time and an abstract philosophical distance rather than the number of inches between naked sex performers and the audiences watching them, so that images on videotape recorded earlier of naked porno models engaging in sex acts have that "distance."

Ferguson's piece, though, is largely a review and criticism of writings and efforts by anti-pornography activists Andrea Dworkin and Catharine A. MacKinnon, and her purpose in bringing up, (1.) the apparent "representational collapse" and, (2.) this distinction between live sex acts and camera-based recorded pornography is to analyze and counter claims made by the two activists.

Both "representational collapse" and the Committee's distinction between live sex acts and camera-based pornography make valid points and raise interesting questions about viewing pornography, whether they have anything to say for or against pornography itself or not.

Are conventional and unconventional sex-acts by naked performers, in front of voluntary audiences, or on-camera presumably for future voluntary audiences, genuinely analogous to traditional acting performances on stage or on-camera?

Or is there a blurring and merging of portrayal with act that differentiates pornographic nudity and sexual portrayal by porn actors/actresses from genuine portrayal and acting by traditional actors/actresses?

Legitimate actors and actresses generally portray fictional or historical personalities other than their own, depict these fictional or historical personalities in staged situations separate from the surrounding reality, and act out their parts while reciting lines of identifiable story. They are thus "representing" something other than themselves and additionally "representing" situations other than the one of the real surrounding world.

Ferguson then hastens to point out that naked sex performers fail to genuinely "represent" personalities other than their own and to imply that the live or camera-recorded sex acts are merely naked people engaging in sex, rather than actors depicting other personalities in other situations.

But this view seems, at very least, too quickly stated and too poorly examined. For instance, in the acting method invented by the Russian actor and producer Constantine Stanislavsky actors/actresses learn to "become" the person portrayed and to genuinely feel his or her emotions and then project them. This may be remote from two undressed porno models seeming less to portray sex than ostensibly enjoying sex on a stage or on-camera, but even here anyone can see similarities. Whether real or portrayed, emotions and feelings are being intentionally conveyed to audiences.

Moreover, the naked porno models always clearly understand that they are on stage or on-camera and therefore virtually by definition offer "performances," even if one wants to claim minimal and attention-getting performances similar to show-off children. But by the very nature of being on a sex-stage or on-camera, they undeniably "perform" for audiences.

A pornography or live-sex-show viewer cannot help but be aware that he or she is watching naked models or actors knowingly "performing" for an audience. Even in those porno movie story lines where audience may be seduced into literary suspension of disbelief about, say, peeping into someone's bedroom, an awareness of naked porno models being intentionally on-camera, or on stage primarily for their nudity and sex-acts, prevails and indeed is some of the amusement of pornography.

A genuinely hidden camera capturing a naked unsuspecting person, or capturing a naked unsuspecting couple engaging in sex, would not offer the same amusement and recreation as a person intentionally portraying himself or herself, at some depiction level, as a whore seduced into publicly stripping naked or engaging in sex acts for presumed compensation. And it would not be, virtually by definition, pornography.

Thus while legislation and its case-law interpretation allows department stores and work places to photograph and videotape naked unsuspecting customers and employees in rest rooms and dressing rooms (yes, sorry to say, it is true!), the resulting photographs and videotapes generally lack even rudimentary entertainment value. If the photographs or videotapes of naked unsuspecting people are shown to unauthorized people, possible criminality might enter. Even if crimes cannot be proven, certainly the tort-law "devaluation" of the unsuspecting naked person would allow him or her to recover monetary compensation "damages."

So commercial pornography is not about the antics and sex acts of naked people, it is about the voluntary and intentionally public antics and sex acts of presumably paid naked porno models.

A viewer of camera-based pornography thus knows virtually for certain that he or she is seeing voluntarily naked porno models voluntarily engaging in sex-acts on-camera or on a sex stage—intentional performers, not recorded journalistic accidents or events. Few pornography viewers are not at least minimally aware, especially after a number of news events like the Vanessa Williams v *Penthouse* magazine affair, that the naked porno had signed "model releases" eternally and unretractably authorizing the public exhibition of their bare flesh, sex organs, and sex acts and thus had freely submitted to surrendering personal value in the global tort-law social rankings and valuations of people.

So a pornography consumer buys a sex magazine, porn videotape, X-rated home-movie film, or goes to a porno movie theater to be entertained by the same elements that one finds in other entertainment like sports, parlor games, books, mainstream movies, and legitimate theater. They are amused at the voluntarily naked porno models' publicly exhibited sex organs, bare flesh, sex acts, and other antics. They are entertained by contemplating the naked porno models' prior-to-performance mental risk-calculations that resulted in devaluing physical deeds of putting their bare bodies on public exhibit on stage or on-camera amid understood storyline "dirty" gossip about their characters. They savor vicarious needling of decision-based consequences resulting in unremitting assignment to lowest class whoredom or pseudo-whoredom in tort-law social rankings, portrayal of the porno models' alternative "selves," and personalities as everyday people who submitted to being seduced, presumably by money, to become public whores of one kind or another. And, of course, they are amused and often stimulated by identification with bodily and mental-excitement pleasures of sexual activities.

In other words, the public nakedness and sex-act performance that porn consumers buy into is the medium more than the message, the genre more than the entertainment, the means more than the end. And consciously or unconsciously they are buying into this form of recreation to be entertained by the overtones, the nuances, the interplays of sympathetic vibrations, the verbal and nonverbal commentary of social protest, the identifications with performers that audience always makes in sports and theatrical performances. Pornography audiences delve into the layers of personality and social complexities of the sex-performers, and how the naked performers may complexly react and respond within the narrower "rules" of the porn stage, set, court, or playing field, some of which—as in all theater and sports—include subsequent post-game or post-performance fame or infame, value or devalue, pride or shame resulting directly from the performance.

The naked porno models may or may not—and for some more than others—find it easier to portray enjoyment on a sex stage or on-camera than an actor would in portraying grief over loss or rage at injustice. Sex on-camera or on a stage would seem to require little or no training and practice, as compared to traditional acting. But by the very nature of it there is some "representation." And one can see in—now second or third generation—protracted porn consumers who have themselves become sex-performers and porno models more relaxed performances, therefore less obvious "acting"—and as a result, porno models expressing more subtle differences in communication from those of one or two generations earlier who had lacked learning and other advantages that accompany seeing others performing in pornography, or sometimes live sex shows.

Moreover, the person often is the portrayal, even in traditional theater and motion pictures. People often choose to see a play or a movie because a known actor or movie star is in it. In other words, they go as much to see the actor, actress, or movie star portraying himself or herself as a great actor or actress as to see the created portrayal.

Is this too greatly different, then, from a person selecting a sex magazine, pornographic video, or going to see a live sex act to see known or unknown naked persons portraying themselves, say, as prostitutes who publicly exhibit their bare bodies and sex organs while engaging in sex acts for pay?

On a city street, a mime may entertain a small audience with his or her mimics of actions. But much of the entertainment is the mime himself or herself, the simple public street-presence of a costumed person mimicking appreciated actions. The mime and the mime act are, in fact, inseparable. How many in the audience stop for a moment to be amused by the abnormally costumed mime himself or herself and how many stop to be entertained by his or her mimics may not be easily testable.

Extending this to camera-based pornography and live-sex-acts, some of the entertainment would seem to be the publicly naked person or people, the unusualness, brazenness, and social defiance of him, her, or them. More may be their audacity in engaging in sex-acts on-camera or in front of a live audience. And some may be the entertainment of appreciating or identifying with the sex acts themselves and the people portraying them.

How many in the audience have sought the viewing experience to be amused by the spectacle of the publicly naked porno model himself or herself and how many have sought to be entertained by his or her sexual antics may not be easily testable either.

There are suggestions—in the popularity of pornography featuring newsworthy names such as John Wayne Bobbitt, or poor quality black-and-white historical hardcore porno movies claiming to feature old movie stars such as Jayne Mansfield—that a known person's bare body has entertainment value in itself, that viewers pay money and take time out of their lives to watch a known person depict himself or herself as a prostitute, a fool, one who has allowed himself or herself to be publicly debauched, or simply as one who enjoys stripping and engaging in sex acts in public—or, more likely, a little of all of the above. There is now a whole Internet category of famous-people pornographic images to support this idea.

But porn is generally not about the rich and famous. A constant need for "new faces" in pornography—sometimes advertised as such in alternative newspaper ads to recruit new porno models—betrays that camera-based pornography is at least as much about porno models' facial identities and their facial emotional expressions. The latter entertainingly range, whether acted or real, from excitement and pleasure to unease, agitation, and apprehension as it is about their bare behinds and sex organs.

Viewers may or may not be looking for that elusive person whom they may actually know and recognize. But they are obviously seeking representational story material as told by the identifiable and expressive faces of nude porno models, if only autobiographical representations by the porno models portraying themselves as prostitutes understood to have agreed to publicly strip naked and engage in sex on-camera for pay and aware of the social and economic consequences.

But even in autobiographical representations of selves as whores, the additional subtexts and complexities conveyed by the naked porno models are as limitless as their personalities, individual identities, and the enormous varieties of on-camera situations they find themselves in. Even if camera-based pornography is produced on the same set with the same naked porno models engaging in the same verbal and nonverbal narratives, each shooting situation is inherently different.

Nowhere was this made more apparent than in the Delphi Palast Theater chain in Germany in the late 1980s, in the basement of whose flagship porn emporium in Nuremberg their amateurish porn videos were made to be shown in the peep-show booths and video-projection theater there and in their peep-show booths and porn theaters across Europe.

In the basement, the Delphi Palast had constructed a simple pornographic studio consisting of a small, roughly fifteen-foot by ten-foot (five meter by three-and-a-half meter) stage elevated about three feet (one meter) above the basement floor. In the center was a roughly nine-foot-diameter (three-meter-diameter) turntable which was rotated with an on-off button by the cameraperson only from time to time to turn the naked porno models to different angles. The video camera, stationary and mounted to allow a full shot of the pornographic stage, was equipped with a zoom lens to allow close-up shots of the porno models' faces, their sex organs and bare behinds, and their sex acts, or full shots of their bare bodies and sex acts.

Very likely the studio had been constructed, so German-like, for maximum ease and efficiency in manufacturing pornographic videos. The naked porno models literally did all the work. The camera person had little to do but watch the sexual activity, press a button to rotate the turntable for new camera angles on the porno models, and press another button to zoom in on or out from the naked bodies, the sex-acts, the facial identities/expressions, or the sex-organs. It was a porn manufacturer's dream.

But this maximally efficient porn manufacturing business's unintended side effect was to completely standardize all of the Delphi Palast's hundreds of commercially sold and shown pornographic video productions.

All porno models always began their productions showing off their complete nakedness on stage and its turntable unambiguously constructed solely to videotape pornography. The videotape viewing audience had no difficulty immediately grasping why the naked porno models were on the sex stage. If however, some might have been slower than others, a large red-white-and-blue sign, DELPHI TV STUDIO, had been sparkle-painted across the back of the obvious sex stage.

Intended or not, it offered the naked porno models as whores know-ingly paid to publicly engage in sex on-camera for audience amuse-ment—as opposed, say, to those bedroom sex scenes with fictitious story lines often seen in porno movies.

Thus the Delphi Palast's porno models always began by presenting themselves to the video camera as naked presumably paid whores knowingly on a sex stage unambiguously constructed to videotape commercially sold and shown pornography.

But in their sex-act portrayals, solely of themselves as nude whores on that standardized sex-stage and turntable, there was infinite repre-sentational variety. If there were not, in fact, the whole enterprise would have collapsed after the first or second pornographic video.

Instead, literally hundreds of different porno models stripped and engaged in sex acts in that ultimately standardized format. Thousands, possibly hundreds of thousands, of porn video viewers paid to watch them. As repeat customers, many paid to watch them and other porno models strip and engage in the same sex acts in more videos with the same monotonous standardized format.

Even if video projection theater customers only sat through a single showing of three different half-hour porn videos, which most did, what they stayed to see were naked porno models—sometimes the same ones—engaging in the same sex acts on the same identical sex stage, illuminated by the same lighting, recorded by the same immobile video camera, with the same inferred nonverbal sex narrative of naked whores publicly engaging in obscene acts on-camera in a sex studio. In same-ness of stage-set, unvarying nudity of porno models, unadjusted angle of the single video camera, and limit of only a few oral and coital het-erosexual sex-acts that could be performed in the context of the small turntable stage, sometimes by the same naked porno models in separate half-hour productions, one might think there would have been an audi-ence-deterring monotony.

Moreover, outside the porno movie theater in the aisles of peep-show booths, customers went from booth to booth to savor different videos of the naked porno models—again sometimes the same ones in different videos—engaging in the same sex acts on the same identical sex stage with the same inferred nonverbal sex narrative. I never saw one single peep-show customer only go into one booth and then leave. All went to different booths and thus looked at several different videos showing naked porno models in that monotonously constrained pornography format. So what variety might have kept these folks from sheer boredom and kept them coming back?

The first and most obvious variety could be seen in the porno models' bare bodies themselves. The Delphi Palast had an obvious interracial sex bias in their porn video production, so there were black men and women, clearly white German men and women, oriental men and women, and clear varieties of other European and Mediterranean men and women. But even so, these different folks were not doing very many different strokes on that same monotonous stage with the monotonous sex narrative recorded by the monotonously anchored video camera. Interracial and international variety of naked porno models could not have by itself kept customers coming back.

So let us focus on a viewing in one of the approximately fifty-seat Delphi video-projection porno movie theaters somewhere in Germany. The porn videos shown there were the same ones shown, apparently later, in the one-Deutschemark-per-play Delphi Palast peep-show booths.

In the porno-movie theater viewers saw these different porno-model folks all begin their porn videos nude on the sex stage. There were no strip-tease undressing ceremonies.

For some minutes into all of the porn videos, the models were required to literally show-off their nudity to the camera prior to engaging in sex-acts. While sitting or standing naked on the stage, they sometimes exchanged brief conversation between themselves or with the unseen cameraperson.

All were, of course, acquainting the audience with their different bare bodies and their different personalities while exhibiting their nakedness on-camera, and sometimes exchanging conversation, even in this standardized beginning.

All engaged in similar sex-acts on the standardized stage and turntable. There were no props, sex toys, erotic costuming. As a result the sex-acts were limited to the few humanly possible coital sex positions, the few cunnilingus positions, and the few fellatio positions, and only rarely to the limited anilingus positions.

The camera person never failed to rotate the turntable and zoom in-and-out on their bare bodies, facial identities and expressions, their genitals and bare behinds, and their sex-acts while they solely portrayed themselves as naked whores publicly engaging in sex acts on camera for audience amusement with no other intervening fictional story lines.

There was only one modification to the format sameness, and this offers a hint of insight into audience's attraction, especially to repeat customers. Early Delphi Palast porn videos were silent, but soon a sound boom was added to pick up sexual slurps, moans, and grunts and spoken words, including directions from the camera person and naked porno models' spoken responses to them, as well as grunts, moans, and background noises.

In other words, if the entertainment of this pornography had been limited to visual nudity and sex-acts themselves, there would not be much reason to add sound. The simultaneously recorded sounds picked up the varieties of human sexual and other interactions. With the aid of the added sounds, including spoken words by the undressed porno models and unseen others observing them, more of their interpersonal interactions, interactions with the recording cameras and camera persons, occasional anonymous spectators, or even with the recording camera itself, were conveyed, understood, and appreciated.

But even with this addition of real-life sound, there was the additional standardization of the unedited Delphi porn videos' "real time." Except for a very rare stopping and restarting of the camera—with an unknown but obviously short interim of time in between—the Delphi TV Studio video camera was simply turned on when the undressed porno models had climbed up onto the unambiguous smut-videotaping stage and turned off when the thirty-minute color videotape ran out, occasionally in the middle of a sex-act.

In between the turning-on of the camera and the running-out of videotape, the naked porno models kept changing poses and postures—apparent to the audience as a result of commands from the cameraperson or porn director—to engage in cunnilingus, fellatio, breast fondling and oral stimulation, and occasionally anilingus, and almost always to engage in coital sex. Since the sex studio lacked props—B & D, S & M, or any other—the naked porno models performed no other sex acts. There was no editing to heighten effect or to shorten scenes if they might become tedious.

Thus the hundreds—perhaps even thousands—of porn videotapes produced in the conspicuously dubbed "Delphi TV Studio" and on its tactlessly self-evident sex-act turntable and stage were in real time, made without benefit of script, and begun without overt story intentions.

Each female porno model was required to perform in at least three separate Delphi porn videos. These videos were all made during the first ten days of each month when the cameraperson set up his equipment in the basement porn-videotaping studio. Generally female porno models performed all three and sometimes more videos with the same male porno models. Some of them were their husbands or boyfriends, and some of them were old Delphi standbys who made porn videos with female porno models. In other words, the same porno models made a number of porn videos, so there was even limited variety of bare bodies and personalities performing the same sex acts in the constrained context.

The lighting was mounted in the same place. The video camera was mounted in the same place. If the turntable rotated the bare bodies to different angles, it did so at the same rotation speed, and the camera zoom lens moved in and out from bare bodies to faces, sex acts, sex organs, and bare buttocks from the same angle and at the same zoom speed.

But if the same old, same angle video camera was always turned-on after the always totally naked heterosexual male and female porno models had climbed up onto the same old sex-stage, this produced intended or unintended effects. The unambiguous smut-videotaping stage under the same "Delphi TV Studio" sign proclaimed not only to the viewers but to the various naked porno models themselves that they knew they were nude sex-performance objects and intending to perform sex-acts "on television" for public amusement. As a result, the denoted "TV Studio" and unmistakable performance context exhorted the nude models, consciously or unconsciously, into concocting pornographic stories with their bare bodies.

While the variety of the always bare porno models' sex-acts was limited to minimal numbers of poses and positions—the same sex-acts in generally the same poses and positions over and over—their bare bodies and their personalities were manifestly different. So each porn video offered at least this intrinsic uniqueness and diversity during the half-hour's half-dozen different sex-acts in several different poses, postures, and sequences as entertainment.

To draw a parallel, there are only eight full tones on a musical scale, but musical possibilities are endless, ranging from the diversities of Beethoven through the varieties of the Beatles and all the countless millions of pieces of composed and uncomposed and performed and unperformed music.

Thus in its simplest statement a given standardized Delphi porn video, lacking any overt intended story other than naked men and women portraying only themselves as paid whores engaging in sex acts for public sport in a "TV Studio," still had a resulting storyline which could be recast as a story in words. "She knelt down in front of him, and…Then she stood up, and he knelt down in front of her…She lay on her back on the turntable, and he got on top of her, and…"

Or, unlikely as it might be, it technically could be duplicated with the same or different naked porno models acting out the same sex acts in the same sequences.

In other words, even in this simplest and most simplistic form, these Delphi porn videos had portrayal and story. By extension, all porn videos, porno movies, or pornographic still photographs tell stories if only because tellable and duplicable stories cannot help but result from the intentional presentation event.

This, keep in mind, is in the pornographic presentation's most basic description-of-sex-act-and-sex-act-sequence form. And yet this, in itself, was an element of created variety in the rigidly standardized Delphi porn video production format that drew repeat audiences.

Even when the same two naked porno models performed the same sex acts in additional videos, there were not only the obvious differences in sequences and precise poses, positions, camera angles, and camera views, there were infinite subtleties in the naked porno models' responses and reactions to one another, in their responses to the cameraperson's commands, in their individual and shared responses and reactions to unique situations within the rigid Delphi TV Studio format, in stories told by their facial and bodily expressions, and even in the graphics of their sex-acts themselves.

Given the rigid format, stage, lighting, and camera-angle standardization, much of the amusement that brought customers back had to have been from perceptions of personality-evolvement before, during, and following sex acts—and the producers and camera person appear to have grasped this. The usually unseen—but due to the amateurishness of the real-time unedited production, sometimes accidentally seen—cameraperson, and sometimes other seen or unseen spectators, often talked to the naked porno models, on-camera, and required them to respond, visually and verbally, during sex acts or while they sat or stood after having engaged in a sex act and in between that one and the next sex act. Thus the Delphi porn video audience was treated to conscious and subconscious shrugs, gestures, facial expressions, interactions, shared or individual responses, and in those after sound was added, words spoken in response, sometimes in protest, sometimes with enthusiasm, sometimes offering reluctance.

And, of course, the undressed porno models revealed a great many other emotional visual responses to being told or questioned, as well as verbal language replies.

During the roughly half-hour in real time that the porno models presented themselves on-camera as naked whores being compensated to perform sex acts for public amusements, viewers saw their feigned cute smiles masking embarrassment, resigned shrugs covering feeling indignant about something. They could note the naked porno models' self-conscious glances at their exposed sex organs, their ill-at-ease scowls and squirms in front of small audiences.

They could recognize, in the nude porno models' glances at the capturing video camera recording their defilement for public exhibit and amusement, guises of vain exhibitionism shielding apprehension for social consequences with family, friends, neighbors, and acquaintances and with expectations of public ridicule. They could see the gawky undressed and sometimes ill-at-ease porno models' attempts to mask all or any of the above with inappropriate polite smiles and strained overly courteous replies from their awkward and handicapped social statuses of blatantly being offered and advertised as porno whores.

Viewers also saw a verbal and nonverbal banter reflecting difference in assigned social value between adequately attired debaucher-producer and nude debauched porno models. As the videos progressed, growing acclimation to and acceptance of subsequent tort-law devalued social status could be discerned. An exposerist-exhibitionist delight at portraying

themselves as naked sluts, narcissistic pleasure from being a focus of attention on the smut-stage and on-camera, pleasure or displeasure in the relationship with the naked sexual partner or partners could be seen. Normal
and unique responses resulting from being questioned or being told what
to do in the context of being on-camera on a flagrant television sex-stage
and disreputably as a naked sex-act performer could be detected. Tensions
resulting from being told to change poses, or to temporarily end this or
that sex-act at the height of sexual pleasures, and a whole slew of normal
human responses and reactions altered by the unique situation of being
naked on-camera solely for purposes of publicly presenting sex-acts could
be seen as mini-stories and were, as such, part of the entertainment.

In other words, even in the severely constrained and standardized
presentation context of the Delphi porn videos made on the sex stage of
the "Delphi TV Studio," there was both entertainment value and genuine portrayal that reaches far beyond the sex-acts themselves. As in all
theater, some of it may not have been consciously intended, but perhaps, due to the sexual content, reached more deeply into audience
being.

As commercial porn goes, however, the Delphi Palast porn videos
were amateurish, often of poor visual quality with bad lighting and
blurry images, and totally unedited for presentation. Their saving grace
as pornography may be due to amazing standardization, use of novice,
non-illustrious, and generally quite average-appearing porno models,
lack of props, lack of contrived set and story that offered the above
instruction and insight.

The vast millions of feet of porn videotape and celluloid porn film
and the millions of pornographic photographs that have been
bought and viewed of course have far greater variety of shooting
location, setting, lighting, camera positions, distances, and angles,
costuming of the porno models before and after stripping naked,
props, and scripted or unscripted storylines and are thus far more
entertaining. Camera-based pornography in general offers viewers

hugely greater very obvious variety than the standardized Delphi Palast porn videos. But, importantly, because it does, consumers' real reasons and motivations may have been largely overlooked.

Porno models and live-sex performers are indeed writing sentences with their bare bodies, but not alone or even in pairs or multiples of porno models. The sentences and stories are always created in conjunction with, and aided by, camera persons, production personnel, office staffs, ticket-takers, stage and set managers, and others without whom the bare-bodied statements would simply be bedroom sex and not public sport and performance presentation.

And what sentences do these bare bodies write? To some extent it is up to the persons who have undressed in public to intentionally write them. Therefore they all may be as different as the naked porno models' earlier premeditated or during-act-for-audience impulsive intentions.

Inherent in or underlying the sentences that most of the bare bodies appear to be writing would seem legitimate social and political expressions of protest, defiance, and rebellion unambiguously protected by the First Amendment.

The vehicle in these portrayals of statements of social protest, like many vehicles utilized in drama, may be the debaucher-debauchee relationship, the portrayal of oneself as a naked whore, the assertion of enjoyment of sex, etc. The point is that it is far more complex than a merging of actor/actress and acted.

Even if one wants to claim that the naked porno models are not actually depicting acts or emotions but simply engaging in sex acts and being photographed and videotaped, there is still, even in live sex acts, depiction. Beyond depicting themselves as naked whores engaging in sex presumably for money, porno models are the material that camera persons, directors, and producers use to tell and thus portray genuine stories, as above, wide ranges of human emotions and responses.

In advertising, for instance, photographers use legitimate living models to tell stories intended to persuade people to buy products. A

"Marlboro Man" is thus a living prop utilized by camera persons and advertising producers to depict not only pleasures of smoking but a hearty rugged persona one might identify with while smoking that brand. The "Marlboro Man" stands on-camera merely himself as a cig-arette smoker. As with porno models there is some minor legitimate acting of "pleasure" (or whatever), but the camera person and advertis-ing producer creates a larger depiction of rugged individualism and wonderful Wild West feelings.

Similarly, two naked porno models may indeed only be depicting themselves as whores paid to engage in sex, but that does not exclude the directors, producers, and camera persons from using them to create larger depictions—even larger spontaneous and unintended depictions delving into human sexuality and emotion.

In the art of portrait photography we see famous, infamous, and never famous faces. They just sit or stand. The portrait photographer creates his or her art from them—using them as raw material, setting up lighting angles, shooting the portrait subject from different angles and distances, verbally provoking a smile, scowl, or reaction from the subject, focusing sharply or hazily, developing light and dark tones, and even cropping the photograph to eliminate distractions from it as art. The face may still be just a face, but the photograph becomes a work of art, a deliberate depiction not by the subject but by the photographer of the subject, a representation that even the subject himself or herself may find communicates and projects something unique and previously unknown.

Depictions, representations, and portrayals are not limited to the actors, actresses, or models. Camerapersons—photographers, cinematog-raphers, videographers, or to the point here, pornographers—are quite free to create and communicate them.

Moreover, directors and producers contribute to them. A production of a dramatic work on a large stage with elaborate costumes may represent the work differently than if produced on a small stage with less elaborate costumes.

A director may have acting people recite their lines in numerous different ways and thus create wide varieties different portrayals even from the "inscribed in stone" lines themselves, not to mention the various gestures, facial expressions, stage movements, poses, postures, and other presentations he or she demands from the acting people.

Thus even the most basic live sex act is not limited to the naked sex models' depictions of themselves as whores or anything else they may project. It is part of a genuine performance production, however elaborate or modest-in-means it may be.

The producer of the sex-show may, for instance, provide the naked sex performers or porno models with a turntable on which to engage in sex acts, may provide a small or large stage close to or farther from the audience, may have the naked sex performers engaging in sex acts behind literal walls with viewing windows as in a peep-show, or out in the open surrounded by audience that can better interact with their spectators while engaging in sex acts on an open stage.

The producer may offer his or her sex-performers totally naked and thus stripped not only of clothes but decency, or mockingly attired in ludicrous scanty costumes like G-strings, or in costumes that expose bare buttocks and sex-organs and thus invite ridicule, or in sexual leather straps, cuffs, and collars to flagrantly categorize them as shameless sex-objects.

The production may offer elaborate public address introductions of implicitly debased sex-performers, or it may just have the naked sex performers walk out on stage unannounced for both shock value and to assert them as just average people, but voluntary degraded for audience amusement.

The sex theater manager, acting more or less as a director, may insert additional depictions.

One live sex show in the Times Square area of New York had the male and female sex performers emerge from the audience superficially dressed in ordinary street attire, strip in front of the stage (as if still part of the audience), climb up onto it naked, and engage in sex acts for public amusement. It made a here-I-am-just-like-you representation, notably different from other live sex shows in the area where sex models emerged naked from behind a stage curtain onto a stage (even properly from stage right), or through a stage door into a peep show arena, and thus portrayed themselves as something distanced and distinct from the audience.

Lighting technicians and background music DJs create additional representations or nuances in representation.

Thus even in the limited context of a live sex show performance there is a variety of both intended and unintended "representation" input from the sex models themselves, from the show producers, and from the sex show director-managers. Add camera persons, photograph, film, or video editors, and camera-based X-rated production directors each offering or modifying depiction and representation input in porno movies and porn videos and it is clearly not just two or more naked human beings simply engaging in sex.

So even in a narrow view that both omits social protest depictions and intended or spontaneous subtleties of expression, naked porno models engaging in sex on-camera or in front of an audience may not be depicting much more than themselves engaging in sex. But even there they are "depicting." Additionally, their cameraperson, porn directors, and porn producers are utilizing them to depict larger contexts and more entertaining stories than the obvious simple views of phalluses plunging in and out of vaginas or mouths and tongues licking sex organs, mammary surfaces, or anal orifices.

The utilization of the naked porno models by camera persons, directors, and producers to convey larger and more subtle depictions than nudity and sex-acts themselves parallels similar uses of actors and models in theater and in advertising as well as legitimate movie making.

But in general, naked porno models are always minorly "acting" on-camera or in front of live audiences. The very nature of what they are doing demands that they "perform." That they generally have come to be called porno "models" rather than "porn actors" and "porn actresses" reflects that as time has gone on and the porn industry has evolved to satisfy audience appetites while lowering costs. Porn audiences no longer seek good acting—if, indeed, they ever really did.

At the dawn of a decriminalized hardcore pornography industry in the early 1970s, a large number of big-name porn stars, like Georgina Spelvin and Harry Reems, had been professional actresses and actors before they entered the slightly more lucrative field of porn acting. Both Spelvin and Reems, in fact, had performed in one or more of Shakespeare's plays.

But image technology evolved and has enormously cut production costs over the last two decades. Producers no longer need the psychological security of having capable actors and actresses in costly productions that require 35 mm cameras and color film, professional camera and production personnel, studios and sets, costly developing of 35 mm (or even 16 mm) color film, additional expensive equipment to make work prints and answer prints, and expensive film editing equipment prior to making costly final prints for widespread national distribution.

All one now needs, in fact, is a fairly inexpensive or even rented video camera, possibly some spotlights, and a couple low paid bare porno models. In addition, tastes and expectations of porn consumers have evolved. The spectacular growth of the so-called "amateur" porn video industry shows that many if not most porn consumers now prefer to see the subtleties of porno models as porno models without contrived overt story contexts. But even in those porn productions with scripted story content, acting requirements have slacked off and much seems simply to have been learned on the set or shooting location.

As a result, naked porn performers have been increasingly used in much the same way as the advertising industry uses legitimate live models—as material for camerapersons, directors, and producers to use in creating depictions and stories.

In this narrower view "representation" is still there. But it is representation the directors, producers, and camera persons are creating to convey to audiences, among other things, spontaneous human emotions, authentic sexual and emotional responses, and unintentional sexual and human feeling reactions out of the given "porno model material," the situations the bare porno models have found themselves performing in, and public sex acts they intentionally perform in given contexts.

In legitimate theater one can find Off-Broadway and coffeehouse improvisation acts where audience pays to see staged impromptu and ad lib performances. In these, "representation" may be little more than actors and actresses representing themselves and their talents of creatively responding to one another and audience, and the audiences themselves expect little in the way of actual "representation" portrayals—generally in and of themselves rather poor—but rather they attend the performances to experience the actors and actresses themselves and their unique talents for unrehearsed interactions. In other words they are attending in order to see the performers "representing" or depicting themselves as clever experts in that kind of acting.

Thus a model, actor, or actress representing himself or herself—representing or recasting himself or herself—would seem to be engaging in a kind of authentic performance "representation" in itself. By extension, a naked porno model, porn actor, or porn actress representing himself or herself in the most base unscripted overt and story-free sex acts as a person who has prostituted himself or herself to strip and engage in sex acts for public amusement or as a social protestor is still re-presenting and recasting himself or herself and thus engaging in "representation."

Moreover, the very exercise of stripping naked on-camera and for an audience is intrinsically a "representation," an act, a statement—all the more so when two or more people not only strip naked on-camera and for an audience but then engage in sex acts for their amusement.

The intention of performing for audience—or future audience as implied by a camera—in itself establishes "representation." One does not "represent" to a brick wall, and a person stripping in private in a bedroom is not, beyond possible narcissistic intentions—portraying or "representing" anything.

But a person who strips naked for an audience is, on the face of it, re-presenting or re-casting himself or herself in the sense of a different character than the one he or she was out on the street, thus creating a "representation," a depiction, a portrayal.

The laws of the land in themselves recognize this. A person suddenly caught naked by the collapse of a building wall is treated quite differently than a person who intentionally "streaks" a public gathering in his or her birthday suit. The first is accorded assistance and given emergency attire, the other is arrested for "indecent exposure." The difference is "representation" and portrayal. In contrast to the naked person taking a bath in a building whose wall collapsed and had no intention of performing in public, the person "streaking" or otherwise exposing himself or herself in public intended it as an act of protest, as an act to offend people, or even possibly a kind of gender overstatement.

Thus the law prosecutes the "indecent exposerist" not so much for being naked in public as for intending to be naked as part of an act or statement in a re-presentation of himself or herself to an involuntary and presumably offended audience.

A person who intentionally strips naked for the entertainment of a voluntary audience, or on camera for future voluntary audiences, and perhaps goes on to further engage in sex acts, is re-presenting himself or herself and making an intended portrayal or "representation." It is indeed a sentence written with his or her body.

In addition, the very nature of camera-based images is that they create stories. Importantly, whenever camera lenses record anything, what has been recorded by them is, in fact, merely "representation" in and of itself. So any given pornographic photograph, motion picture, or video is in itself a "representation" of a reality that had previously taken place and was recorded and intrinsically contains a wealth of story material waiting to be read and interpreted.

There would, then, seem to be no more of a "representational collapse" in live sex acts and camera-based pornography than in any other dramatic or theatrical portrayal. In writing sentences of protest, defiance, clowning around, erotic interest, or whatever with their publicly naked bodies engaging in sex acts, sex actors/actresses and porno models express a number of ideas, conceptions (perhaps sometimes literally!), impressions, and emotions, abstractions, and representations beyond those inherent in the nudity and sex-correspondence itself, many of them, as in all drama, unfathomable in and of themselves, but nonetheless communicating to something all too deeply human.

One may then begin to question the wisdom of the Committee on Obscenity and Film Censorship in suggesting that live sex shows should be banned because there is insufficient distance between the naked sex performers and the adequately attired audiences. As in live legitimate theater, performer responses to audience reactions, and vice versa, act to communicate powerfully and affect deeply.

A naked woman in a live sex act looking at a member of an audience while engaging in fellatio with a naked man will communicate a wide variety of complex ideas, concepts, impressions, and emotions, abstractions, and representations beyond the simple movement of a penis between her lips. If it is done with obvious relish, it communicates something. If it is done with a dull stare, it communicates something. If it is done with a defiant glare, it communicates something else. If it is done with pretended obliviousness to amused spectators, it communicates yet something else. And there would seem considerable, if not endless, possible additional variety.

Needless to say, the same naked woman looking into a camera lens while engaging in fellatio with a naked man will have options to communicate in the same way, but lacking live audience feedback may do so less powerfully. In either case, what the naked sex performers ultimately portray may not be, as happens in theater, what they intended consciously to portray.

The naked woman and naked man engaged in this sex act may indeed merely conceive of themselves, to put it in the terminology of their profession, as paid and prostituted public cocksucker and paid and prostituted public recipient of a cocksucking. But entirely unintended identifying chords may be struck in spectators viewing these on-stage and on-camera depictions of the sex act.

To suggest "representational collapse" is to fail to thoroughly examine wide varieties of intended and unintended potential representation inherent in any public nudity or sex-act portrayal. The sex act, almost like a stage prop, is merely a vehicle to aid the naked sex performers in their own recasting of themselves, their own re-presentation. A better analogy might be a gesture by an actor—which one could claim was the actor representing himself waving his hand and nothing beyond that. To narrow one's analytical view and only, to take the earlier example, see the obvious penis plunging between the obvious lips is to miss the whole point of the given sex act portrayal itself and the meaning and motivations of pornography in general.

In viewing pornography one is thus experiencing an art form. As an art form, pornography probably falls lower than farce, science fiction, cartooning, or street miming. But it is low art and contains or at least utilizes elements of these.

As farce it is a plotless satire on human pretensions, including sexual pretensions, and the social subterfuges and pretexts that accompany civilization. As science fiction it explores human sexual and personality interactions with and responses to technologies involved in image capture, image publication, distribution, and broadcast, social responses and changes in response to these, and personal and social consequences resulting from all of the above. It is an authentic cartoon, by nature superficial and limited, graphically conveying simplified story, and in this cartoon the intended and unintended mimes of bare body language take precedence over spoken words, indeed if there are any at all. No viewer really misses any of this even if those viewers who find pornography objectionable will probably blot most of it out. Like spectators at a sporting event who may focus on the score and the action but nevertheless must appreciate the physical grace and talents of the athletes, pornography viewers may focus on the "score" and the sex action but nonetheless cannot help but be at least subconsciously aware of all the intended and unintended subtexts.

It is unlikely that a person being introduced to pornography for the first time will grasp many of its subtleties any more than a person seeing a sporting event, hearing a symphony orchestra, or attending a theatrical production for the first time will fully appreciate them.

CHAPTER TEN

Participating As Viewer

My reminiscences of viewing pornography now come nostalgically to mind. Memories of viewing and emotional inputs, from seeing the first black-and-white "stag films" when it was illegal to even do so, to viewing early "girly flicks," to a look at a Danish sex store in the late '60's, to watching early public porn in old downtown theaters and 8 mm and 16 mm peep shows are probably tempered by that nostalgia.

I continue to drop into "adult bookstore" peep shows—now color video, not 8-mm or 16-mm color film—and video projection porn theaters. There have been changes, not only in camera-based technology but, possibly as a result, subtle changes in pornographic substance.

I went to northern Europe the mid-'80's and saw the scene there. It was amid the transition to videotape that was in the process of dooming the large-audience 35-mm color film porn theaters. In Germany I saw the precocious beginnings of an amateur porn video industry which developed into a phenomenon for home TV screens and small video-projection theaters both in Europe and here.

But to return nostalgically to those long gone days of the early 1960s, I saw my first motion picture pornography when I was still a sexual virgin on leave after completing Army basic training. I went back to visit a former coworker at the workplace where I had done the graveyard shift.

Graveyard-shift work involves a lot of sitting around, and that was the case there. But my coworker-friend, whose cousin was a cop, had temporarily acquired two black-and-white sixteen-millimeter porno movies from a police raid on a local whorehouse. They probably belonged in the police property room, but I never asked. He made it plain, though, that he had gotten them only for the night, and he was terribly anxious about being in possession of them.

In 1961 possession and even viewing of hardcore porno movies was a crime, and my friend was acutely worried about getting caught with them, all the more so if they had been "borrowed" from the police property room. This not only illustrates the folly of criminalizing pornography—that cops are all too human when it comes to enforcing frivolous and unrealistic laws—it also illustrates one aspect of pornography that nullifies legislation against it—that it can be "borrowed," shown, and returned or sent on to another viewer. It is not a one-time consumed commodity like dope or one-time spent like money. Raids on suppliers and users would inevitably fail to seize all copies that have been manufactured, and those not seized could be used to make more copies.

Even more importantly, it is story material, and stories cannot be snuffed out even by brutal authority. Even if all copies of camera-based pornography are somehow miraculously seized, the pictorial stories remain in minds for lifetimes and beyond, and at first opportunity to utilize camera-based technologies to remake them, some will. The most hard-nosed opponents of pornography may appreciate an impossible policing problem and a resulting terrible undermining effect on police morale if attempts are made to enforce unenforceable legislation.

Not only has mass-publishing of copies become easier and cheaper as a result of printing and xerox technologies, the minimal material needed to create pornography does not come from the jungles of South America and involve difficult refining processes. Following the invention of the Polaroid camera and then the home video camera it became totally impossible to know who was creating it. Polaroid film does not need lab development. Videotape comes out of the video camera ready to use on home television sets. And with xerox machines and tape-copying options on VCRs both can be copied and in effect "published" with great ease and in total secret.

An amateur pornographer with a home video camera and one, two, or multiple eager and low paid or unpaid bare porno models can create hours of salable pornographic material and even retail it out of his or her home with Polaroid photographs of the porno models—taken live or from the TV screen, used as is, or color-xerox copied—on videotape carton covers. Legislation and law enforcement become laughable.

In addition, wide distribution of adult pornography—as of this writing—can take place legally on the Internet, either in the form of still photographs, or a strung-together series of still photographs called M-PEGS that mimic motion pictures, or for those with adequate computer memories, the videos themselves. Given legislation's and law enforcement's poor record in halting the distribution of child pornography on the Internet and the much larger appetite for adult pornography, pending Internet anti-pornography legislation is doomed to not only fail but to create much larger and more profound social problems than the Internet pornography itself.

Pornography may be as old as the human species, certainly as old as civilization. What we are seeing now is not a sudden new human interest in pornography, but enormous new levels of effectiveness for widespread and inexpensive production and distribution of pornography that have leapfrogged traditional social controls and are assisting in initiating social change to our hyper-technological progress in general.

The transition from across-the-board illegality of pornography to legal and quasi-legal adult pornography began in Denmark between

1967 and 1969 and spread with near simultaneity to other places in Europe and the United States.

Like many others still around to remember it, I first saw an explicit-sex porno movie when they were called "stag films" or "blue movies" and still illegal and thus was able to appreciate the transition. The process of viewing an illegal porno movie in 1961 involved getting hold of a sixteen-millimeter movie projector and a home or classroom movie screen. But my friend had already done that.

He threaded the first silent film into the projector, and we watched as it clattered away in the wee hours of the morning.

The film itself was not bad quality. I had seen worse in school classroom films, and this was still the heyday of black and white television and black and white movies were still regularly showing in theaters, so the lack of colorization meant little.

The black and white images flashed somewhere between adequately and vividly on the home movie screen. Facial expressions and identities of the porno models were certainly clear in the context of image quality of the time.

The porno models were attractive females and average males. The lighting was semi-professional. And there appeared to have been some professional direction. I would guess that both films had come out of underground—and in those days criminal—professional New York or Hollywood porn suppliers.

It was a genuine thrill to watch human beings strip naked on-camera. It was an even bigger thrill to watch them then engage in sex-acts on-camera.

As a literal sexual virgin I still had a "pedestal" concept of women and had never seen an adult woman totally naked, so I ogled their bare bodies.

It came as a shock when they began engaging in sex-acts on-camera. In the first of the two porno movies the guy began eating pussy. I had vaguely heard about eating pussy standing silently in groups of males. But all the sudden I was seeing a naked guy lick an attractive young woman's twat—that I had been ogling and privately snickering at the public on-camera exhibition of—in front of me.

The whole idea of someone putting his or her mouth on someone else's genitals had been almost totally alien to me, an idea profoundly loaded with contempt, a suggestion that you might make to childhood playground associates and later adult associates only at the risk of getting beaten up or otherwise badly punished.

And there—on-camera no less—was this guy licking the young woman's sex organs.

An even greater surprise came when the naked-on-camera couple reversed themselves. I looked in a mixture of awe and derisive amusement as the naked pretty-faced young woman inserted the guy's penis into her mouth and began sucking cock on-camera.

The term "cocksucker" had, until then, been reserved as a pejorative with innuendo of then publicly forbidden male homosexuality. My mind had not yet conceived of a woman "cocksucker." All of the sudden I was seeing one, and I was thus literally introduced to the performance of oral sex.

They of course fucked on-camera, too. It was also a surprise, but less of one, almost an anticlimax.

It was not until some months later that I lost my virginity to a pretty and sexy young woman in a Thai whorehouse. I would venture that well over half of the first-time male military enlistees and draftees who were sent to Asia following World War Two lost their virginity to plentiful and inexpensive Asian women prostitutes.

Be that as it may, I had been sexually inexperienced, pre-sexually naive, and psychologically unprepared when I had seen that first black-and-white 16-mm stag film in the BMR room of my former hospital laboratory workplace just after Army basic training. Quite likely as with most first-time viewers of stag films when camera-based pornography was illegal and underground, it had its profound impact from shock-value.

Dredged up decades-old memories are, to say the least, fuzzy. The first important thing that stands out is the stark anxiety of my former laboratory coworker that we might get caught. Photographic pornography showing explicit sex-acts was very illegal in the early 1960s.

I naturally did not understand what he was so afraid of until after I had seen the first graphic sex-act on the home-movie screen.

"I've got something I've got to show you," he had told me.

I watched puzzled while he carefully locked the door to the laboratory's BMR room, and then sat patiently while he set up the fold-out home movie screen and tediously threaded the first can of black-and-white sixteen millimeter film through the home movie projector.

There were two. I remember the first largely because of the shock value, but I may indeed be mingling memory of it with the other or others shown that night.

My coworker turned on the projector and doused the overhead lights. In the dark room with the projector clattering away, an image of two decently dressed men and two decently dressed women came up on-screen. They were playing cards, possibly sitting around on a living room rug. I recall that one of the women had dark hair and had on a dark typical dress. The other seems to have been a blond in a typical era skirt and blouse. The men had on slacks and shirts with collars.

They were all reasonably good-looking average decent-looking people, and I was wondering to myself why my friend was so anxious and why he had bothered to invite me and go through all the trouble of setting up a home movie showing.

As with all moviegoers at the start of a movie, I was reading what I could into the actors' expressions and trying to pick up the story as it began to unfold. And as I look back over all those years, it is instructive.

I had never seen hardcore pornography, and I was not expecting it. In fact, since mere possession of pornography, especially hardcore pornographic motion pictures, was a crime, the shock of the unexpected may have been an integral part of these "stag film" themes and hence the actors and actresses began these films in normal situations and normal attire. Some of the pleasure derived from a "stag film" may have been witnessing the surprise or shock of an audience person being introduced to it for the first time—in those days before porno movie houses and adult bookstores when few people could have imagined that such things as hardcore pornographic movies even existed.

It was a genuinely different era with very different expectations from those that just about anyone will have now. I cannot imagine that someone being introduced to a hardcore porno movie or porn video for the first time in the 1990s does not have at least a vague inkling of its ubiquitous presence. But as a young adult just out of Army basic training three decades earlier, there were not even the faintest clues, and my expectations and experience probably cannot be completely understood by those who went into a public porno movie theater or were shown a porn video on a TV set in a living room for the first time.

I was simply—unconsciously, of course, as with moviegoers—reading facial expressions, body language, meanings in the costumes, meanings in the movie set, meanings the camera angles and focuses were trying to convey, and following the story as it unfolded.

I vaguely recall expecting to see a silent-movie story about a card game, maybe a silent sitcom sort of thing. In other words, there was, indeed, a story unfolding. As it turned out, it quickly developed into a hardcore pornographic story. But this anecdote illustrates the inherent story material in all pornographic material. Strip away the pornography and there is still story. And at that point in the movie, pornography was effectively stripped away, having not yet appeared and not even the faintest bit in my imagination-derived expectations. In my lack of worldly experience I was putting together, following, and anticipating a story, but a different story from the one the movie producers had intended. It is something that perhaps can only happen once in one's lifetime, because once one has seen hardcore pornography, story expectations will forever after include its possibility.

I sat there following the unfolding story naive and inexperienced. Here were these people sitting around in a living room playing a parlor game of cards. I had heard, some time back into my childhood, of "strip poker." But it was a kid-joke, not something real, and it did not even vaguely occur to me what was going on. My coworker had never let on that he was going to show me a porno movie so all I could do is wonder why he was showing me a home movie of a family playing cards.

But it was not for long.

Into no more than the third hand it was clear that the four card play-ers were taking off clothes in response to the card game. I thought this might be interesting and that I might be able to eventually see some almost naked ladies, or at least down to scanty bathing suits, their underpants, or even G-strings as in the one and only burlesque show I had seen up until that time. So I kept looking on with interest as more garb came off.

I cannot remember with desired clarity who was down to nothing first, or even if anyone was. But I vague recall that it was the blond woman, and then some animated discussion ensued. She volunteered to receive another hand and apparently lost. Seeing her now naked and down to nothing in the way of an offering in a game of strip poker, I wondered whether they were arguing over whether she would go for her purse and pay up.

Alas, I was that naive and unschooled in the art of pornography.

But the animated discussion slacked off with the blond's resignation, and I believe she was guided naked by the guy, now in briefs, feeling her bare behind toward a back room.

The average man and the average woman appeared to exchange some words, but it was a silent black-and-white film. Even with her naked, the exchange seemed to portray fairly normal needling that happens from losing in parlor games.

Then they sat on the bed and did some rather average Hollywood movie kissing. It went into necking and breast fondling. I watched quite amazed.

The losing of this card game had already led to more than cute needling for the naked lady, and it was clearly going to go further. How much further, I had no experience to even guess.

When the man's hand slid up the woman's leg, it did not even dawn on me that this would end up in explicit sex acts.

But the man slipping his finger around the woman's sexuality gave me clues that this was perhaps something quite a bit more than I had ever expected to see, especially on permanent celluloid in a film. The couple was kissing, and he was finger-fondling her.

I recall that my coworker friend made some snide comments at first, but after the action really got going on-screen, both of us were silent until the reel finished and flap-flapped around on the projector.

I think he made a snide macho remark about the way the guy was feeling the woman. He had probably seen it before and knew the story-line and was commenting on what he was anticipating. That is to say, there was clearly a story line and the naked woman and the almost naked man were far more actors than present amateur porno models. They, of course, had to be. Film was expensive. Film developing and printing was expensive. It required expensive developing, printing, and editing equipment. And the market was extremely limited in those days when porno movies were still criminalized. So they had to be good sex actors, if only because the budget probably would not allow retakes.

I was so lacking in experience with not only explicit-sex pornography but the rigors and costs of filmmaking in those early days that I thought, while I watched the guy fondle the naked lady's twat, the porno movie might be a local home movie.

I had not expected to see her slip off her panties to publicly (as it were, even on privately shown on film!) expose her cunt in the card-game scene.

I never expected to see the guy grab her cunt in the bedroom scene and then watch her expression and sexual reactions on-camera and for an audience while he fondled her publicly exposed female sexuality.

I think they had a further animated discussion, and I think my coworker had a comment which I again failed to grasp.

They resumed necking, and he fondled her breasts as well as her twat.

It was more mysterious to me than erotic at that point. I was having a difficult time believing what I was seeing. There she was on naked camera and in public with her breasts and cunt being stimulated and reacting sexually to it.

The guy in underpants stopped fondling her twat and orally stimulating her tits.

And then it cut to her sitting naked on the edge of the bed with him kneeling on the floor between her legs with only his underpants on.

And here again my friend may have made an anticipating snide remark, but again I failed to understand it because I did not believe that the man would publicly on camera press his face into her female sexuality and begin stimulating her twat with his tongue. The very sex act itself was only very vaguely known to me.

So I watched with amazement while the guy ate pussy in public, while the nice naked lady succumbed to sexual stimulation and silently showed moaning and groaning, while she grinned dirtily at the guy with his face in her crotch licking her female sex organs, and while the camera moved around capturing the public nudity and "dirty" perverse sex act.

I think I remember watching him fondle her bare breasts while he ate pussy. She was either a good sex actress or really succumbing to her stimulated sexuality at that point.

Then, as best I can recall, the scene changed. He either slipped off his underpants on-camera or the next take showed him lying naked on his back on the bed.

She crawled over him kneeling on the bed, her face above his sex organs. For a few seconds she looked at his limp penis and balls. Again I could not have imagined a nice lady like that naked on-camera, let alone allowing herself to be filmed while a half-naked guy first fondled her sex organs and then ate her pussy. So I did not expect to see her suck cock. I vaguely remember wondering why she was inspecting the guy's sex organs.

It came as something of a shock to see her get her pretty face down into his crotch, make contact with his penis with her lips, and then insert it into her mouth.

The whole idea of a nice looking woman putting some guy's sex organ in her mouth was totally foreign to me. Minutes earlier I would have thought that I would ever see such a thing, and if I had dared to think it, I would have dismissed it immediately as a very "dirty" thought. But there I was seeing it—seeing the pretty and nice naked woman sucking cock in public on-camera—not only seeing her with a phallus stuffed into her mouth, but seeing her bare ass and cunt as the camera person moved around for a view from her bare behind while she sucked the guy's cock.

When the camera came around to focus on her pretty face with her sweet lips moving up and down on the phallus slipping between them, and her cute nose going down to the guy's hairy balls, it went to a close up so no one could possibly mistake her facial identity while she sucked cock, or her stupefied expression while the now stiff cock plunged in and out of her mouth.

After a time the scene shifted. The naked guy mounted the nice naked lady, and they fucked on-camera in public, I believe until the guy had a climax. I think the camera gave us one more view of the naked couple and then zoomed into their faces looking foolishly into the lens after having stripped and engaged in sex acts in public on-camera.

The next sequence showed the other lady down to nothing in the way of garb and losing a hand at cards while her male partner, in his underpants, grinned widely.

By then I was beginning to know what to expect. I was quite sure I would at least see the two of them fucking. Most likely I would see him eat pussy and her give him a blow job.

The shock of it had worn off. For the first time—the first time in my life—I was looking forward to seeing two naked porno models publicly engage in sex acts.

And they did not disappoint me. I vaguely recall he ate pussy, she gave a fine blowjob, and then they fucked. The fine points of it may have slipped by me because I was still in a partial state of disbelief.

The normal needling that goes with losing a parlor game had been acted out to a sexually explicit end. Twice the debaucher had acted out debauching the debauchee, but it was clear that both the naked men and both the naked young women had been debauched in the real world by the cameraperson and by the porn producers.

Four of my fellow human beings had stripped on-camera and publicly engaged in sex acts to their eternal degradation—although I did not have the faintest idea of tort-law social rankings way back then, the reality of what had taken place and had been captured on film was quite clear.

For months afterward I looked at people to see if they might be the ones who had stripped and engaged in sex acts on film.

The next film was less of a shock—but still one—and more of an erotic experience.

My friend had to rewind the previous one and then tediously rethread the projector. I do not recall much comment. These were not only illegal movies, but they were genuinely, in the terms of the time, dirty movies. They were genuinely embarrassing to have seen and people did not talk about such things. So that may explain my memory of silence.

The next one began in a 1950s-style motel with a swimming pool, probably taken in California. But I was thinking it was filmed somewhere nearby in Ohio and struggled to identify the motel because I did not even imagine that there might be a nationwide underground porn industry.

The girl was prettier. And I thought to myself the age-old male question: what was a pretty girl like that doing in a porno movie?

After seeing the first porno movie, I pretty much knew what the second might be about—although I could not be sure.

The very attractive and shapely blond young woman and her dark-haired male companion both wore bathing suits by the poolside.

He appeared to invite her into his room, and the next scene showed them entering a motel room and closing the door.

I believe he poured drinks for them, and they sipped for a moment.

Then they began necking, with him feeling her twat through her bathing suit. It was clear at that point that this would probably be another sexually explicit movie. And I thus wondered even more at that point about the pretty young woman who would allow herself to be in one.

Her bathing suit came off, and he publicly fondled the pretty naked lady's revealed twat on-camera, kissed her and her titties, and turned her on.

Then his bathing suit came off. The naked man got his face into her female sexuality and ate her pussy, and it went on for some time while she squirmed and writhed her bare body in sexual stimulation, some of the time while he fondled her breasts with his hands while he publicly ate her pussy.

Then he attempted to change positions. He got his dong up to her face, and appeared to coax her to suck cock. She refused. She appeared, in fact, to show considerable distaste for getting a penis anywhere near her face, let alone her mouth. It became clear that she was not going to suck cock even while he continued to graphically insist that she do so.

So she got up and went to the motel telephone beside the bed. And we could see her standing there naked talking insistently on the phone. Decades later an underground magazine entertainment columnist reviewing this or a similar period stag film would point of that the telephone was a clever artistic metaphor for the juxtaposition between the restraints of the "outside world," represented by the telephone call, and the sexual abandon of the pornographic scene in progress.

The scene changed. The naked blond young woman opened the motel room door and in came a brunette Hispanic-looking woman in, possibly, tight and revealing but decent attire.

The naked blond and she had a quick animated conversation while the naked guy looked on.

The brunette undressed. The guy returned to eating the blond's pussy, this time with her sitting on his face.

The brunette began sucking the guy's cock while the pretty blond sitting on his face reacted to his oral stimulation of her female sexuality and watched the naked Hispanic woman suck her guy's cock.

I don't remember too clearly, but I believe he eventually fucked one or the other of the two ladies, possibly both. I think the Hispanic licked the blond's clit while the guy fucked her.

Then the movie projector went flap-flap-flap as the dirty movie ended. I believe there was another along the same lines, but it is less memorable.

After we had taken down the screen, folded it up, and put the projector back into its black suitcase-like box, my friend carefully took the films and equipment out to his car. He his the film cans under a rug, and put the projector and screen on top of them, then carefully locked the trunk.

I left the parking lot and took a bus home steaming with sexual arousal and wondering with great interest at the people I had just seen who had no only stripped naked in public on-camera, but had then engaged in public sex acts, including unheard of, except in the dirtiest and often pejorative contexts, pussy eating and cocksucking.

A few days later I left for regular Army duty, and from there, a year later, I was shipped to Southeast Asia where amazingly plentiful whorehouses were filled with pretty inscrutable screwable inexpensive oriental girls. I would call my stint there the staging phase for the Vietnam War, and over the next decade-plus millions of young, naive, and worldly inexperienced American boys and men would be shipped to Southeast Asia and uncritically partake of the strange exotic non-Western culture. It was a culture recognizably different assumptions about women and related prostitution phenomenon. Add to these the millions of American young men who had only a decade earlier taken part in similar Asian experiences during the Korean War, and World War Two veterans from a few years prior to that, and it is clear that a largely ignored and unstudied psycho-sexual and cultural upheaval began taking place in American male population in the early 1940s.

I both returned from Southeast Asia and got out of the Army within a two-week period just prior to Christmas 1962, lifelong inculcated attitudes changed, structured military society gone, and a young adult with future unknown. Free as a bird and with a small severance pay in hand, I bought a bus ticket to San Francisco.

When I got there I tried out my new freedom. In 1962 Market Street was a sleazy drag with numerous girly peep-show joints and there was one just around the corner from the Greyhound Station. For the first time in my life I went into a girly "pre-beaver" peep show, and I found it curious, fascinating, and arousing. I visited the town's burlesque theater, then in the middle of downtown. I had been dragged down to one by the boys in the dorm during my brief stint in college prior to the Army, but this time I strode in voluntarily and watched the women undress from gawdy gowns to G-strings and pasties and cavort to live band music, interspersed with sexual innuendo comedy acts.

And shortly before I left for places south and then home, I visited the Peerless Theater on run-down Third Street surrounded by honky-tonk bars. In a beautifully concise and illustrative two sentences, Kenneth Turan and Stephen F. Zito describe the films shown there a few years later when restrictions on showing full female nudity were being slowly relaxed. The only difference is that the "girls" in 1962, as best I can now recall, stripped to bikinis, sometimes topless. According to *Sinema*:

> The performers were not strippers but rather young girls who were earning a little spare cash to put them through San Francisco State (then College) or (the University of California at) Berkeley. It was easy money, and there were no strings attached: no sexual activity; no lines to remember, just fifteen minutes of slowly taking off clothes, parading about, and going through a series of suggestive gyrations on the nearest bed.[23]

I have found it charming to go to public libraries to research this book and read about these places that in my youth I had so surreptitiously slipped into for scurrilous enjoyments and films I had, decades ago, considered to be always risqué, often "obscene."

I have to take Turan and Zito to minor task in this, however. They appear to be acutely aware of the pornographic scene, and I would be tempted to unquestioningly take their word on the "college girls" observation, but I have had to ask myself: Were these really predominantly "college girls"? Reportage of the era would sometimes snickeringly allude to "college girls" doing it. Possibly as a result, popular mythology had it so. But is this not more of the debaucher-debauchee syndrome—the diversion of seeing upper middle class "college" girls debauched, thus far more socially devalued than lower class girls, who would seem far more reasonable as the majority of these nudie and semi-nudie performers?

Watching these attractive young women suggestively almost bare it all with visual innuendo of sexual invitation in the darkness of the great old Peerless Theater, by then a sleazy turn-of-the-century downtown theater relic which probably had shown silent movies and then the new "talkies," lacked the graphic explicit sex that I had seen in the "stag films" almost two years earlier. Nor did it substitute for the varieties of real sex with pretty young women that I had just come from experiencing in Southeast Asia.

But the dark vast theater with its few scattered patrons offered the imagination a freer run than the burlesque theater with its comparatively well illuminated and more rowdy audience, its noisy live band, and its intended and unintended interactions with nearly bare live women. In short, the girly movies gave free rein to fantasizing, a term that might otherwise be called personal story creation. Prompted by the young women's depicted on-camera striptease and sexually suggestive gyrations, audience members like me could create additional layers of their own "whore stories," not unlike what happens in imaginatively filling out printed fiction or drama and mainstream movies, but with less structure and allowing more personal story creation, or fantasizing.

In *Sinema* (page 98), Turan and Zito say that one of these on-camera strippers, Marsha Jordan (albeit in slightly later "soft-core" exploitation films) got between a hundred and a hundred twenty-five dollars per day for generally one-day shoots. This pay-scale loosely corresponds to the high end of my vague recollections from talking with people connected with the genre and from news stories, but a hundred dollars in the early 1960s had four or five times the purchasing power and was enough to pay fees and tuition for a quarter or semester at San Francisco State and Berkeley.

In 1967 "girly-movie" theaters like the Peerless and the downtown "girly-movie" arcades began showing full nudity "beaver" films with bare breasts, bare behinds often showing anuses, and glimpses of the naked female pubis. This quickly evolved into "split beaver" with full displays of female genitalia, and "action beaver" with the naked young women fondling themselves.

But in 1962 when I dropped in at the Peerless Theater it was all left to the audience imagination. Patrons paid to have "whore stories" vaguely suggested to them by young women undressing down to bikinis or G-strings and pasties and cavorting slowly and erotically on beds or other furniture. Some of it featured female performers featured as being from exotic Mexican border towns with known wild sexual entertainment reputations, as if to enhance patron imagination and story creation.

Economic viability of early 1960s offerings in movie theaters like the Peerless and similar arcade peep-shows gives further indication that pornography is not so much about bringing to light hidden or obscured genitals as it is about storytelling, including inducing those personal created stories in processes we call fantasizing.

Explicit-sex pornography merely leaves less to the imagination and therefore not only more accurately depicts bare bodies, sexual poses and acts, and genitalia, but conveys more constructed "whore story" material that is closer to authors', producers' and performers' intentions. Even so, much is still left to spectator imagination.

Five years after that first experience with what was then considered "pornography" (and still is in a more general way) I would see my first legal public sexually explicit photographs in Denmark.

To again quote Laurie Taylor recalling her visit to sexually liberated Sweden, "Perhaps...it is the juxtaposition of pornography's explicitness and the restraint of other public conventions which is so much more intriguing than its actual content."[24]

Other than the seminude "girly" movies in seedy theaters like the Peerless in San Francisco and peep-shows there and in other American cities—actually little different from the present commercial broadcast television presentations on *Baywatch*, or its satire off-shoot the *Babewatch* bikini show—my previous experience with anatomically correct and uncensored sexually explicit camera-based pornography had been in the shrouded clandestine atmosphere of the hospital laboratory seven years earlier.

One attraction of pornography stems from, among several other things, its juxtaposition with, and therefore protest against, social conventions. Sexual and other interest in the bare bodies, sex organs, and explicit sex acts themselves may stimulate hormones but could not sustain the kind of interest seen in a quarter century billion-dollar pornography industry. A pair of boobs, a cock and balls, a cunt, and a bare ass, taken out of the pornographic (whore story) context would soon lose interest and become medical anatomical breasts, penis and testicles, vaginal area, and gluteus.

That juxtaposition and the implied story material intrinsic solely to it remains vaguely in mind about the small Danish pornography shop. The very public nature of the anatomically correct and sexually explicit photographs and magazines there caught me by surprise.

Through the window just outside the door I could see decently dressed people walking to and fro displaying the restraint of public conventions. Inside the pornography shop were racks of displays clear color photographs of literally hundreds of different men and women who had publicly stripped naked and were flaunting them in photographs of couples engaging in sex acts or orgies of group sex, in the words of pornography, naked women sucking cocks, naked men eating pussy, naked men and women fucking, and other fine points of human sexuality.

In the black-and-white porno movie I had seen, no more than seven different porno models had stripped naked and engaged in sex-acts on-camera, and while the black-and-white film quality was adequate, the Danish sex shop's color photographs had captured far more accurate and realistic images of the porno models, their shooting locations, and their attire, skin, and sex organs. And displayed across the racks while decently dressed people walked by outside were all these clear color photographs of hundreds of different naked porno models fucking, sucking cocks, and eating pussy with their facial identities and facial expressions perfectly clear.

A whole wealth of stories of protest, lust, greed, debaucher jubilation and debauchee degradation, lewdness, shame and shamelessness, and lasting blot and tarnish presented themselves across the racks, not only the contrived sex storylines of the various pornography magazines and photograph collections showing bedroom situations or sex parties, but the veiled ones about the real stripped porno models and their anxieties and anticipations of future life-options that were authentically represented by the merciless objectivity of the camera.

I bought a couple of the glossy sex magazines if only because there was nothing like this yet available in the United States, both of them, as I recall, with multiple male and female porno models in group-sex or swinger-type-parties. But I went on from Denmark to Asia and was there for two years while great changes unfolded in the United States.

I took a small chance and "smuggled" my two Danish sex magazines into the United States when I returned in 1970. It was not difficult because I had returned working on a merchant marine ship, and no one checked seamen's bags in those days.

Curious and sentimental after being out of the country for almost three years, I stopped in at an old familiar "girly" peep show called the Fun Terminal across the street from the Trans-Bay Bus Terminal in San Francisco (now torn down and replaced with condo skyscraper apartments) where when I left two years earlier they had just upgraded from showing bare-breasted young women in bikini bottoms to sometimes showing them bare-assed, but still largely concealing the anatomy of their female sexuality.

To my surprise I found bare men and bare women engaging in explicit sex acts interspersed with the more usual fare of now fully naked young women suggestively cavorting on beds or living room furniture. That is to say, for the first time in my life I saw color motion pictures of women sucking cock, men eating pussy, and naked men and women fucking. Also for the first time in my life I saw these images in a quasi-public setting.

It was all the more public because the greater share of the Fun Terminal's business came from pinball machines which mostly teenage-and-younger boys and girls played wildly. Probably not that day but some other I dimly recall, a few about fifteen years old had slipped past the cashier into the peep-show area and were hissing and whispering sneers.

The kids saw me and grinned anxiously. I was not about to get them in trouble, so I kept it to myself. I looked at a few more "loops" and went on my way with the teenagers still hissing and whispering sneers.

The underage teenagers in the porno movie peep show part of the Fun Terminal were an aberration but it raises questions about age-definitions of adulthood in this age of pervasive public sexuality and whether children should be protected from it or instructed in best ways to deal with it.

But the juxtaposition was not the teenagers. It was the apparently legal and public normality of the color explicit sex films in juxtaposition with everyday decently dressed civic pride and restraint walking around on the sidewalks.

I remember that I found the Peerless Theater on Third Street no longer in business, maybe demolished by then, and stopped at the Paris Theater not far away on Sixth Street and watched more explicit male and female sex-act pornography. It was both liberating and entertaining to sit and watch color film of naked males and females engaging in fellatio, cunnilingus, and coital sex in a public movie theater in a downtown American city. Nine years earlier I had been queasy with fear of being found while surreptitiously watching a couple black-and-white stag films behind a locked door in a hospital laboratory around midnight.

Back then I had wondered aloud to my friend and coworker about what kind of people stripped naked and publicly engaged in sex-acts on-camera for those illegal and thus limitedly distributed black-and-white stag films which very few people saw.

After I emerged from the movie into the lobby, a disheveled ticket-taker with a two-day growth of beard struck up a conversation with me. I wondered the same to him, only now it was what kind of people stripped and engaged in sex acts on-camera for widespread public viewing in downtown porno movie theaters.

He knew what I really meant. He told me that if I wanted to strip naked and be in an explicit sex porno movie I could go over to an address in Berkeley, which he wrote down for me. "The girls are a little harder to find, so the guys hang around the stairway," he said. "You hang around, they'll get to you."

I took the address and toyed with it, but I had to be somewhere else in the country in a few days and never tried—to my regret now a quarter of a century later in my upper middle age years.

In northern Ohio, center of the old New England puritan culture transplanted into the near Midwest, I was again surprised to find at least three explicit sex porno movie houses doing a booming business. Moreover, a number of peep-shows showed the same kind of color-film explicit-sex pornography.

It was not only shown in liberal and avant guard San Francisco, it was literally legally and publicly shown in cities all over the country. Times had changed. In theaters where in my boyhood I had watched second-run black-and-white matinee films like "The Sands of Iwo Jima" starring John Wayne, I now sat and watched high quality color film of naked men and women fucking, engaging in cunnilingus, and engaging in cunnilingus and was entertained by all the subtleties of their bare-body-language implications of shameless acts and resultant social scandal and tarnish.

I went into porno movie theaters and peep shows showing eight-millimeter and sixteen-millimeter color porno movies over the next decade. Expectations that some had that the porno movie business would reach a saturation point and then dry up never materialized.

I think it was probably based on mistaken presumptions. Those who saw porno movies as just the same old sex acts done over and over had presumed that it would lose its novelty and appeal. But there are those who see baseball games as just the same old hitting of a leather-covered ball by a big stick and running around to touch carefully placed sand-bag cushions. You might think something like that would soon lose its appeal, too. Or that the same might be with that other spectator sport where they throw and kick and inflated oblong ball around a gridiron-marked stadium field. Bunch of athletes chasing a football around a field for a couple hours cannot hold too much interest.

But that is not why people pay big money to sit and watch spectator sports. There is a spectator-identifying with the game-playing pleasures of the players. And there are subtleties of interaction between not only players but between players and the spectator crowd, niceties of exhibiting dexterity, individual shows of concern for reputation as published in sports pages, grandiose displays of human ego as in end-zone dances after scoring, and the whole interplay of the game with bodies banging and swirling, running and sliding, all to a set of internal rules of behavior for the sport.

And similarly, that is not why people pay money to watch the kind of spectator sport inherent in camera-based pornography. There is a spectator-identifying with the game-playing as well as with the sexual pleasures of the players. And there are subtleties of interaction between not only the naked sex-performer players but between players and the spectator-viewers and audiences. These include niceties of exhibiting sexual dexterity in the limited playing-field of the camera-view and with an audience watching.

There may be individual shows of a porno model's concern for his or her reputation as a glimpse of awareness that may or may not have been anticipated before or after stripping naked and performing sex-acts for public amusement. There may be displays of human ego. These may be when a naked porno model is observed successfully debauching another. Or they may be more entertainingly seen and inferred when the unknown and hidden camerapeople and directors/producers—effectively the audience—have their sport with the naked on-camera porno models, sport including successfully and permanently debauching the now tort-law-devalued porno models. And there is a whole interplay of the on-camera game, with bodies banging and squirming, humping and sucking, all of it to a set of internal rules of behavior for the sport of pornography.

In other words, there would seem to be all the elements of entertainment that one can find in spectator sports as well as entertainment found in depictions and portrayals of mainstream theater and movies. And that would seem, on the face of it, why commercial pornography failed to fade and go away.

The large porno movie theaters began to fold and shut their doors one-by-one in the mid-1980s. But that was not due to a declining interest in camera-based pornography. Costs and upkeep of large theaters had something to do with it. Union projectionists got a fair paycheck. Ticket booth personnel got minimum wage but it still took a chunk. The old theater buildings required large outlays to keep clean, to physically maintain and repair, and to heat in winter. Moreover, the thirty-five-millimeter color film shown in these porno movie theaters—and even the sixteen-millimeter color film shown in many of them—and all the expensive processes involved with color film production required large initial capital outlays and thus called for large billing fees.

Video camera and videocassette technology, on the other hand, required very little.

It was not only that video cameras began to proliferate and pornographers turned to making cheap porn videos, though. It was the content of the pornography, made possible at first the far less expensive costs of professional video equipment and professional videography personnel, and then virtually next to nothing with high quality home videocams and home VCRs in every household.

The professional and generally feature-length porno movies of the 1970s required large investments to pay for not only the expensive film and its processing and professional editing but professional movie-making personnel on the sets or locations. This, in turn, called for professional and known-quantity porno models. This allowed the same old faces and personalities to strip and engage in sex acts in front of professional cameras with increasing sexual and acting skills and in competitively more elaborate porno movie productions.

It was the era of the genuine porno star and the big-bucks elaborate porn production, even those that were merely three or four "loops" strung together as with the Swedish Erotica and other porn productions.

They were good, and the porno stars attracted their followings. But some of the excitement of pornography slipped from it as slick film editors cut to, say, close-ups of blow-jobs, then closer close-ups, then back to other angles in a visually artistic flashing montage of aspects of the sex act by famous porno women who had become literal fellatio experts on-camera and had done the scenes in front of a number of cameras operating simultaneously and had stripped and sucked penises in a number of takes for the same scene.

The arrival of cheap porn video production and then literal amateur porn video production returned the genre to its early decriminalized days when viewers were entertained by new average faces with their average bare bodies and porn producers experimenting with them as pornography camera subjects rather than engaging in experiments in the art of filmmaking with all the expensive film and editing equipment to make slick artsy porno movies.

The subtleties of interaction on the porn video set "playing field" returned to pornography productions. That which was not edited out, including all the unintended foibles, refusals, and mishaps, was seen as some of the interest.

Videos took hold and big professional porno movie productions slipped away. If porn viewers wanted to see an old famous professional production, it could be found on videotape. Every abode soon had a cheap VCR to show them on a bedroom or living room TV set. And one could "own" the porno movie and show it over and over on the TV set at will.

So the old porno movie theaters that had been outstanding features on American cityscapes for a decade-and-a-half closed their doors. But camera-based pornography was booming.

Mass circulation magazines delivered by the US Postal Service to millions of homes every month like *Penthouse* showed glossy color photographs of naked males and females engaging in sex acts and lesbian couples engaging in oral and coital sex acts, ever slightly short of totally explicit but leaving only the subtleties of interaction to the imagination. By the 1990s glossy full-page color photographs in *Penthouse* showed naked male-female and female-female couples engaging in anilingus (an example, *Penthouse*, December 1995, spread that includes page 62). In 1961 few people might have dreamed that magazines delivered by mail to a great segment of American homes would show, to put it in blunt pornographic terms, sharp clear glossy color photographs of people licking other people's assholes.

To some, probably the same ones who claimed that people would soon tire of seeing naked people perform the same old sex acts, it seems to show that camera-based pornography must get ever more "dirty" and outrageous to hold its audiences. But it may also be that pornographers simply follow a market to satisfy appetites of low-population sexual minorities.

In the old expensive porn productions it took a great amount of courage to include takes of anilingus in a porno movie. Various local pressure groups might react with outrage and have the expensive movie banned. Costs required a certain prudence even if the word may sound strange in the culture of pornography.

Cheap video technology allows experimenting with consumer appetites. And anilingus clearly has a porn market, as does S & M, B & D, and piss-porn (in Europe, the last still censored in America). In fact, the cheapness of video production allows it to turn a profit with small sexual markets.

Anilingus is nothing new to American pornography, even in American literature. William Borroughs's 1959 novel *The Naked Lunch*,[25] which had to be published in Paris, France, by Olympia Press, first because it was legally banned in the United States until Grove Press dared the restriction in 1962, is now considered part of American literature.

In the roughly ninth chapter titled "a.j.'s annual party," the novel describes a "blue movie" (porno movie) of an obvious underground porn producer named The Great Slashtubitch, a personality and happening that may have been loosely fictionalized from the author's experience.

In the novel we see: "*On Screen*. Red-haired, green-eyed boy, white skin with a few freckles…kissing a thin brunette girl in slacks."

The novel continues narrating the porno movie as it unfolds, describing the two porno models, an unnamed girl and a guy named Johnny, as costumed and made-up to appear like people seen in existentialist bars, and then describes the bed they are seated on. The girl fondles Johnny and tells him to strip. When they are both naked and sitting on the bed she whispers, "Darling I want to rim you."

Johnny doesn't want her to "rim" him, but relents and says he'll go wash his ass, but she hastens to volunteer to wash it. After some banter they go to the bathroom and she washes his ass with "soap and hot water" and sticks her finger up it.

Next she leads Johnny to the bedroom. "He lies down on his back and throws his legs back over his head, clasping elbows behind his knees. She kneel down and caress the backs of his thighs, his balls, running her fingers down the perennial divide. She push his cheeks apart, lean down and begin licking the anus, moving her head in a slow circle. She push at the sides of his asshole, licking deeper and deeper. He close his eyes and squirm. She lick up the perennial divide. His small tight balls…"

It goes on to describe her giving Johnny a blow job on-screen.

Through this vignette we catch a glimpse of a stag films and pornographic filmmaking in and prior to the 1950s and sex acts very likely depicted in one of them as fictionally retold from memory by Borroughs. And we may safely conclude that anilingus was performed by naked porno models in underground illegal porno movies prior to case-law legalization.

This would appear, at least in its own small part, to debunk the theory that porno movies gotten "dirtier" and more outrageous because saturation-point appetites for more "normal" pornographic sex acts have been reached. A wide range of sexual portrayals and explicit sex acts seem to have been in camera-based pornography long before it was decriminalized in the late 1960s.

And even while the deciding cases were still being heard, the second or third "*Mona*" feature-length porno movie was being made with graphic scenes of anilingus. During this time peep-shows regularly showed eight millimeter and sixteen millimeter "loops" showing anilingus, mostly lesbian-lesbian anilingus, but some males licking female assholes and an occasional female licking a male asshole, as in the early 1970s loop "Amazing Grace," produced by the Film Festival Theater group.

In other words, porn really did not get any "dirtier" as such. New cheap camera technologies simply made greater varieties of small porn productions possible for the same old limited-population sexual minorities and appetites.

As a result of inexpensive video production and less expensive high quality still cameras and film, camera-based pornography continues to flourish as a large segment of the Gross Domestic Product more than a quarter of a century after its case-law virtual decriminalization. Those who are waiting for a "saturation point" to be reached appear doomed to wait for a long time.

As home video camera technology spread, amateur porn videos spread into adult bookstores and video projection porno movie theaters. Some of these "amateur" porn videos are, in fact, very professionally produced. But with home camcorders in most suburban houses the illusion of just-plain-folks stripping and engaging in sex acts on home video cameras for public sale and amusement made a credible thesis. And the showing of these at home on the living room TV set only added to the aura of perhaps seeing a potential neighbor's sex organs while he or she engages in obscene acts for public entertainment. If not him or her, then why not?

Amateur porn videos may have alleviated a lot of sexual anxieties that gorgeous and voluptuous professional sexual dynamo porn megastars could have produced in average people. The amateurs look average and do it clumsily like the average folks do out there, surely part of the entertainment of it.

The first "amateur" porn videos as a genre hit the market in the late 1980s. Now near the end of the 1990s the adult bookstores still do a booming business in them. There must have been a considerable appeal to keep these often poor quality porn videos so viably on the market for nearly a decade.

I remember seeing for the first time what I believe was one of the early amateur porn videos in a peep show place in Missoula, Montana, in 1988. I recall it because shortly after seeing it I discussed it with a small porno movie producer in California.

It was run-of-the-mill porn. A fortyish white man and a thirtyish white woman began on a couch decently dressed. They were, I believe, told by someone unseen to strip and unceremoniously undressed on-camera.

They went through all the requisite scenes of cunnilingus, fellatio, and coital sex in a number of poses and positions.

The interest was real time. There was little of that all too clever film editor's cutting. The couple just awkwardly went from being dressed to undressing naked to this sex act and then the next and the next, and so on. No one cut out their clumsiness and self-consciousness while in transition from one sex-pose and sex-act to another on camera, or their narcissism-betraying and future-stigma-misgivings-revealing looks at the camera, or even their self-conscious uneasiness at being naked on-camera when they asked an off-screen camera person or director for clarification about a sex act they were told to perform. In addition, sometimes the camera would pick up the lighting wires and the spot-lights themselves.

Video viewers saw real people as they undressed and performed sex acts on-camera, their human apprehensions and clumsiness, their awareness of being on-camera for a commercially sold porn video, and the many authentic stories of their personalities responding and react-ing to the fact of being porno models on-camera and all the small pleas-ures and unpleasantnesses of being naked and publicly engaging in sex acts at someone else's direction and for pornography viewers' interests first and their own sexual and other pleasures somewhere below that.

When I got back to the Midwest shortly after that trip in mid-1988 "amateur" porn videos were finding their way into local adult book-stores and peep-shows. Even a local video projection porno movie the-ater showed them sometimes.

A unifying feature was "real time" and little cutting or editing. Video cameras rolled. Porno models undressed. Porno models engaged in sex acts and then were shown moving around between sex acts to get into poses and positions to perform other sex acts. Off-camera porn pro-duction personnel and sometimes invited audiences exchanged conver-sation with the porno models before, during, and after engaging in sex acts. Unintended views of lighting and production wiring reminded the viewer that the porno models were voluntarily on-camera and were not, after all, your average people, but a small wanton fraction of the population that will strip and engage in sex acts for public amusement.

And in the virtually journalistic reportage of the amateur porn videos, viewers can see and amplify with imagination stories of why the porno models are there submitting to tort-law devaluation, being literal fools on camera for public amusement—like circus clowns to some extent. Viewers can see them finding sexual pleasure in sex-in-public for public amusement, watch the feelings and interactions that the porno models show with each other and others on the set or location with them. These may sometimes include uncut suggestions of resentment or regret, unctuous knowing acquiescence to producer, director, and camera person demands that they literally degrade themselves for others' profit and public amusement in degrading naked poses and sex-act view positions. In short, they see very normal human interactions of all these separate authentic stories, and they may see others synthesizing larger stories when porno models' individual personalities are factored in.

The "amateur" porn video will never have the interaction potential of a live-sex-act, but it has the "real time" authenticity that permits much subtext and underlying story to be revealed.

CHAPTER ELEVEN

Debaucher Audiences and Debauchee Live Sex Performers

It was not until the late 1970s that I saw my first "live-sex-show" in the raunchy Times Square area of New York City. I came away wondering, among other things, what these people felt like during and after stripping and performing sex-acts in live-shows in front of audiences.

Here there were no—at least not legitimately—cameras to record the female and male sex-models who stripped and engaged in sex-acts in front of paying male and female customers.

While I was too far back into the audience to directly interact with the naked sex-show performers, much of the entertainment that I felt and could gather that the rest of the audience felt was derived from the performers' awareness of us spectators. They could see us viewing their bare bodies and sex-acts, and their resulting interactions as sex-objects and reactions to us in audience in general was the genuine entertainment.

They were the equal-under-the-law bare sex-objects depicting themselves as tort-law devalued whores engaging in explicit sex-acts for paying audience's amusement. In a duality relationship far more evident
than in a porno movie theater, there were the debaucher members of
the audience who had paid to see the two bare debauchees.

And there was a low-level flow of intercommunication between these
two forces, from aware naked debauchees' nonverbal sucking, sexual
grunts, and suppressions of shame, including expressions of feigned
indifference, to amused debaucher audience's undertone verbal commentary of generally polite innuendo razzings and counterfeit chidings.
In addition, there were the audience-participatory nonverbal snickers,
sneers, and exchanges of snide glances. It has always seemed—looking
back—that the occasional women in the audience were the greater participants in these exchanges than the men who came more to watch and
partake of the show. But male audience intercommunication with the
live sex-show models may have been more experienced and therefore
more sophisticated in addition to being less shocked at the anti-social
audacities, and thus less in need to express responses. Always, however,
whether male or female audience members, a low-level interaction
went on between the debauchee naked sex-act performers and the paying debaucher spectators.

But the long term consequences of "live sex show" models' public
debauchery and literal tort-law degradation were different from those
of porno models, who stripped naked and performed sex acts in front
of recording motion picture, video, or still cameras. Live-sex models
have an option to literally and figuratively walk away from it, to disappear unremembered and unbranded into mainstream society.

Paradoxically, porno models who strip and engage in sex-acts on-
camera to be seen by tens of thousands, sometimes millions, do it in
front of almost no audience, sometimes only a camera person, and in a
largely private set or location. Live-sex-show performers who may vanish back into mainstream society after having stripped and performed

in front of forgetful spectators, engage naked in sex-acts in front of significant numbers of paying people, genuine audiences.

Nevertheless, at least on the face of it, live-sex-show performers can subsequently go on out in the world to wallow in social respectability, hold important and powerful positions, bask in public fame and prestige, and be able to conceal their earlier debauched public embarrassment.

Theoretically they are able to quit, filter back into "reputable" society even in the city where they had performed, take other jobs, and in a short time anyone who might have viewed their bare bodies and sex acts on a stage or in a peep-show will have largely forgotten what their facial identities actually looked like. Moreover, quite often sex-show audiences may have slight difficulty recognizing the performers after they have their clothes on, even immediately after the sex-shows. I found this to be the case at least once. It seemed partly a result of those sex-performers having been "costumed" in naked flesh in the make-believe spotlit on-stage world and reentering a "real" world as two average decently dressed people.

The few, and therefore poor sampling of, live-sex-show performers that I talked with, either after shows or some length of time after they had slipped back into "normal" society, betrayed little or no concern about repercussions. They had slipped off clothes, slipped on stage, publicly performed sex-acts, slipped back off stage, slipped back into clothes, and slipped unrecognized, unremembered and unblemished back into society. Almost no one knew, and for some there was a deliciousness of having a gossipy little secret to carry around.

Unless there is a familiarity arising out of constant contact and seeing people, or powerful poignant reasons to remember people and their facial identities, the human mind has a capacity to forget old faces and personalities, possibly for reasons of mental economy, as a constant stream of life's new ones displace and replace them.

But unlike a live-sex-show model's quickly forgotten facial identity, a face captured on film or videotape, like a spoken comment captured in writing, retains its accuracy and authenticity. It can be viewed a second, third, or hundredth time to remind the viewer of an appearance and an identity. And it is "permanent." Years, decades, and even centuries later a photograph and videotape, like a printed or written account, is still there.

Whether the viewer sees the person first or the person's photographed or videotaped image first and subsequently recognizes the real flesh-and-blood person, the person's and his or her image likeness can be compared and verified, virtually over a lifetime, for inevitable human commentary. And why else capture an image of anything or anyone, even a porno image, except for later spoken, written, or private mental commentary?

Thus a naked porno model's accurate and authentic facial identity, captured—to put in terms of status-ranking vocabulary licensed by the Great Social Beast—while shamefully and disgracefully exhibiting sex organs and bare behinds and degradingly and humiliatingly engaging in sex acts on film or videotape for public amusement, lingers for comparison, verification, and scurrilous comment as minutes become hours, days, months, and years.

Unlike a live-sex performer, if a porno model should come into someone's life with past unknown, scandalous images authenticating facial identity of his or her bare body engaging in public sex-acts may be revealed later. If, on the other hand, a porno model is introduced to someone without his or her past "shame" being revealed, the other party in the introduction may recognize him or her after having earlier seen pornographic photographs, films, or videotapes and may go back to an image to verify an identity.

So porno models just have to live with it. Someone who dimly thought they might have recognized a reputable person, or even a friend or neighbor, naked and performing in porn can retrieve an old sex magazine, porno movie, or porn videotape and compare image facial identity with the real flesh-and-blood person's to see if their vague and faulty memory served them correctly. There they may be, captured on film or videotape.

In addition, because the films and tapes are generally mass-produced, much larger audiences than those who could have viewed even a prolonged series of live sex shows by a performer will have viewed the porno models' debauchery and degradation, creating hugely greater probability of recognition.

Even over a year period of time, a comparatively few people, probably numbered in the hundreds, will have watched a live sex show. But public commercial pornography is literally manufactured for widespread sale. Thousands—and usually tens of thousands—of even low-sale commercial "amateur" porn videos or sex magazines are going to be distributed and sold. Sometimes literally millions of copies of more professional porn photo, motion picture, and videotaping sessions are distributed, sold, and viewed.

The facial identities of naked debauched porno models seen in X-rated movies shown in theaters may be as quickly forgotten as the live performances. But even in the case of "amateur" porn videos they will have been seen by porn video, sex magazine, and porno movie multitudes. It increases the odds of recognition.

A "debauched" live-sex-show performer is only temporarily "disgraced." The pseudo-disgrace may have been part of the show's amusement, but when the show is over, it is over. When the performer goes on to other things in life, the live-sex-show performances will not necessarily follow her or him. The debaucher-debauchee social contract can conceivably be revoked after a performer quits. Viewing or performing in a live-sex-show has that disclaimer attached to the great unwritten contract.

The physical and psychological effects of viewing a live-sex-show are slightly different from viewing a pornography photograph, motion picture, or videotape. For one thing, the latter has already been done. It is past tense, history. At the time a viewer watches "debauched" naked porno models' taped, filmed, or photographed performances, the real flesh-and-blood porno models have by then gone on to other things.

To the contrary, naked live-sex-show models perform in the present in front of people. By the very nature of it, even in the enclosure of a peep-show, but certainly quite clearly on a public sex-stage, there is that interaction between viewing respectably attired customers and the naked "debauched" sex-performers.

Of course by the very nature of capturing camera-based images, a small audience, maybe an audience of one debaucher cameraperson, interacts with the naked and debauched porno models engaging in sex on-camera. The very rare exception is those very rare amateur productions where a camera is remotely operated by one of the porn performers.

But in the vast, probably ninety-nine percent, majority of commercial, including "amateur" commercial, porn productions, one or more production personnel participate in image capture and porno model directing. And some shrewd pornographers have been quite clever in capturing the interaction between naked "debauched" porno models on-camera and properly clothed "debaucher audience" photographing, filming, or videotaping them, directing them, or even just interacting while watching the porno models' socially stigmatized implicit disgrace being recorded for widespread public showing, sale, and distribution.

Even this, though, is merely recorded. The event of the porn performance is already history even if shown and viewed mere minutes later. There is no way for a viewer of a hard-core pornographic photograph, film, or videotape to interact with the images of the sex performers on magazine pages, theater screens, or television sets, even, it must be asserted, in "interactive" pornographic material now on sale in adult bookstores and on the Internet.

The only way a viewer-debaucher can verbally, nonverbally, inferentially, or sometimes even physically interact with naked sex-performer-debauchees is in their real live presence.

In any live public performance, and not limited to sex performances, there is an interaction and psychological identification process going on between performers and audience. That is why legitimate theater is far more emotionally powerful than movies, or why live concerts have stirring impacts that even the purest-sound CDs can only minimally provide.

So an audience member watching a live sex performance tends to identify with the performers. There is, and it cannot be helped, a tiny level of embarrassment for the audience and of course slightly more so for the performers.

Even a jaundiced camera-based pornography producer once told me that he was genuinely embarrassed when interviewing new prospective porno models for his on-camera sex performances and at times found himself momentarily unable to ask certain necessary questions of them. So one may extrapolate that less experience-hardened sex show spectators identify with and feel tinges of embarrassment.

Nevertheless, a shared embarrassment seems to be a part of the amusement, perhaps some of the genuine titillation of a live-sex-show audience and the reason they inconvenience themselves and pay more to see a live sex show rather than settling for viewing a porn video on a TV set in the comfort of a living room. That the naked sex-performers experience at least some minimal embarrassment probably goes without saying.

Additionally, observers seem to enjoy a slightly Sadistic glee of observing the sex-performers' debauched self-degradation—live while interacting with them at some level. Amid these and other quite human feelings, audience and sex performers react to one another.

But rather than analyzing live-sex-performers and their public sex-acts, it seems best to relate a viewer experience. I viewed explicit live-sex-performances in New York, Hamburg, and Amsterdam, but the ones in Hamburg strike me as the juiciest, and the following one had that quality. The Reeperbahn area of Hamburg, at that time shortly prior to German reunification, was perhaps the most blatant, free, and garish sex-entertainment center in the world.

On top of bars or on small stages attached to the bars in numerous cocktail lounges along the Reeperbahn naked male and female couples lay in sixty-nine positions and engaged in oral sex for the amusement of customers right on top of the bars, a few inches away from them.

Other drinking establishments had small sex stages where naked heterosexual couples engaged in oral sex acts and copulated while customers sipped their beers and watched.

Still other sex entertainment establishments had live shows on turntables in arenas surrounded by peep-show booths with viewing windows. A viewer dropped a one-mark coin into a coin box, and a blind covering a viewing window in a booth was raised to permit a casual examination of the spectacle of a brightly spotlighted naked man and woman engaging in fellatio, cunnilingus, sometimes anilingus, and copulating.

In those, the viewer was safely behind a glass window, often a silvered one-way-visible mirror so the debauched and disgraced naked sex performers would not have the slightest chance of ascertaining who had been amused and entertained by what the socially accepted would call their humiliation and shame.

Interspersed with these sex entertainment establishments along the Reeperbahn were the more usual porn video arcades, porno movie houses, and naked female strip shows.

The gaudy sex-strip stretches for about a mile along a wide main street called the Reeperbahn and then turns and goes some blocks up a street aptly named Gross Freiheit (Great Freedom), where there are some lavishly presented sex shows like those a sex entertainment palace called Salambo involving dozens of sex performers, orchestras, professional lighting, and professional choreography of acts of fellatio, copulation, and cunnilingus.

On the periphery are several giant office-building-size whorehouses and a street (blocked off to "proper" women) of whorehouses. Prostitution is legal and carefully monitored in Germany.

One has to really see the district to appreciate it fully, and perhaps one has to experience a live sex show act in order to understand it. But let me sketch one of a number of them here to give an example of a live sex show viewing. And to provide a feeling and ambiance, it seems indispensable to understanding to relate it in pornographic terms utilizing some obscenity.

There was one peep-show about midway down the Reeperbahn where, at the time, the viewing booths were, apparently deliberately, left well lit.

In addition, the padded blue turntable that the standing viewers looked out onto from their viewing-booth windows was raised to just below the level of the windows. The outer edge of the rug-covered turntable itself rotated only an inch or two from the windows, and either the thin wood-veneer walls allowed transmission of much of the sex-act and human sound, or small openings had been deliberately constructed to let the sounds through from the turntable sex-stage to the viewing booths.

There was clearly a desire on the part of management to allow this interaction between satisfactorily garbed spectators and naked sex performers.

Several months later, for whatever reasons, they redesigned the peep-show turntable stage and lowered it almost to the floor level. But I was lucky to see it the old way, and to my mind the better way, before they did that.

This live-sex-show storefront was only one of a number along the Reeperbahn. Competition for spectator money was fierce, with most joints hiring barkers to lure customers in, but there was never a shortage of spectator-customers. In the most basic law of economics, supply simply grew to fill demand.

In this live sex show joint the small turntable sex-show arena was itself surrounded by a circle of about fifteen to twenty viewing booths which had viewing windows facing the turntable and doors on the opposite side going out into aisles in the storefront.

All of these live-sex peep-shows also had dozens of video booths showing commercial European porn videos, and in this one the walls were lined with about twenty of them.

The live-sex-show "arena" was constructed halfway down the main aisle leading to the street, the Reeperbahn itself, and conveniently located near a cashier's cage. The fifteen-or-so viewing booths had been built of some thin light-colored wood-veneer only for a minimum of privacy they offered the customers and to make certain that only those who paid could watch the sex-show.

Like all the peep-show booths up and down the Reeperbahn, the ones for viewing the sex acts there covered only a minimal floor area, no more than two-feet by two-feet. One either dropped one-Deutschemark coins or a five-Deutschemark brass token into a coin box mounted inside the booth wall, and this activated a small electric motor that raised a blind from the window to allow viewing of the turntable sex-stage and the naked sex-performers.

The deeply padded red-carpeted turntable was about eight feet in diameter and rotated slowly around.

In this live sex show, the two sex performers, a slightly portly thirty-something blond, blue-eyed, apparently Slavic, woman and a middle-age well-built large apparently Turkish man had climbed up on it naked from a tiny "dressing room" in back of the cashier's cage and had been offering themselves on display that way for some seconds when I stepped into one of the viewing booths and deposited coins which raised the blind from the viewing window.

Without some terminology of pornography, one may find difficulty in communicating the ambiance and attractions of the unique Reeperbahn. While the naked blond Slavic woman was rotated around standing literally above me on the turntable I could see that she had pale northern European flesh, large slightly sagging breasts, blond pubic hair, a big bare ass, and a large fleshy juicy cunt. The hefty muscular dark complexioned Turkish guy had black pubic hair and a fat limp dong.

Both had bland matter-of-fact expressions as they stood naked on the turning turntable with their bare asses and sex organs on exhibit and preparing to engage in sex acts for our entertainment. They were, by then, experienced sex performers who had done live sex shows several times per day for weeks if not months, and part of the sex act was to offer this preliminary exhibit of their bare bodies for peep-show spectators' inspection and amusement.

I could see across the turntable into other viewing booth windows and adequately make out faces looking out through them. Most were, of course, men. But I remember two couples had squeezed into a couple viewing booths, and I could see both the men's and the women's faces in the well-lit booths as they looked out through the viewing windows at the naked blond woman and naked Turkish man.

Like me, they could see that the Slavic woman's bare ass showed a moderate middle-age spread, and when the turntable rotated her around facing the opposite way, they could see her tuft of brownish-blond pubic hair and the split bulge of her twat and its thick fleshy lips.

And for that matter, the naked Slavic woman could not help but see them and all of us gawking through the windows at her. But she betrayed no emotion at it. She had a lady-next-door look to her, albeit a naked lady-next-door. She betrayed a tinge of self-consciousness that one might expect from standing naked on exhibit as a sex show performer for all those fifteen or twenty spectators she could make out in the viewing booths, but she also had a look of just doing her job.

The first thing this naked Slavic and Turkish couple did was struggle clumsily in their nudity and on the comparatively small turning turntable to get down.

The Turkish guy lay on his back across the diameter of the turning turntable.

The naked "lady-next-door" Slavic woman straddled him and lowered her large fleshy bare ass over his face. She moved her naked Slavic female flesh matter-of-factly and with an apathetic expression as if she had a job to do, a pose to get into, a sex act to perform.

As she squashed her body down on top of his with her head over his crotch, he pressed his lips against her cunt and began licking to stimulate her female sexuality while we all watched.

He ate pussy while the turntable rotated them around past the windows so all of us viewers could see from any angle.

With the turntable raised to window level, the sex action was taking place right in front of my eyes. The blond woman's ample meaty ass and Turkish guy's head was a foot of two from my face as he came around licking her cunt. I looked above his cunt-licking mouth the Slavic lady-next-door's large exhibited anus as her behind was rotated by my viewing window. Her buttocks squirmed and undulated as she reacted to his oral stimulation of her cunt.

I could also see both of the ladies in viewing booths across the turntable from me pointing and smirking. The men, theirs and the lone ones in the other booths, looked out at the presented sex act blandly.

The naked blond woman's head was starting to be rotated around in my direction.

Her lips were wrapped around his saliva-lubricated stiffening meaty penis and her head was pumping up and down to slip it deep into her throat and let it back again.

The naked lady-next-door continued to publicly perform fellatio while her sex-partner continued to perform cunnilingus. Her face came around to my viewing window, inches in front of my face, and she looked straight into my eyes with the Turkish guy's large stiff penis stuffed into her mouth.

We exchanged knowing eye contact while she clearly sought to amuse me by pumping the penis down her throat several times while fondling his balls with her fingers.

I deliberately grinned at her degradation, but she seemed pleased with it and kept looking at me with her big blue eyes while sucking cock. Her attempts at nuances normally communicated by facial expressions lapsed into ludicrous enigmas with her lips wrapped firmly around his meaty male member. I had seen numerous different women engaging in fellatio in both pornography and live sex shows, but I believe this was the first one who ever directly attempted to communicate something exclusively to me by facial expression with her mouth wrapped around a penis. As a result, I may have failed to comprehend the intended communication. But then again, I may not have. Among the things she seemed to be looking at me and narcissistically saying was, "This is what I look like sucking cock."

She seemed to like it. With a large fat penis stuffed in her mouth she could not return a smile. But before she had been completely rotated by my viewing window, she stopped cocksucking and just looked at me through the window with a fleshy cylinder of male sex meat stuffed in her mouth. I have to admit it was amusing.

The next time her face came around, however, she was licking his hairy balls. She looked at me while licking his nuts. We made eye contact, and again I grinned at her public self-disgrace and she clearly saw me. The naked sex-show lady-next-door, on public exhibit as a cocksucker and crotch-licker, licked a hairy nut with an unashamed nod at me. She did not smile, but that may have been part of the sex act.

The naked Turkish guy also glanced at me while he licked twat. I think that if I had been one of the numerous female customers who stopped in the view the sex show, almost always accompanied by a man or men, he might have winked at them while they watched him lick female genitalia.

In fact, I heard one of the female voices in the booths across from me cackle tauntingly—either frustrations at his oral technique or what she perceived as his public disgrace—when his face came by.

When I looked over at her, she was giggling and pointing at the act of cunnilingus. But the Turkish guy just kept licking pussy, knowing that was why he was performing.

There had been very clear exchanges between sex performers and audience. If it was not quite that clear in other live sex show situations, there were certainly similar kinds of exchanges of communication and responses in all of them.

The Slavic lady-next-door and the muscular Turkish changed positions and sex acts several times before I left. I watched her sit on her haunches in front of him and engage in fellatio. I watched him kneel in front of her and engage in cunnilingus. And I watched them copulate, both in the missionary position and doggy-style.

I wondered and wondered how it felt like from the other end of the sex-performer and audience thing. What might these sex performers really feel like. I asked some of them, but I got either crisp quick answers with no depth or jocular laugh-it-offs as they went on their way, apparently bothered enough by such questions from people who had viewed what society would label their shame and degradation.

One young woman who "danced" nude in a peepshow and had in the past performed in live-sex-shows talked briefly with me. She claimed not to be or have been ashamed of it, and it may have been true. She was deeply involved in the culture of the sex-show industry. Her friends and peers were in it. Her life revolved around it.

I sensed that to her there were those "real" people with whom she associated and those fleeting "spectator" people who came and went almost like images and therefore may have seemed unreal. One could hardly feel embarrassed in front of these "images."

Nude dancing and live sex show performing paid her bills. It was a job. The income gave her freedom—far more than those of a lower class *hausfrau.* She lapsed wistfully into daydreams of better options, but don't we all. She seemed pleased with herself and with things as they were.

Degrees of individual liberties and freedoms have been misapprehendingly stifled as our era of technology-caused hyperchange has forced the great social beast to blunderingly and blindly react to its threats.

Porno models and pornographers are just some more people caught up in the swirling eddies of this social and technological change. In fact, in many ways I feel that they are among the best and most honest of all of us people caught up in it, and I would prefer to associate and share friendships with them than most others.

Stirred by the swirling change to consciously or unconsciously put their bodies, reputations, and lives on the line, they have given us opportunities to look at ourselves in new ways. Ancient stigmas continue to define them, castigate them, and limit their human potentials. But they have done it to and for our benefit, and it cannot be retracted.

If some day I may be proved wrong, and it turns out that the fervent opponents of pornography were right in calling it a cancer on society, I submit to them here that a serious disease like cancer must be objectively studied with no allowances for dishonesty, and subjectively examined to ferret out unrealized tendencies toward dishonesty, as well as to discover new avenues of understanding.

Specifically, we must seek to understand not only porn consumers but shed some figurative light on porn participants and their reasonings and motives for participating in pornography for consumers. And, if one believes that pornography must be brought under some kind of control—which I do not—understanding these reasonings and motives might bring into being benign social controls for the satisfactory management of pornography rather than legislation and criminalization which terribly erode intellectual freedoms, civil rights, and civil liberties so necessary to the healthy functioning of a free society.

I do not believe for a moment that pornography is a cancer or any other disease metaphor. Human sexuality will be with us as long as there is a human race, and pornography is not going to go away until something technologically "better" comes along to replace it. It would seem, therefore, that it should be studied in an atmosphere with as much honesty and willingness to discard ancient preconceptions and prejudices as possible.

Stigmatizing and castigating the participants in it may have short term social control purposes, but even then only when underlying social values remain valid. And we will not know whether they are valid or not unless we poke and probe into theses social controls and society's goals and directions in general.

If public live explicit sex shows exist in northern Europe and North America, private ones seem to exist everywhere that they are not public. In Asia and in our more puritanical places in mid-North America, one with the means can find illegal "private" live sex shows staged in hotel rooms by low-class males and low-class professional female prostitutes. The only real difference between these and the public sex-shows in Europe and New York is the cost to the viewer and police risk to both viewers and sex performers.

Where there is an appetite and money there will be performers and shows, and it would seem that there always have been during the span of civilization. It is difficult to say that live sex shows are more or less interesting than camera-based pornography. The former offers the excitement of interaction and communication. But the latter offers audience a certain permanence to the performers' debauchee relationship and a potential for multiple showings to examine subtext story and performer intent.

But low-cost camera-based pornography has brought naked performers engaging in explicit sex acts to millions of spectators, if not billions, and has created, for the first time in history, a virtual record of explicit human sexuality. The performers in many cases cross over into both genres, on-camera and live sex shows, but "doing it on-camera" has its differences and its own viewer and spectator enjoyments as well as its own performer consequences that may motivate additional spectator pleasures. "Doing it on stage" may allow a performer's anonymous life-experimentation with subsequent disappearance back into mainstream society in ways the capturing camera and permanent images will not allow.

CHAPTER TWELVE

On Camera

Experiences of live-sex-show performers have obvious parallels with those of porno models who strip naked and engage in sex-acts on-camera and in front of camerapersons and other assistants and observers. But there are, naturally, differences.

In camera-based pornography, the observers are usually coworkers working together to create a product as well as coconspirators participating in production risks with the porno models. They share some mutual interests in the outcome. Not all observers may be actual coworkers. Often the production personnel will invite guests to watch, and sometimes these guests will have paid to be spectators. But even in situations where observers have paid to watch pornography being photographed, filmed, or videotaped, they become, in a sense, "coconspirator spectators" in the porn production.

Seldom, if ever, do either live-sex-show performers or porno models invite genuine friends or "guests" other than fellow porn-industry personnel to watch them strip naked and engage in varieties of sex-acts in a live-show or on-camera. Friends of production personnel may be there out of curiosity or to be helpful. But most come to watch a debaucher-debauchee act played out and even take some enjoyment in minorly participating as transient "debauchers." "Debaucher" paying spectators are virtually always there to effectively snicker at and ogle the "debauchee" naked sex-performers or porno models at the invitation of porn-industry or production personnel.

They are more than paying audience because they are in a context of sharing the situation with the porno models, rather than participating as audience from behind the psychological safety-barriers of off-stage seating or in back of partitions, as with members of the public paying to view naked live-sex-show performers. And they have in-group allegiances of one kind or another to the porn production personnel and thus have a stake in a resulting "good product."

Production personnel themselves may be titillated by what they see, but they have jobs to do photographing, videotaping, and directing the porno models. Like workers in a factory, they are all doing it to produce items with sale value, commercially sold porn videos.

But in photographing and videotaping session the debaucher-debauchee dichotomy is quite evident, and it continues afterward.

The debaucher camerapersons, directors, and other production people will leave the set or location, like any factory production worker would, and go home or go play after doing his or her job, returning to work to photograph or videotape in the next session.

Unlike these coworkers, the debauched porno models know that later they will indeed have to deal with it. Prior to having gone on-camera, even prior to having arrived on the set, naked first-time models engaging in sex on-camera had been be forced to consider the consequences of large audiences seeing their permanently recorded and publicly sold photographs and videotapes. They therefore have feelings related to consequences before and during their "work." In the good-byes that follow having gotten dressed again, the porno models may part company with their production coworkers with tinges of uneasiness, if not faint smatterings of shame and embarrassment.

Not only must a porno model personally deal with those who will have seen her or him naked in hardcore porn, but she or he must deal with her or his own new social standing, subsequent related job and employment limitations, and other reputation-based realities.

By definition, porno models have posed to publicly expose bare flesh and private parts and have consented to being positioned, photographed, and/or videotaped in conspicuously debasing postures and defiling public sexual acts for exhibit and commercial publication in camera-based "whore stories."

Once having been photographed and/or videotaped naked and performing sex acts for public amusement, a porno model is driven to re-adapt her or his self-image to resultant realities. She or he has been permanently and publicly debauched and degraded, and everyone who knows of it, knows it.

So a porno model is, from then on, branded a debauchee-half in the great social debaucher-debauchee compact, an indelibly tainted servant-player in the social entanglements of complex master-servant, buyer-seller, debaucher-debauchee relationships. In the great commercial bazaar of social interactions, she or he has been permanently condemned to a "seller" category—by not only the buyers of porn, but by those who are aware of her or him being on lasting social exhibit as one who has "sold" her or his own sexual flesh, a socially marked "whore."

Over and above pornography, in a shadowy illusory world of "buyers" and "sellers," the "buyers," whether they have intentions to buy or not, wander through the great social bazaar constantly inspecting their fellow human being "seller" goodies. Some "sellers" have art, music, or industrial designs for sale. Some have their labor for sale. When a "buyer" comes upon a first-time porno model stigmatized by having sold her or his bare sexual flesh, the "buyer" sees marred merchandise, a "seller" perpetually for sale cheap.

Thus when cameras are packed, and everyone is dressed and ready leave a pornographic shooting site, the debaucher camera persons and producers gleefully exit with merchandise of value, but debauched first-time porno models go out with their persons now socially and economically devalued and doubtlessly suppressing some cynicism.

In tort-law economic valuation, these new porno models have fundamentally valueless indemnifiable reputations. In regard to upward social mobility, low ceilings have been erected and direct earning prospects, and social power prospects related to these, have been given unmistakable caps. In those less tangible personal valuations where esteem and self-esteem play roles—including roles where self-regard for one's own standing relate to assertiveness, which can be of economic and social value—these porno models are now socially esteemed "whores," licitly debased and ordained to have been corrupted, debauched, and perverted. They are limited to reorganizing self-worth, self-regard, and self-respect around the new psychological, social, and economic boundaries.

Among the boundaries, porno models' reputations are reduced. Invariably as a result, their long-term accesses to easier livelihoods, respect, and community standing are, generally speaking, undermined. Status in society is reduced. Pay and position, with associated levels of comfort and insulation, are generally sacrificed. There is a measurable tort-law social and economic devaluation, and the "seller" may endlessly "sell" self more cheaply.

But near the bottom of the social-economic scale—from where virtually all porno models come—it may matter very little. They are already "sellers" born to "sell" selves cheaply. Living in that context, in addition to pay for modeling services, the uniqueness of having stripped naked and performed sex acts in commercial pornography may at least set them apart, give them some anomalous individuality, and earn them if not respect then a certain amount of admiration for their audacity from their peers.

Even so, the word-based Social Beast is in control and requires conservative conformity. In the great national and now global group as a whole that includes rich and poor, powerful and powerless, buyer and seller, debaucher and debauchee, they are censured. The Great Social Beast's individual human integers retreat in fear, cower and comply. The Eric Berne game "Ain't it awful" both feeds the fear and supports the censure.

Anyone who dares elect or appoint a porno model to a position of power or influence risks a confrontation with the Social Beast and a fallout.

In short, once having performed on-camera for national publication exhibiting her or his bare flesh engaging in sex acts, a porno model is cast into a permanent "servitude" class and regarded as certified social sport. It used to be reserved for "fallen women," but now male and female porno models fall into that category.

Society has evolved and both porno model genders are represented in these losses of "respect" and status. Lower class female whores have known it for eons. Now male porno models have joined them.

This is not to say it is without choice. Just as in ancient times a person could temporarily sell himself into legal slavery, virtually all of the porno models now seen and ever seen in sex photographs, porno movies, and porn videos have voluntarily offered themselves into the new effectively permanent low-class servitude and regarded-as-public-sport status.

Virtually all naked porno models have intentionally—rashly or calculatingly, mostly for pay—submitted to photography, filming, or videotaping sessions that demanded they publicly and permanently shame themselves, and as a result surrender to its social consequences and social ranking aftermaths of their literal public degradation. Most of them, however, were going nowhere, socially or economically, anyway. But now they must additionally acquiesce to social outgrowths of their present and future debased status.

But "doing it on camera," might be regarded as a new and different form of sexual activity in itself. Certainly the yuppies with video cameras in their bedrooms know that.

Perhaps a branch of "doing it on-camera" may be: "doing it on-camera for widespread publication and sale." "Doing it on-camera" seems to be a form of sexual activity and enjoyment in itself.

"Doing it in front of people," as in the live sex-shows, is interesting and different. But throughout history it has been done. In some primitive tribes there are marriage rituals of "doing it in front of people." And in our modern society significant populations belong to "swingers clubs" where members strip naked and engage in sex acts in front of other members for both the sex-performers' and the viewers' enjoyments.

"Doing it in front of people" is not at all new to historical and prehistorical human experience, but "doing it on-camera" is. The social consequences of "doing it on camera," as a result, are too new for the Great Amorphous Social Beast.

Thus "doing it on-camera" as a new form of sex calls for some comment in itself, and "doing it on-camera for widespread publication and sale" begs elucidation from a participant's angle.

Quite often male porn producers and directors are also themselves porno models. The debaucher-debauchee relationship would seem blurred, but male porn producers and directors who are also their own male porno models are both enjoying this new form of doing-it-on-camera sex and debauching (but to a much lesser extent than non-model producers and directors) their female porno models. And the same would seem to be true with the small but growing numbers of female porn producers and their male and female porno models.

There are some female porn video and porno movie producers now. Candida Royalle and Tyffany Million come to mind. Even the second or third "Mona" feature-length porno movie of the 1970s directed by Mona Watson comes to mind. They began as debauched porno models themselves. Yet one can note in their productions the same delight in debauching male and female porno models that the male producers and directors betray.

No natural law forbids the debauchee from becoming the debaucher, though of someone else besides the person who debauched her or him. It is, for instance, highly unlikely that Candida Royalle or Tiffany Million will ever debauch the early male producers and directors of their porno movies by having them strip naked and degrade themselves (literally in tort-law valuation, and psychologically subversive of their self-respect) performing sex acts on camera for commercial distribution. But they have debauched numerous female and male porno models in their X-rated productions.

A porno model, as opposed to a yuppy with a private bedroom video camera, arrives at a set or location with at least some level of certain knowledge of the consequences of stripping naked and engaging in sex acts for widespread commercial publication and sale.

The first-time porno model arrives at the videotaping or photographing set or location knowingly prepared to literally sell herself or himself into the modern analogy of a permanent servant category, if not something close to a slave category.

Amidst glad-handing and back-patting that accompanies arrival on-set or on-location of a decently dressed—and still at that point "respectable" and "reputable"—first-time porno model, she or he knows beyond doubt that nakedness, disrespect, disrepute, degradation, disgrace and permanent stigma will shortly begin and forever follow.

Producers, directors, and camera people thus put some effort into charming and fawning over the porno models as a diversion prior to shooting. Their naked flesh and their disgrace will be the bases for valuable for-sale commodities, and a certain temporary masking of it may aid in obtaining a good "dirty" porn product.

In choosing a porno model for an explicit adult film, video, or sex magazine spread, an amateur or professional producer or photographer will invariably speak the phrase, "I can use you."

"Use" is the key word. *Use* the naked model he or she will.

But there is a flip side, and that is protest. Beyond the pay, the novel sexual enjoyment of "doing it on-camera," the promise of unique individuality and scurrilous admiration for audacity in the eyes of peers, the porno model uses her or his recorded naked sex-act performance as a profound statement of protest and glaring rejection of social values. The protest may be tantrum, but even that is a protest.

In that, the porno model, at some level, even tantrum-analogous, is knowingly and actively participating in fomenting social change.

So, too, of course, is the porn viewer, but more passively.

So a porno model who strips naked and engages in sex-acts, on-camera and for future widespread publication, not only does it with the thrill of this new kid of sex "on-camera for publication," but with a delicious tingling excitement of being on the vanguard of social change.

A factor in any porno model's image capture is that the permanent pornographic images do not change, and there may be unconscious "fountain-of-youth" motivations in this. Over time, the living porno model's body continues to age and change.

Though probably never considered on-set and on-camera, a real result is that a facial identity captured and published in a porno movie or sex-magazine a quarter-century earlier will appear different than the porno model's living facial identity twenty-five years of natural aging later. Slowly—far more slowly with lasting images, but similar to forgetting facial identities of live-sex-show performers after nude performances—the facility to discern, recognize, and remember a porno model's facial identity fades. If the rampant anonymity of modern urban culture does not achieve it earlier, after a decade or two even a popular and widely known porno model will blend anonymously into a crowd.

The Great Social Beast is a living organism, and it adapts. Defiant though a porno model may be of it, she or he is an integer or single cell of the amorphous living organism and knows that it will by degrees slowly respond.

The mass of individuals that make up the great social beast may hold the disgraced porno model in mild contempt and give her or him lower value, but the definitions of disgrace, contempt, and value are subject to slow evolution and eventual change. Even the most frivolous bimbo who strips and gives blowjobs on-camera has at least a tiny and fleeting inkling of being part of an undercurrent of change.

But the social beast responds over lifetimes, even over centuries. No porno model participating in present porn production is going to be suddenly relieved of her or his personal cheapening effected by institutionalized notions of societal disgrace and degradation and legal tort-law devaluation and debasement.

So a porno model knowingly approaches a pornographic production set or location prepared to strip naked and be permanently degraded, disgraced, and devalued on-camera as a consequence of subsequent widespread publication. He or she does it willingly, and quite likely with a thrill of participating not only in a "new form of sex" but with intuitions of being part of a vanguard of social change.

This potpourri of social protest, being in on making social change, enjoyment of sex itself in addition to a "new kind of sex" on-camera, and other operative motivations in addition to needed pay may help to explain why so many people have voluntarily submitted to becoming porno models. And there are a whole lot of them.

Valerie Kelly points out at the beginning of chapter ten of her book *How To Write Erotica* [26] that in 1984, at the beginning of the commercial videotape revolution in both "legitimate" entertainment and porn, there were 1,192 X-rated videotapes produced in the United States alone. In the following year, 1985, there were 1,600 porn videos produced and nationally distributed in the United States. My 1996 projection, based on Kelly's decade-earlier figures, wildly guessed that an average in excess of 2000 porn videotapes per year had been produced and nationally distributed annually over the subsequent decade, and therefore 20,000 hardcore pornographic videos had been produced between 1986 and 1996. It turned out to be about 40,000 too low.

A few months after this guess, a 1997 *US News and World Report* feature[27] revealed that in the United States "Since 1991, the number of new hardcore titles released each year has increased 500 percent." My guess was a terrible underestimate. The article continued: "Last year (1996) nearly 8000 new hard-core videos were released." There would seem more than a linear annual increase, from 1,192 hard-core videos produced and distributed in the USA in 1984 to about 8,000 in 1996, and those who had projected an eventual slackening of appetite for hardcore porn have thus far been proven wrong.

Not only does this suggest an average annual hardcore pornographic video production of approach 5000 over those twelve years, or a total of maybe 60,000 hardcore porn videos produced in the United States alone between 1984 and 1996, it shows hardcore porn video production growing at a rate of around 150 percent a year.

Moreover, in the half-decade since, Internet porn mushroomed. Hundreds of thousands of porn websites have erupted into the marketplace. Most porno models now find employment and exposure on these. Some are live-sex-show sites, by their very nature employing new and current porno models, as opposed to reshowing old videos. Some are still semi-video MPEGS and use current live porno models. Most are video sites or have videos amid thumbnail still photographs of naked models engaging in sex-acts. It is literally impossible to count them all, but the offerings are huge beyond anyone's imagination even a decade ago.

To go back to the adult bookstore video age in 1996, when things were still calculable, one can at least get an inkling of the scope. Even if a few high-rated porno models appear in dozens of porn productions, at least two porno models perform in each video. In addition, each video usually has several episodes involving several different porno models in each episode of a typical commercially sold porn video. So the number of repeats by high-rated models may approach being canceled by several episodes per commercial video.

Moreover, in some videos there may be as many as ten or fifteen porno models in each gang-bang, inverse gang-bang, and orgy episode of a several-episode porn video. Five episodes per video may require over fifty different porno models in that one video.

With the constant demand for new porn personalities in the form of "new faces" in pornographic videos, one can make an educated guess that several thousand "new faces" appear in commercial videotaped pornography every year. If we take total approaching 60,000 new hardcore porno videos produced and nationally distributed during the last twelve years and conservatively figuring a net of at least one new naked couple performing in each, it seems reasonable to assume that at very least 120,000 new porno models stripped and performed sex acts on-camera during only that dozen years in the USA.

A look at any adult bookstore shelves suggests that the number of new videos cranked out using old porno stars is outweighed by the ones using new raw meat. So I would guess that since each new porn video has several episodes involving a total of around ten different and generally new porno models, and possibly as many as fifty different porno models spread over several episodes in orgy and gang-bang porn videos, a more realistic estimate would be that in porn videos alone over the twelve years between 1984 and 1996—and not counting sex-magazines and Internet pornography—at least 10 x 120,000, or over a million new porno models stripped and engaged in explicit sex-acts on-camera for national porn video distribution.

Add an estimated 20,000 new videos for 1997 and 1998 and maybe 200,000 new porno models in them, and way over a million of our fellow Americans have stripped naked and engaged in sex acts in front of commercial video cameras for nationally distributed public amusements. And this notably large population only includes the people who did it in front of video cameras.

Additional different individuals would have done it in front of still cameras for sex-magazine spreads and in front of commercial motion picture cameras for the remaining eight and sixteen-millimeter film peep-show "loop" porno movies and the thirty-five-millimeter film big-screen feature-length porno movies.

Many of those stripped and engaged in sex-acts on-camera over the previous undergoing-decrimalization decade in commercial celluloid porno movies. Large numbers of amateurish, but commercial and professionally manufactured, ten-to-twenty-minute eight and sixteen millimeter color-film peep-show "loops" were made then. Loops were notorious for using new porno models only once, thus requiring at least two new porno models for each new hardcore loop, and loop orgy and gang-bang productions with averages of maybe six new porno models in each were quite popular. Even underguessing a national production of an average of about 2000 new hardcore 8 mm and 16 mm loops per year between 1968 and 1984 when videotaped pornography began to replace them, one can safely add about fifty-thousand fellow Americans who had stripped and engaged in explicit sex-acts in these widely distributed and shown hardcore films.

And an additional number of people did it in illegal but widely distributed and shown black-and-white "stag" films in the years previous to decriminalization, starting a century ago and continuing up to the effective decriminalizations of pornography taking place around 1968.

Add all those together, and a conservative estimate would be that at least a couple million different people, probably more, in the United States alone, have appeared naked and engaging in sex-acts in hardcore pornographic movies, videos, magazine stills, and now Internet porn.

With a U.S. population of around 250 million, two-and-a-half million hardcore porno models would mean that one out of every hundred of us Americans have stripped naked and engaged in sex-acts in front of cameras for commercial public distribution. If a few from the early days of this century have died of old age, most explicit-sex porno models would still be living at the beginning of the new century and second millennium. Only very recent names few are known to be no longer with us, male porno star John C. Holmes (who was bi-sexual and also appeared in gay pornography) died of AIDS in the early 1990s. Female porno star Savannah, who appeared in 78 porno movies and liked to date rock-music stars, died, like so many rock-music stars and yet very few other porno models, of drug-related suicide on July 11, 1994. And male porno star Cal Jammer committed suicide on January 25, 1995. The fact that their deaths made news may give an inkling of the fact that so few of the estimated two million other porno models have died of natural or other causes.

Given the numbers of living present and former porno models in this country, an average American almost cannot help having met, knowingly or unknowingly, at least one hardcore porno model. Walking in a downtown area of a large American city at lunch hour on a nice day, one would rather quickly walk past five hundred people. Statistically, five of them would be former or present American hardcore porno models who have appeared in nationally distributed pornography in this country. In addition, thousands more American porno models, and millions of non-American porno models worldwide, have appeared in commercial camera-based pornography produced and distributed outside the United States—from Sweden and Denmark, where legal camera-based pornography has been commercially produced since the late 1960s, to Germany and Holland where enormous quantities have been produced for decades, to elsewhere in Europe, and now in former Iron Curtain countries—and a few of these have immigrated here. One might be tempted to speculate that well over a three or four million different living people have stripped naked appeared engaging in sex-acts on-camera in commercial pornography.

And a traveling person thus has an even greater chance of knowingly or unknowingly meeting one.

But that may be the paradox of the era of ubiquitous quasi-legal camera-based pornography. So many productions of pornography have been created that there is no shelf-space or any other kind of commercial room to put them all at one time. The result is that the constant demand for "new faces" in pornography keeps the porn production mills humming, but the lack of retail shelf-space allows only a short shelf-life for any given porn videotape or magazine.

The "new faces" rapidly disappear to make way for yet newer faces. Of all those millions of facial identities that one may walk by who have stripped naked and engaged in sex-acts on-camera for commercial distribution, very few of them will be currently seen in the pornography retail stores at that moment. And the retail space of Internet sites turns over faster than in the retail stores. Porno models' images ever more quickly vanish into the sands of pornographic archaeology, to be resurrected only by determined pornographic researchers.

There is a small probability of an odd-chance encounter between a porn performer and someone who has just viewed old images of her or him. But it will be very rare. Some of the old big-name porno stars of the breakthrough era of the early 70s are still around and would be recognized as widely known superstars except that they have aged by decades while their images continue to show them young. It would also be rare for any of them to be spontaneously recognized on the street after all these years.

So except for in-group recognition by people who had taken part in the on-camera porn production, their business and friendship associates, those whom the in-group may chose to tell, and those who had found out while that particular piece of pornography was current, porno models now have a degree of anonymity simply due to the massive weight of camera-based pornography that has been made and continues to be made. Indeed porno models' scandalous pasts can catch up to them, and this has an effect of limiting their life-options and permanently reducing their tort-law valuation. But comparatively few outside the in-group are going to know that they are porno models unless someone points them out as such. As a result, we are unknowingly passing people on the street who have been hardcore porno models—millions of them living right now in this country alone.

Additionally in her book *How To Write Erotica* [28], Kelly offers an appendix of corporate names and addresses of forty porn "Video Distributors/Producers" in business and looking for porn video and porno movie scripts in 1986, probably a small number of the total because most of the low budget producers used no written story script and depended solely on impromptu sex performances.

In 1996 five of these hardcore porno movie and porn video producers/distributors are still at (or close to) their addresses of a decade earlier, all of them "big names" in the porn industry. The computer pulls up a number of others that may still be in the porn video business at their old addresses but not surprisingly under different corporate names. But the great majority are gone, even the addresses themselves are gone because these were rather clearly low budget operations in inner city addresses whose marginal buildings now seem to have been torn down.

The one-eighth still in business, operating quite openly and publicly and obviously doing quite well, and the great numbers of new porn producers, largely of "amateur porn videos," points to the remarkable demand for hardcore pornography that these suppliers have acted in the most basic law of economics to fill. Those who predicted "saturation points" and a drying up have not yet come to realize their predictions—and have not done so over a quarter of a century.

While a number of porno models engage in repeat performances, at least two porno models participate in each explicit sex porn episode in a porn video, and an average video will three to six episodes. With a continuous level of over two thousand new porn videos being added every year, that would infer an annual increase in explicit sex porno model population of perhaps three or four thousand new porno models.

A large turnover in both porno models and porn production people reflects a pornography demand that is looking not only for new naked porno model facial identities and personalities but differences in both scripted and impromptu pornographic story material. In the impromptu and innuendo story material, it is the camerapersons, directors, and producers who offer much of the creative input for this consumer demand.

But the naked porno models are not limited to being sex-objects manipulated by producers/directors for a manufactured porn product. They are themselves, by the conscious and unconscious projections of their performances, creative inputs to that porn product—and generally quite enthusiastic ones. Needless to say, without their bare bodies there would be no porn product.

But captured bare bodies is not all that attracts viewers to pornography. Without the cooperative efforts, resourceful role-playing poses and performances, and conscious and unconscious creative inputs of naked porno models in their own pornography sessions—of course as well as creative input by camerapersons and directors—the booming pornography industry might be left with drab, monotonous, and markdown products. Personalities and faces of porno models and their own creative inputs to photo sessions and motion picture and video productions are thus as vital as their publicly submitted naked bodies, sex organs, and sex-acts.

Audience asks, and then imagines answers. What might they have been thinking prior to, during, and following stripping and engaging in sex-acts on-camera? And what might they say about consequences of that in the real, tort-law valued, world after the commercial release of the pornographic material they appear in? How might they have been responding to people directing, capturing, and watching them? How are they interacting with one another, sexually, romantically, and otherwise? And so on.

Participating as a naked performer in camera-based pornography has lost more than a trifle of its stigma as a result of widespread dissemination and public acceptance. In fact, so many people now actively seek to be seen and known as naked commercial pornography performers that new scams have emerged. On the Internet and in alternative newspapers one can find advertisements for porno models. In and of itself, these are not unusual. Porno models have been hired this way for decades. But many are blatant scams. One new scam offers to "package" promotional materials to get someone into "high-paying" commercial pornography for a fee of somewhere between two hundred and a thousand dollars. A singularly attractive female may find "employment" through one of these ads. Ninety-nine percent of these ads, however, are simply rip-offs similar to the old legitimate model schemes of the past. A prospective model pays up-front money and waits, and waits, and waits, and never gets that magic call.

So pervasive is porn that it has generated a large popular appetite to become a porno model. Scam-artists, as scam-artists will, have jumped in to milk the urge, whatever its motivation.

Attractive young woman who seek to be porno models are always in demand and can find themselves on-camera rather easily. It is not entirely unlike pre-pornography days when attractive young women who sought to be whores could easily get into it.

After one or two hardcore smut videos, however, only the strikingly attractive and unusually "talented" women—and men—remain literally in the picture. The women and men who have done one or two porn videos and/or related pornographic magazine spreads may cash in on their sexual and social notoriety in prostitution-related undertakings. But it would seem that there is only a small gain from being in commercial pornography to be made that way. Most of it would seem personal satisfaction. The porno models did what fewer others would have dared to have done.

In talking to a limited number of women and men who had appeared in only a few small commercial pornography productions, I found very few who were able to genuinely cash-in on their fame or infame. Many of the woman worked as strip-joint "dancers" and may have picked-up a little extra from prostitution on the side. But in this they were little or no different from the other strippers in their joints who had not gone on-camera in commercial porn. The men who had performed in only one or two heterosexual commercial porn videos or magazine spreads were harder to find. They had no strip joints to fall back on for continued sex-industry employment and gravitated back to the great mainstream underbelly.

The women, even as public strippers, were a little more secretive about their having "done it" on-camera, the whore-stigma and its related social pressures still pressing somewhat harder on women than men. But with hardcore pornography now widespread and effectively socially accepted, the women turned out to be somewhat prideful about having done it on-camera once it seemed safe to say it to a guy. None of them showed regret like Mona had. Unlike Mona, who had performed in studios in front of commercial movie cameras and numbers professional movie production personnel and as a result had become literally world-famous as a porno model when it was far less socially acceptable, they had been in a few of a literal multitude of low-quality and high-turnover amateur porn video segments in an era when adult bookstores selling them had been in the same spots for decades. After a few months their videos had been removed from the shelves and new ones had replaced them. No one knew that they were porno models unless they chose to tell them.

The Internet is offering new possibilities in porn. There are a number of "amateur exposurist" sites where women and couples can broadcast images of their bare bodies and public sexual activities worldwide. A fairly large number of people contribute to these without pay, obviously for the pleasure of "doing it on-camera" and being publicly seen. But here again, the images are fleeting. Even the downloaded ones are fleeting. A week or a month later, many if not most disks and CDs are recycled. Something always remains, of course, to "catch up" with the naked sex-performers and tort-law degrade them should there be a good reason. But for most, there is none. They did it on-camera, showed themselves off, and were quickly forgotten amid a plethora of others doing it.

In this way, they are not much different from live-sex-show performers. They vanish anonymous into an ever-growing crowd. There are billions of pornographic images in the vast Internet memories. Fewer and fewer care.

Only the actuality of their naked public sex performances remains. Within a group they are forever known as the debauchees in a debaucher-debauchee game. Within that group they have a reputation. But it is not a "bad" reputation, just one that advertises their proclivity to be a low socio-economic class debauchee and fact of having been one.

Technology has spread the consequences of being one fairly thin. Social change has reduced those thinly spread consequences. Over two million Americans, most of them living, have stripped naked and performed public sex-acts on-camera for commercial sale and distribution, and more have done in on-camera in private. Clearly a new sexual-social context has emerged.

CHAPTER THIRTEEN

Summary: The Pornographic Looking Glass

A generation or two has now grown to adulthood with quasi-legal public pornography all around. The demand remains and even grows year-by-year, indicating that the interest is something more than a passing curiosity.

New technology like the Internet has created such marvels as instantaneous porn production and dissemination for a gigantic new business and social demand.

While voters, legislators, law enforcement professionals, judges, and juries were wrestling with management and regulation of film-based pornography, cheap and easy video camera and video projection technology skirted around them. As this was going on, the vast, massive, international, and virtually unregulatable Internet pornography industries suddenly sprang up. Pandora-in-the-buff is now out of the box camera and projector and digitized into the worldwide web.

An interesting result of the camera-based pornography revolution and its quasi-legalization is a wealth of data now available for psychology and sex researchers. One of the more obvious findings from free-choice pornography purchases by consumers is that the great majority of people's sexual interests revolve around what might be termed "normal" heterosexual pornography.

Most of the filmed, videotaped, or digitized pornography sold uses one heterosexual couple engaging in various poses and positions. They open with excruciatingly normal foreplay and quickly continue on to coital sex, fellatio, cunnilingus, and more recently occasional anilingus. There is an appalling visual sameness of bare human bodies doing the same old things. Story generation explains the continuing appetite. The photographs, films, videotapes, or digitized productions are only made different by that and the multitude of different naked on-camera porno models and a variety in behind-the-scenes directing, image-making, and production personalities.

The next largest selling variations use nude threesomes, foursomes, and larger orgies engaging in the same heterosexual sex-acts, again only made different by the naked personalities and behind-the-scenes production people involved. If these threesomes, foursomes, and larger orgies also have same-sex acts, they are lesbian and are not the majority of the total sex-acts.

Lesbian pornography by itself finds acceptance with mainstream heterosexuals and is often included in mainstream porn video and magazine packaging along with episodes of heterosexual couples. But male homosexuals are virtually the only purchasers of male homosexual pornography, and this accounts for a small percentage of the total porn pie.

Sales of heterosexual and lesbian bondage-and-discipline pornography and Sado-masochistic pornography account for a small segment of total heterosexual porn sales.

Pornography involving underage children had a brief quasi-legal status and mingled with the rest of publicly sold and shown pornography in some areas during the mid-1970s. But during that time, sales of "kiddiporn" appear to have been notably unspectacular, indeed far lower than "normal" porn. Only a small group of pedophile consumers demand "kiddiporn," which unlike all other kinds of pornography is by its very nature coercive of involuntary underage performers.

This less than scientific assessment of porn sales—that average citizens could easily have seen and may continue to study by dropping into adult bookstores and porno movie theaters from time to time in most of Europe and North America—would appear to make its own statement about the range of sexual interests and appetites. More recently, those with Internet computer connections can quickly and easily survey the insatiable appetite, enormous demand, huge numbers and varieties of willing porno models, and inexhaustible supply of pornography.

The creation, publication, and distribution of nude images in pornography has become a major industry, a significant part of the Gross Domestic Product. Profiting from publicly stripping people naked is big-big business. People obviously pay a lot of good money to see other people submitting to publicly being stripped naked and having their nakedness widely seen and published for commercial profit.

Commercial pornographic images are so widespread in western Europe and North America that one might be hard pressed to find anyone over fifteen years of age who had not seen some. In about an hour on the Internet—and without any credit card or so-called membership—one can find not only numerous clear color images of explicitly naked males and females, one can see numerous clear color images showing unmistakably naked people unambiguously engaging in a variety of positions of explicit coital sex, fellatio, cunnilingus, and anilingus, and a whole category of urinations onto faces and into waiting mouths.

A rank amateur, quite unfamiliar with Internet use and certainly not up there with the agile bright kids who use the hardware and software with great ease and flexibility, can quickly and easily put these images on-screen. Many of these images of naked human beings engaging in sex-acts and socio-sexual degradation were enticements to enter pay-per-view sites. One need not pay to see the plethora of not only entice-ment images of effectively naked people, but nude explicit sex enticement images. Any adult or kid can do it, and undoubtedly much more, and it is difficult to imagine that kids would not.

It is clearly too late to bother about what should be done about it. It has already been done. Adults and children alike, and even those with even minimal access to computers in homes, homes of friends, libraries, schools, and other institutions, have seen the multiple images. A picture is worth a thousand words. An objective camera-created picture tells more and is far more effective, descriptive, and convincing in telling it. While the actual photographic image may fade and blur in the mind after time, the story told by it and the instruction acquired from it does not. It remains for a lifetime.

And since the mid-1960s, when camera-based images of graphic nudity and explicit sexual activity were effectively decriminalized and widely published and shown, generations of people have literally been born into that new freedom. They had these images, and their resultant stories and instruction, brought to mind one or more times, lived full and fairly long lives, and by now some have even died of natural causes in the new millennium—after having lived their whole lives immersed in a world of easy access to images of nudity and nude sexual activity.

For probably most of the world's population, and certainly most of combined European-American populations, it is plainly too late to do anything about public images of nudity and pornography. Even if all the images could miraculously be confiscated and destroyed, the story mate-rial and instruction that they generated would stay fixed in minds for more than a generation or two. This would seem to suggest a need to work from within pornography in order to supervise its social direction.

Given that it would be literally impossible to gather up all the presently-created nude and/or pornographic images, even if no more would be added day-by-day, a plethora of these images will exist for centuries, and all of them can be multi-duplicated. Ease in creating and distributing objective camera-based nude images—not only naked people, but naked people engaging in all varieties of sexual behavior—has overtaken any method of control, even the most draconian and harsh.

The reality is that not only does a large percentage of population like to view these images, a significant population likes to participate in creating them—on both sides of cameras. Therefore, what might be done now is to critically and honestly analyze the effects and then to construct entirely new political, social, legal, technical, moral, and perhaps religions resolutions to any socially detrimental consequences that may be revealed.

As a result of public pornography, we have at least this slightly better understanding of ourselves. People in general might sometimes have a momentary curiosity about same-sex, bondage-sex, sado-masochistic sex, and sex among children or between adults and children, but it is clearly not their overriding sexual interest. Pornography consumption numbers show the prevailing appetite. Most patrons want pornography involving a single bare male and a single bare female engaging in sex-acts. And the small population percentage of each sexual minority appetite remains surprisingly stable.

Commercial figures from sex on the Internet have revealed a long suspected division between male sexual interests and female sexual interests. A 1998 front-page article in the *San Francisco Chronicle* [29] reviews a study by "cybersex" expert Alvin Cooper whose 9000 Internet user "click-and-tell" poll found that: 1. five out of six people who cruise the Internet for sexual material are male. 2. Men prefer sexually explicit Web sites twice as much as women—in other words, men want "a look," not a relationship entanglement. 3. Women were twice as likely as men to participate in "chat rooms," but more than half claimed they do not download sexually explicit material. 4. Female adult cybersex surfers are generally younger than their male counterparts. 5. Eighty percent of men and women polled had viewed erotic material on their home computers.

The article goes on to note that there is an "insatiable" appetite for steamy Web sites. Relevant Knowledge, a Washington DC research organization, said 9.6 million Net users, about 15 percent of the total, logged on to the ten most popular sex sites during a one-month period. It adds that there are approximately 70,000 Web sex-related sites, accounting for a considerable part of what they claim is a four billion dollar annual US porn industry.

There has been an enormous change in sexual attitudes in the last three decades of quasi-legalized camera-based pornography. It would seem to have been reflected in the healthy "ho-hum" attitude to the recent presidential sex scandal and the explicit pornographic Starr Report on it, approved for publication by the U.S. Congress and printed by the U.S. Government Printing Office. A quick look at the president's subsequent approval ratings seems to show that the only people deeply concerned about his unremarkable human sexuality seem to have been from the Republican Christian Right, people clinging to the old ways of The Great Social Beast even while The Beast appears to be evolving in the interest of its own self-preservation. Perhaps history will point to the U.S. Government's Starr Report as a point of demarcation, where we either enter an era of dealing with our overpopulation, our biosphere limitations, and our psycho-sexual being, or wallow in that which worked so well for so long to preserve us while ignoring its growing pernicious creep toward catastrophe.

Population continues to grow out of control and threaten all of life itself on this planet, and it generally grows most rapidly where pornography is not only illegal but severely punished. These areas are also notable for extreme religiosity, sexual hyper-puritanism, and regard of women as essentially baby-factories and child-rearers and always less-than-second-class citizens.

A movie actor was recently elected to the presidency for two terms, ending an ancient stigma going back at least as far as the Elizabethan stage. Porn performers, too, have been elected to office. These may have been largely in jest so far.

But as this millennium draws to a close, we are now faced with the results of literal explicit-sex pornography about a sitting President of the United States having been published by the Congress of the United States. In addition, we the people have been besieged with a videotaped sexually explicit interrogating of that president, broadcast for hours on not only national, but world television.

There would seem a very small step indeed from that point—which we have now reached—to the public showing and publication of hard-core pornographic images of our office-seeking candidates or elected officials, including candidates for president and sitting presidents.

Thus we may ask in all seriousness: will a porno actor ever be elected president? Will it matter anyway?

Alternatively, will the growing demand for salacious details about sexual activities of public figures and elected officials eventually dry up? Will camera-based pornography eventually dry up?

Will this happen before all chaos breaks out from overpopulation and destroys the delicate biosphere, leaving just another big bare rock hurling through the great dark void of space?

The invention of the preserved authentic visual image by Daguerre and others was probably the most powerful influence on thought, opinion, and social change of all inventions since language, tools, fire, and clothing.

Camera-based pornography—that at once and without historical delay sprang out of Daguerre's invention—was destined to play with and play on millions years of augmentations to these original four horsemen of our animal apocalypse and disconnect, proto-human inventions of language, tools, fire, and clothing. In doing so, camera-based pornography has afforded mental relief not dissimilar to laughter and humor and growing out of an ancient anthropological continuity of "dirty" jokes and ribald stories.

Camera-based pornography plays with and plays on the grunts, groans, and moans of proto-language interspersed with interplays of "proper" and "obscene" language. It plays with and plays on the human use of tools, especially the modern tools of image capture, projection, and publication. It plays with and plays on the crucial human-differentiating manipulation of fire, as for example symbolized by utilization of heated filaments for light and artificial lighting. And lastly, it plays with and plays on the demarcating human adoption of clothing by flirting around and focusing on the lack of it, on ceremonial undressing, on defiantly flaunting nudity, and on social disparities between the naked and the attired.

In playing with and playing on these four cardinal human inventions, camera-based pornography performs a liberating function, psychologically regurgitating hundreds of millennia of social adaptations to them, but especially the social adaptations of the last five or six millennia that we call "civilization."

With civilization came the invention of writing and money, social stratification, assignment of monetary values to human beings, and written laws governing social interactions and financial transactions between them. Just as the millions of years earlier invention and long gradual development of spoken language had created a "virtual" living organism I call the Great Social Beast, the invention of written language gave it corporate and corporeal form and massive power to dominate the planet.

Within civilization there developed systems where there were people who were users and people who were used, people who had more value and people who had less, people who were born with social advantages and people who were born to be taken advantage of. If some see a problem with pornography, that would be the key, and thus to all the anti-pornography crusaders I have to say that radical social restructure would appear the sole realistic solution to work toward.

For millions of years of proto-human and human evolution, sexuality served procreation. The "virtual" organism subsidized sexuality-for-procreation for the continuous replacement of its human integers and for its own growth and well being. As civilization gave it form and increasing power, it created and defined the female whore as both a caution to fertile women to bear and raise its integer humans and simultaneously to offer its male defenders from internal and external threats sexual user-privileges and pleasures. These included the invention of the sexually "bizarre," which added fear-inducements to keep "proper" women in their child bearing and child-rearing places, most especially lower strata women. Only among very upper strata women were sexual pleasure entertainments possible, and these were mostly in the form of word-based story material with carefully disguised implied warnings and therefore yet another form of social manipulation.

By whatever designs there may be in the universe, the invention of photography came at a point in time when the virtual beast's very success was about overwhelm its biosphere support base with overpopulation.

Photography permitted the creation of non-language pornography, and as the virtual organism struggled with its own excesses of population and power success it also had to respond to this sudden new form of sexual pleasure and entertainment.

The very demands for whores and "bizarre" sexual entertainments it created for its male-integer defenders and sexual innuendo story material for its female childbearers and child-raisers grew to confront it as technology grew out of its control. In a mere century and a half—as compared to several million years of proto-human and human existence and the word-based virtual organism's growth with it—an explosion in camera-based pornography and appetite for it has overwhelmed word-based social controls and forced reevaluations and relaxations. The word-based "virtual" organism is alive, and living creatures adapt to internal and external changes or they die and become extinct.

On one front it continues, perhaps too slowly for its survival, to adapt to reduce population growth. On another it continues to adapt to the sudden new phenomenon of camera-based pornography. In the mix of these two adaptations appears to be a partial survival solution. An evolution of our view of sexual activity has given us a public honesty and consciousness of sexual pleasure for its own sake even while we ponder the looming monumental disaster caused by sex for procreation.

But it is only a consciousness. Effects of pornography on human sexuality and society seem not to have been well studied, and may need to be as population continues to spiral haywire out of control, threatening civilization and possibly all life on the planet. Given the ubiquitousness and inexpensiveness of image-capture technology and the amazing demand for pornography, literally nothing short of annihilation of the human species will make it go away. That leaves few alternatives to accepting and living with it, and the only realistic legislation dealing with it must be derived from social and scientific examination of causes and effects to ends of accepting and living with it.

I offer this motley collection of anecdotes, theories, and experiences for its own interest but with hopes that it may generate additional honest and uninhibited thought, debate, and examination.

Notes

Introduction Notes:

1. "Cultural Ecology and Mathematics," by J. Peter Denny, in *Native American Mathematics*, ed. Michael P. Closs, 1986, Univ. of Texas Press, Austin, p 155.

CHAPTER NOTES
"ADVENT OF PHOTOGRAPHY"

2. *L. J. M. Daguerre; the History of the Diorama and the Daguerreotype*, by Helmut and Allison Gernsheim, 1968, Dover Publications, New York (page 2).

3. Ibid (page 80).

4. In the George Eastman House Collection, Rochester, New York. Published in *The History of Photography*, by Beaumont Newhall, 1982, New York Graphic Society Books, Little Brown and Company (page 31).

5. In the Webb Collection (location unknown). Published in *The Birth of Photography*, by Brian Coe, 1977, Taplinger Publishing Company, New York (page 111).

6. *Reading, Writing, and Rewriting the Prostitute Body*, by Shannon Bell, Indiana University Press, Bloomington, 1994.

"DEBAUCHER-DEBAUCHEE"

(no notes)

"BIRDS, BEES, AND BARE BEHINDS"

(no notes)

"PEDESTALS, PROSTITUTION, AND PORNOGRAPHY"

7. "Pornography: the Theory," by Frances Ferguson, in *Critical Inquiry*. Spring 1995.

8. *San Francisco Chronicle* San Francisco, California, columnist Herb Cain's daily column, early 1996, exact date unremembered. [ms page 68]

9. *New Yorker*, October 30, 1995, article by Susan Faludi

10. *Across the Board*, May 1991 issue, page 75.

"FACSIMILE AND REALITY"

11. *Mona; The Virgin Nymph*, feature-length porn film produced mid-to-late 1970 by Bill Osco.

12. *Storyville Portraits*, photographs by E. J. Bellocq, published by The New York Museum of Modern Art, New York, 1970.

13. *Sinema; American Pornographic Films and the People Who Make Them* by Kenneth Turan and Stephen F. Zito, Prager Publishers, New York and Washington, 1974, page 3.

14. *Hardcore; Power, Pleasure, and the "Frenzy of the Visible"*, by Linda Williams, University of California Press, Berkeley, 1989.

"CHASTENED AND EXHIBITED"

(no notes)

"SHAME SHAME SHAME"

15. *Sinema; American Pornographic Films and the People Who Make Them*, (previously cited, exact page of this quote unremembered).

16. Jenni Bidner, editor of *Petersen's Photography Magazine*, in an article or editorial in that magazine, circa 1980s, exact issue, page unremembered.

17. *The Filmmaker's Guide to Pornography*, by Steven Ziplow, Drake Publishers, New York, 1977, page 126.

"PORNOGRAPHY CONFRONTING RACISM AND SOCIAL STAGNATION"

18. *A Completely New Look At Interracial Sexuality; Public Opinion and Select Commentaries*, by Lawrence R. Tenzer, Scholars' Publishing Company, Manahawkin, New Jersey, 1990.

19. *Sally Hemings*, by Barbara Chase-Riboud, Viking Press, New York, 1979.

20. Movie review of "Jefferson in Paris," see *Newsweek*, April 3, 1995.

21. *Bottom Feeders; From Free Love To Hard Core; the Rise and Fall of Counterculture Heroes Jim and Artie Mitchell*, by John Hubner, Doubleday, New York, 1993.

"SEEING PORN FOR WHAT IT IS NOT"

22. "Diary," by Laurie Taylor, in the British magazine *New Statesman and Society*, December 2, 1994, page 6.

"PARTICIPATING AS VIEWER"

23. *Sinema; American Pornographic Films and People Who Make Them*, (previously cited) page 77.

24. "Diary," (previously cited)

25. *The Naked Lunch*. by William Borroughs, also published by Corgi Books, Div. of Transworld Publishers, London, 1969.

"DEBAUCHER AUDIENCES AND DEBAUCHEE LIVE SEX PERFORMERS"

(no notes)

"ON CAMERA"

26. *How To Write Erotica*, by Valerie Kelly, Crown Trade Paperbacks, New York, 1986, beginning chapter.

27. "The Business of Pornography," *US News and World Report* feature, February 10, 1997, pages 42-50.

28. *How To Write Erotica*, appendix,(previously cited).

"SUMMARY CHAPTER"

29. *San Francisco Chronicle*, June 10, 1998, front-page article, reviews a study by "cybersex" expert Alvin Cooper.

www.ingramcontent.com/pod-product-compliance
Lightning Source LLC
Chambersburg PA
CBHW061339280526
45784CB00001B/69